IMAGINING AN AUSTRIAN NATION

JOSEPH SAMUEL BLOCH AND THE SEARCH FOR A MULTIETHNIC AUSTRIAN IDENTITY, 1846–1919

by

Ian Reifowitz

East European Monographs, Boulder
Distributed by Columbia University Press, New York

2003

EAST EUROPEAN MONOGRAPHS, NO. DCXXXI

ISBN 0–88033–529–7
Library of Congress Control Number 2003109664

Printed in the United States of America

TABLE OF CONTENTS

ACKNOWLEDGMENTS

I want to acknowledge and thank the many people in academia who have supported my work over these past years. First and foremost is my mentor, Aviel Roshwald, without whose guidance on innumerable questions over the last decade I could never have accomplished this extremely difficult task. He has given his time and energy to an incredible degree, offering advice on questions far and beyond what advisors are typically asked, and I greatly appreciate all he has done for me. I also want to thank Marsha Rozenblit and Roger Chickering for the countless hours both of them spent advising me on my research and on the writing of this book. Thanks also to Steven Beller, for his crucial help over the years, in particular during my research fellowship in Vienna. I have benefited from the efforts of a number of other scholars who have taken the time to read what I have written and to offer constructive suggestions and feedback, including Sam Albert, Emil Brix, Gary Cohen, Thomas Fröschl, David Good, Malachi Hacohen, Charles Ingrao, Jeremy King, Nicholas Miller, James Shedel, Gerald Stourzh, and Nancy Wingfield.

I also want to thank Georgetown University and the Woodrow Wilson International Center for Scholars in Washington, DC, for their financial support of my work, as well as the Internationales Forschungszentrum Kulturwissenschaften (IFK) for awarding me a generous fellowship as well as office space that allowed me to conduct my research in Vienna. At the IFK, Lutz Musner and Sonja Egger deserve special thanks for their extraordinary assistance and support. I am also grateful to Hadassah Assouline, Director of the Central Archives for the History of the Jewish People, Jerusalem, and her staff for their help with the Archives' collection of Bloch's private papers.

I want to thank Volker Berghahn, who first inspired me to pursue a career in history and for more than ten years has been watching over my progress. I am also especially grateful to my uncle, Professor Leslie Schuster. His professional and personal advice in all aspects of academic life has proven invaluable. I want to thank my family and especially my parents, Helaine and Jerry Reifowitz, for their love and support from the start.

Finally, and most importantly, I want to dedicate this book to my wife and best friend, Jane Kaufman, whose life has been most impinged upon by my work, and who has been my inspiration to complete it.

Ian Reifowitz
New York, NY
SUNY-Empire State College

INTRODUCTION

"Today, from all of the nationalities of the state, a holy, great and irresistible Austro-Hungarian nation has come into being,"[1] declared Joseph Samuel Bloch (1850–1923) on August 14, 1914. He was mistaken; the outbreak of war in 1914 did not lead the many nationalities[2] of the Habsburg Monarchy[3] to see themselves as a single nation. His

---

1 "Der Kaiser Franz Josef I," *Oesterreichische Wochenschrift*, Nr. 33, Year 31, August 14, 1914, p. 561.

2 When discussing the Habsburg Monarchy's various ethnic groups (Czechs, Jews, Germans, et. al.), this book will use the terms 'nationality,' 'people,' 'ethnic group,' or, on occasion, the German term 'Stamm,' which politicians, including nationalists, used during the period under examination (along with '*Volk*' and '*Nationalität*') and can be best translated as 'tribe.' While there may be subtle differences among these terms, for the purposes of this study they describe a group of people who, without respect to any political or territorial claims of sovereignty, claim to share (or are identified by others, such as the state, as sharing) a language, cultural and literary traditions, a religion, descent from an earlier people, or any combination thereof. This book will not refer to these groups as 'nations,' or Austria as a 'multinational' state because in current English usage, 'nation' and 'country' are often conflated, i.e. The United Nations. This conflation implies that the term nation carries with it a political significance, namely the right to a nation-state. To call the groups into which the citizens of the Monarchy divided themselves 'nations' is a political statement in and of itself.

3 As always in a discussion of the Habsburg Monarchy, a note about terms is necessary. 'Austria-Hungary' refers to the polity that came into being after the 1867 *Ausgleich* or Compromise, also known as the Dual Monarchy and, in more common parlance, the Austro-Hungarian Empire. Before 1867 the term 'Austria-Hungary' is anachronistic. When talking about politics or government after 1867, 'Austria' refers to the non-Hungarian half of the Dual Monarchy, an entity also known unofficially as 'Cisleithania.' Before 1867, the term 'Austria' stands for the whole of the Monarchy. This book will also use the term Austria to refer to the Habsburg state in the abstract without reference to any specific time in history, i.e. 'the idea of Austria....' Bloch, who began his career almost a generation after the 1867 *Ausgleich*, focused his ideas for a common civic consciousness on the Austrian half of the Monarchy, although on a few occasions he seemed to be speaking about the entire Habsburg polity. These inconsistencies were perhaps tactical, or perhaps simple lapses as a result of having to write a weekly editorial in addition to his other manifold responsibilities.

statement, however, reflected the hope of its author, an Austrian Jewish writer and politician who sought to cultivate a sense of civic nationalism to unify the peoples of multiethnic Habsburg Austria. This study is an intellectual history that explores the ideas of Bloch as well as those of other Austrian political thinkers of various ethnic and political backgrounds in order to discover how these individuals conceived of a supraethnic Austrian nation. In particular, it examines the ideas of Adolf Fischhof, another Austrian Jewish politician and reformer, whom Bloch considered his mentor. Finally, it compares Bloch's ideas to those of other reform-minded Austrian politicians, including Frantisek Palacky, Karl Renner, Otto Bauer, Joseph Eötvös, Aurel Popovici, and Iakiv Holovatskyj.

Bloch's call for a dual-layered Austrian consciousness that respected the desire to protect pre-existing ethnic, cultural, religious, and linguistic communal bonds while building transethnic ties based on citizenship resonates in multiethnic societies throughout today's world. From North America to Africa to India to Europe, countries are wrestling with how to define membership in their national community in light of the diversity of their populations. Many European states are attempting to integrate into the European Union while absorbing unprecedented numbers of immigrants from non-European lands. Both tasks require states to adjust their definition of national identity. Societies on every continent can learn something from Bloch.

The successful creation of a common civic identity defined the viability of multiethnic states in the twentieth century, and will continue to do so in the future. In Central and Eastern Europe alone, the breakup during the 1990s of the Soviet Union, Yugoslavia, Czechoslovakia, and even tiny Moldova, itself a former Soviet republic, have demonstrated that a multiethnic state in today's world requires a state idea that legitimizes its existence to its constituent ethnic groups, and an identity that binds the citizens of those groups to one another and to the state they share.

Although the Habsburg Monarchy is long gone, the concept of a supraethnic sense of nationhood remains relevant for contemporary Austria because it can serve as a reminder of a pluralist tradition within Austrian history as that state adjusts to being a member of a united Europe that will soon embrace many of its former Habsburg cousins. In fact, the questions faced by the rulers and politicians of Habsburg

Austria still exist for most of the countries of contemporary Central and Eastern Europe, where, for example, significant ethnic Hungarian minorities in Romania and Slovakia and the presence of ethnic Russians in the Baltic states as well as Ukraine defy the traditional notion of nation-states. The Yugoslav wars of the 1990s proved that exclusionary national identities cannot peacefully exist in ethnically mixed societies.

The relations between peoples in multiethnic Balkan and East-Central European countries have the potential to weaken not only the domestic stability of these states, but also, as in the case of Kosovo, to worsen relations between the host country (Serbia) and the ethnic homeland of its minority (Albania). Instability and bloodshed both within and across the borders of these countries may, in addition to the human cost, reduce their likelihood of joining NATO and the European Union, institutions that many see as vital to solving the age-old problems of security and stability in the region. As during the 1920s and 30s, ethnic tensions could destroy the possibility of regional cooperation and once again subject the peoples of Central and Eastern Europe to domination by a powerful outsider.

The leaders of contemporary multiethnic states in the region face many of the same dilemmas as did the leaders of Austria-Hungary. Today's societies have a clear choice. They can follow the path of Serbia under Slobodan Milosevic and place ethnic minorities outside the defined boundaries of the nation. Such an exclusivist vision of a nation can lead a country only to bloodshed and pariah status within the international community. The states of Central and Eastern Europe must create inclusive citizenship-based identities in which the majority accepts the cultural differences of the minority, and the minority proclaims loyalty to the state and participates in the political process as full members of the society. Only by developing these civic bonds will these societies be able to integrate their minorities politically, peoples who have no interest in either abandoning their cultures and traditional identities or leaving what they have come to consider their homelands. These countries will have to separate membership in the civic nation from membership in the ethnic nation.[4] Such an achievement

4 See Chapter 1 for a broader discussion of differences between ethnic and civic forms of nationhood.

would lay the groundwork for the long-term stability and regional cooperation that will enable the area between Germany and Russia to flourish and take its rightful place within a united and secure Europe.

The challenges posed by diversity do not solely exist on the other side of the Atlantic. In recent years the debate in the United States over how to conceive of the American national community has grown increasingly shrill. The loudest voices are often those on the extremes. On the one hand there exist xenophobes who have no tolerance for cultural diversity and anything other than a 100% American identity, and, on the other, there are extreme multiculturalists who reject out of hand the concept of a common interest or a sense of belonging that can unify all Americans. Only a definition of Americanness that seeks a balance between these extremes can succeed. The cultivation of a civic national identity to bring together all groups within a multiethnic society remains one of the great tasks of our times.

This book considers the question of how, to borrow a phrase from Benedict Anderson, one political thinker tried to 'imagine a community.'[5] Bloch helped to cultivate a civic Austrian nationalism among Austrian Jews that formed a major part of their overarching political identity. An examination of his ideas thus contributes to the exploration of how national and political identities are constructed, further demonstrating Anderson's point that national identities are made, not born.

This book broadens our understanding of the vexed relationship between liberalism and nationalism by assessing the potential for the survival of a liberal political culture and civic identity in a society riven by nationalist tensions. A study of Bloch demonstrates the connections between ethnic consciousness and civic identity in a diverse society, and counters the view that one can only survive at the expense of the other. Such an analysis thus connects to the larger discussion of the relationship between ethnic and civic nationalism and the prospects of what Yael Tamir has called 'Liberal Nationalism.'[6] This book addresses the meaning of nationalism and identity in a pluralistic society, issues that certainly have followed us into the twenty-first century.

---

5 Benedict Anderson, *Imagined Communities: Reflections on the Origin and Spread of Nationalism* (London: Verso, 1983).

6 Yael Tamir, *Liberal Nationalism* (Princeton: Princeton University Press, 1993).

This book fills a major gap in Central European historiography. Most of the attention paid to Bloch has come from historians of Habsburg or Viennese Jewry who have emphasized his political activism in the battle against antisemitism.[7] Although they have mentioned his call for Jews to be loyal Austrians and to embrace their ethnic Jewishness, these historians have not examined in detail his concept of a civic Austrian consciousness. Furthermore, Bloch has rarely appeared in general histories of Austrian identity. These have focused on the creation and roots of contemporary Austria, which is built around a mostly homogeneous German-speaking population.[8] This historiographical imbalance has distorted our understanding of the development of ethnic and national identity in Austria, and it ignores the once-vital concept of a pluralistic Austrian consciousness.

On the other hand, broader scholarship on the Monarchy is finally beginning to recognize the importance of Bloch's ideas for Habsburg

---

7 The most detailed analyses of Bloch have been: Katja Lander, "Joseph Samuel Bloch und die Österreichisch-Israelitische Union: Initiativen zur Begrundung einer jüdischen Politik im spaten 19. Jahrhundert" (Ph.D. diss., Universität des Saarlandes, 1993); Robert Wistrich, *The Jews of Vienna in the Age of Franz Joseph* (Oxford: Oxford University Press, 1989), pp. 270–309; and Jacob Toury, "Josef Samuel Bloch und die Jüdische Identität im österreichischen Kaiserreich," in Walter Grab, ed., *Jüdische Integration und Identität in Deutschland und Österreich, 1848–1918* (Tel Aviv: Nateev, 1984), pp. 41–63. All three of these, although they discuss Bloch at some length, focus almost exclusively on his political activities on behalf of Jews, not his analysis of the larger Austrian question. Bloch also received some attention in: Malachi Hacohen, "Dilemmas of Cosmopolitanism: Karl Popper, Jewish Identity and 'Central European Culture,'" *Journal of Modern History* 71, 1 (March 1999), pp. 105–49, see pp. 115–16; William McCagg, *A History of Habsburg Jews, 1670–1918* (Bloomington: Indiana University Press, 1989), p. 184; Marsha L. Rozenblit, *The Jews of Vienna, 1867–1914: Assimilation and Identity* (Albany: SUNY Press 1983), pp. 181–4; Robert Kann, "German Speaking Jewry during Austria-Hungary's Constitutional Era (1867–1918)," *Jewish Social Studies*, 10 (1948), pp. 239–56, see pp. 253–55; and David Rechter, *The Jews of Vienna and the First World War* (London: The Littman Library of Jewish Civilization, 2001), p. 35.

8 On Austrian identity, see Ernst Bruckmüller, *Nation Österreich* (Vienna: Bohlau, 1984); Peter Katzenstein, *Disjoined Partners: Austria and Germany since 1815* (Berkeley: University of California Press, 1976); Friedrich Heer, *Der Kampf um die Österreichische Identität* (Vienna: Bohlau, 1981). One counter-example can be found in Jacques LeRider, "Hugo von Hofmannsthal and the Austrian Idea of Central Europe," in Robertson & Timms, eds., *The Habsburg Legacy*, pp. 121–35, see p. 127. LeRider devoted two sentences to Bloch. General surveys of the Monarchy are too numerous to list here.

history. In the most recent survey of modern Habsburg history, Robin Okey noted that Bloch's "supra-national Austrian patriotism" had a major impact on how Austrian Jews identified themselves.[9] A full-scale analysis of Bloch's call for a civic Austrian consciousness is due.

Bloch served from 1884 to 1895 in the Austrian *Reichsrat*. In 1886, he co-founded the *Österreichisch-Israelitische Union*, a civic organization charged with the mission to fight antisemitism and defend the civil rights of Jews. He also published and edited the weekly newspaper, the *Österreichische Wochenschrift* from 1884 until 1920, and wrote a number of books and essays. These, as well as his published memoirs, speeches, and private papers serve as the primary source material for the analysis of his ideas.

Throughout his career Bloch sought to cultivate a dual-layered Austrian identity that contained two components, one based on an individual's ethnic, cultural and/or religious background, and a second based on being an Austrian citizen. He imagined an Austrian nationhood that centered on the shared rights and interests of individual citizens but also recognized the equal worth of the Monarchy's cultural groups as collective entities. In addition, Bloch demanded democracy and full civil rights for all the Monarchy's citizens. He linked the creation of this new civic consciousness to a transformation of the Austrian state into a true state of nationalities that enforced real equality among the peoples.

Bloch's conception of a civic Austrian consciousness grew out of the particular circumstances Habsburg Jews faced in the last decades before the First World War, a time when antisemitism threatened their legal rights and physical security. Jews, perhaps more than any other Habsburg people, had to think actively about their identity and their loyalties in a society in which it was unclear whether they belonged. Bloch reasoned that Jews needed a multiethnic, anational Austria because they would always be a minority in any European state defined by ethnicity, culture, language, or religion. He recognized that Austrian Jews needed a definition of community that could include them on equal terms. Only a civic Austrian nation, in his view, could do so. Bloch sought to define what it meant to be Austrian in such a

---

9 Robin Okey, *The Habsburg Monarchy* (New York: St. Martin's Press, 2001), p. 296.

way that no one could claim that Jews, because they were of a different *Stamm* and religion, were somehow 'less Austrian.'

Not only would Habsburg Jews benefit from the development of a supraethnic Austrian nationhood, Bloch also contended that it was crucial for the very survival of Austria-Hungary in a Europe characterized by the growing strength of racial or racist nationalism. Racial nationalism is an exclusionary form of nationalism based on the idea that each nation ought to consist of a single people united by so-called 'blood ties,' i.e. a perception that the members of this 'race' share descent from a common set of ancestors and also share common biological or physical characteristics.[10] Proponents of racial nationalism created political and/or ideological movements that emphasized those perceived biological ties and, more dangerously for those within a society who were designated as outside the majority 'race,' embraced a belief that the members of the majority group were superior to all others as a result of the characteristics inherent to their 'race.' Simply put, racial nationalism is nationalism centered on racist prejudice and hatred. Racial antisemitism is anti-Jewish prejudice or hatred based on perceived biological and/or racial differences. Bloch recognized the rising tide of racially defined nationhood and the virulent prejudice that almost always accompanied it as a profound threat both to Habsburg Jewry and to the Monarchy itself. He believed, nevertheless, that if the Austrian state could introduce reforms that satisfied the various nationalities, and those peoples then developed a sense of unity as citizens of a state that treated them equally, such developments would not only ensure Austria's survival, but also reduce ethnic hatred in general, and antisemitism in particular.

---

10 In the US today, people most commonly use the term race to distinguish among human beings of European, African, and Asian origin (among other groups); it is basically a proxy for skin color, and a poor one at that. In Bloch's time, many Europeans and those of European origin also divided themselves into so-called races, the major ones being: Germans/Nordics, Latins (French, Italians and Spaniards), Slavs, Gypsies, (who now identify as Roma or Sinti), and, according to some, Jews. The fact that the very definition of 'white' (i.e. anyone with predominantly European ancestry, including Jews) that most people use today did not exist one hundred years ago makes clear that race, like ethnicity, culture, and religion, is a form of identity that people construct and that lacks a meaningful basis in physical or biological reality. The fact that race is constructed makes racial prejudice no less real or damaging.

Some Habsburg Jews claimed that assimilation would save them from antisemitism. Assimilation is an incredibly complex term and requires a definition. According to *The American Heritage Dictionary of the English Language* (4th ed.,: 2000), assimilation means "to absorb (immigrants or a culturally distinct group) into the prevailing culture." One can then ask what specific processes define absorption, and at what point has it occurred, which of course must be different in each individual society under discussion. For the purposes of this book, assimilation is defined as a process with many stages, a continuum-like spectrum of behavior that, in the particularly complicated case of Austrian Jews, ran the gamut from, as an initial step, having German language—or Czech or Polish—as a mother tongue (as opposed to Yiddish), to full acculturation, another difficult term that is defined here as the absorption not only of the language but of all outward cultural forms of another ethnic group in an attempt to 'blend in,' and, finally, to religious conversion, an act independent of other aspects of culture. In theory, the final end point on the continuum was full assimilation, defined for Habsburg Jews as complete absorption into another ethnic community through full acculturation, conversion, intermarriage and the abandonment of any identification by the individual with a separate collective Jewish existence. However, Habsburg Jews as a group could not achieve full assimilation because the other peoples had no interest in absorbing them in such a manner. Many Jews in Bloch's time either supported or opposed Jewish assimilation without actually defining it other than as a vague notion of fitting in.

From the outset, Bloch asserted that Jews' attempt to assimilate, to find acceptance as members of another ethnic group, had not only failed but had also increased the enmity that they themselves faced. Instead, he called on Austrian Jews to regard themselves not as Germans, Czechs, or Poles of the Jewish faith, but as members of a separate ethnic group based on religion and a shared history. In addition, Jews were to define themselves as part of the Austrian civic nation. Bloch hoped the other Austrian peoples would embrace a similarly hyphenated conception of their own ethnic and civic identities. His call for a renewed Jewish ethnic consciousness thus related directly to his idea of a civic Austrian consciousness. This book examines these concepts and demonstrates the close relationship between them.

Bloch did not use the phrase 'civic consciousness' to describe his concept, nor did he offer a formal definition of civic culture. Civic consciousness, as it applies to Bloch's vision, refers simply to a sense of unity that people feel based on the fact that they are citizens of the same state, as opposed to ties that link members of an ethno-cultural or religious group. His concept of civic consciousness, which he referred to as 'Austrian state patriotism,' resembles what Jürgen Habermas a century later called constitutional patriotism, namely "a form of patriotism crystallized around the democratic constitutional state."[11]

This Austrian civic consciousness bears some similarity to ideas put forth by Austro-German liberals, particularly in its commitment to the principles of the *Rechtsstaat*, namely civil equality, the rule of law, and constitutional government. However, among several differences, one stands out. Bloch's vision for Austria was free of any notions of German cultural superiority. He viewed all the Habsburg cultures as having equal worth and deserving equal treatment from the state. Pieter Judson has shown that Austro-German liberalism, which on the surface claimed cultural neutrality and argued that ethnic and cultural identities were purely secondary, private forms of awareness, also contained a firm belief in the pre-eminence of German *Kultur und Wissenschaft*, and envisioned a profoundly German mission for Austria.[12] Bloch, however, recognized that such an orientation was inconsistent with the principles of equality upon which the Austrian *Rechtsstaat* he envisioned could rest.

Bloch sought a solution to the 'nationalities question,' which he believed threatened the existence of the Habsburg Monarchy. Why the Monarchy collapsed is one of the primary questions of Habsburg historiography. Some historians have argued that in 1914 Austria-Hungary remained a viable, functioning state that retained the loyalty

---

[11] Jürgen Habermas, "Historical Consciousness and Post-Traditional Identity: The Federal Republic's Orientation to the West," in Habermas, *The New Conservatism: Cultural Criticism and the Historians' Debate*, Shierry Weber Nicholsen, ed. and trans. (Cambridge: MIT Press, 1989), pp. 249–67. Quoted from p. 257.

[12] Pieter Judson, *Exclusive Revolutionaries: Liberal Politics, Social Experience and National Identity in the Austrian Empire, 1848–1914* (Ann Arbor: University of Michigan Press, 1996).

of most of its citizens. Thus, outside forces, above all military defeat in a major war caused the Monarchy's destruction in 1918. Other scholars have characterized the Habsburg state as a rotting anachronism that imploded under the weight of its internal contradictions and could not have long survived in an age of nationalism under any circumstances.

This book seeks to shift the focus of the debate. It links the issue of Austria's viability to the question of identity, rather than to the strength of the regime. The long-term viability of a state rests not on the vitality of its governmental system or the support it possesses in a given moment, but in its ability to create a sense of community among its citizens. As Robert Kann has argued, Austria-Hungary disintegrated in large part because its peoples lacked a common consciousness independent of the Habsburgs.[13] Kann contended that the history of the Habsburg Monarchy was marked by this "imperfectly developed sense of community."[14] According to Kann, Austria disappeared in large part because its peoples possessed an "insufficient sense of community...the monarchy failed to develop a concept of a typical Austrian man. Success in this respect might have possibly prevented dissolution, and would certainly have boded well for future reunion."[15] This book examines conceptions of a common Austrian identity proposed during the crucial last decades of its existence. It thus tackles an issue at the center of Austrian historiography.

Historians have debated the causes of Austria-Hungary's destruction virtually since the day it happened.[16] Until the 1980s, most Western historians argued that nationalism and the drive of its peoples for independence weakened the Dual Monarchy and made its disappearance likely, if not inevitable. These forces, in the view of this interpretation, rather than the First World War, were primarily respon-

---

[13] Robert A. Kann, *The Habsburg Monarchy: A Study in Integration and Disintegration* (New York: Praeger, 1957).

[14] Ibid., p. 6.

[15] Ibid., p. 193. See also pp. 6, 120–1, 124, 189, where Kann made similar statements.

[16] For a more detailed chronology of the Monarchy's historiography over the last century, see Steven Beller, *Francis Joseph* (London: Longman, 1996), pp. 3–9.

sible for the dissolution of Austria-Hungary.[17] Yet, as late as 1917, almost none of the nationalist leaders in the Monarchy sought independence or the overthrow of the dynasty.[18] Historians cannot assume that the forces of nationalism doomed Austria-Hungary to be vanquished. The Monarchy fell after suffering defeat in a long, destructive war.

In the last two decades, historians have identified a number of institutions and ideas, including the Catholic Church, the supraethnic spirit of the Habsburg officer corps, the Monarchy's success as a free-trade area, the Austrian bureaucracy's commitment to upholding the law, and the strength of the Austrian *Rechtsstaat*, whose vitality has altered the traditional picture of Austria-Hungary as an anachronism destined for destruction.[19] These and many other recent works echo Alan Sked's thesis that the pre-1914 Dual Monarchy remained viable. Defeat in war, not national enmity, destroyed it in November 1918.[20]

---

17 See, among others: A.J.P. Taylor, *The Habsburg Monarchy, 1809–1918* (Chicago: University of Chicago Press, 1948); Oskar Jászi, *The Dissolution of the Habsburg Monarchy* (Chicago: University of Chicago Press, 1929); Robert A. Kann, *The Multinational Empire: Nationalism and National Reform in the Habsburg Monarchy, 1848–1918*, 2 vols. (New York: Columbia University Press, 1950); C.A. Macartney, *The Habsburg Empire, 1790–1918* (New York: Macmillan, 1969). Arthur J. May, *The Hapsburg Monarchy, 1867–1914* (Cambridge: Harvard University Press, 1951) provides an early exception to this pattern, arguing that the war itself, not nationalism, destroyed the Monarchy.

18 Alan Sked, *The Decline and Fall of the Habsburg Empire, 1815–1918* (London: Longman, 1989), pp. 230–2.

19 John Boyer, *Political Radicalism in Late Imperial Vienna: Origins of the Christian Social Movement, 1848–1897* (Chicago: University of Chicago Press, 1981), *Culture and Political Crisis in Vienna: Christian Socialism in Power, 1897–1918* (Chicago: University of Chicago Press, 1995); Gary Cohen, *Education and Middle-Class Society in Imperial Austria, 1848–1918* (West Lafayette, IN: Purdue University Press, 1996); István Deák, *Beyond Nationalism, A Social and Political History of the Habsburg Officer Corps, 1848–1918* (New York: Oxford, 1990); David Good, *The Economic Rise of the Habsburg Empire, 1750–1914* (Berkeley: University of California Press, 1984); Waltraud Heindl, *Gehorsame Rebellen: Bürokratie und Beamte in Österreich 1780 bis 1848* (Vienna: Böhlau, 1991); James Shedel, "Fin de Siècle or Jahrhundertwende: The Question of an Austrian Sonderweg," in Steven Beller, ed., *Rethinking Vienna 1900* (New York: Berghahn Books, 2001), pp. 80–104.

20 István Deák, "Comparing Apples and Pears: Centralization, Decentralization and Ethnic Policy in the Habsburg and Soviet Armies," p. 239; Conference Remarks, by Tofik Islamov, p. 12; Dennison Rusinow, "Ethnic Politics in the Habsburg Monarchy and Successor States: Three Answers to the National Question," p. 255, in Richard L. Rudolph and David F. Good eds., *Nationalism and Empire: The Habsburg Monarchy and the Soviet Union* (New York: St. Martin's Press, 1992).

According to this 'revisionist' school, on the eve of the First World War, the dynastic idea, buttressed by the rule of law, the granting of universal male suffrage at least in the Austrian half of the Monarchy, and the conclusion of nationality compromises on the provincial level in Moravia (1905), Bukovina (1910), and Galicia (1914), retained the strength to keep Austria-Hungary together at least under relatively normal circumstances.[21]

These revisionists provide an important correction to the older school by arguing that the rising tide of nationalism in the twentieth century had not made the Monarchy's demise inevitable. Gary Cohen provided an excellent summary of this revisionist trend and rightly called for an abandonment of the traditional, hyper-negative picture of pre-1914 Austria, arguing "it is long overdue that we abandon the old portrait, which envisioned a rigid governmental structure that could not adapt significantly to changes in society after the 1870s and 1880s."[22]

Sked, however, claimed that it required a long and particularly devastating war to destroy an otherwise stable and sound Austria-Hungary.[23] He ignored the fact that military defeat alone does not explain why the peoples rejected the multiethnic state along with the dynasty. For example, although the German and Russian monarchies also fell as a result of defeat in the First World War, Germany and Russia continued to exist, albeit in different forms, as territorial states while Austria-Hungary disappeared from the map. Nationalism in Germany

---

21 On these compromises, see Gerald Stourzh, *Die Gleichberechtigung der Nationalitäten in der Verfassung und Verwaltung Österreichs, 1848–1918* (Vienna: Österreichische Akademie, 1985). In another article, Stourzh described how conflicts over improper voting (i.e. a German voting in the Czech curia or vice versa) in Moravia after the compromise in that province led to a 1907 decision by the Imperial Court that the state had the right to use 'objective criteria' to determine a citizen's nationality. He argued that these compromises, thanks to the above court case and similar rulings, led directly to what became the interwar racial policy of Central European states, namely that the government determined the ethnicity of individuals. This policy brought the most horrible consequences for Jews after 1933. See Gerald Stourzh, "Ethnic Attribution in Late Imperial Austria: Good Intentions, Evil Consequences," in Ritchie Robertson & Edward Timms, eds., *The Habsburg Legacy: National Identity in Historical Perspective* (Edinburgh: Edinburgh University Press, 1994), pp. 67–83. On the 1907 court case, see p. 74.

22 Gary Cohen, "Neither Absolutism nor Anarchy: New Narratives on Society and Government in Late Imperial Austria," *Austrian History Yearbooks* 29 (1998), pp. 37–61, quotation on p. 61.

23 Sked, pp. 264–5.

and Communism in Russia (perhaps aided by Russian nationalism) provided a legitimating ideology so that enough of their respective peoples either fought for or at least passively accepted their continued existence, even without their dynasties. Austria-Hungary disappeared as a state along with its dynasty because it failed to provide itself with an ideological legitimacy to exist without the Habsburgs.

The breakdown of the state machinery that accompanied the Monarchy's military defeat in the fall of 1918 crippled the existing *Staatsidee* (idea of the state). Practical reasons for the Habsburg state's existence, such as the *Rechtsstaat* and the provincial compromises so carefully crafted before the war, lost their validity with the collapse of the functioning institutions of government around which they had been constructed. The dynastic idea was all that remained to justify the continuation of Austria-Hungary. No longer pushed along by the inertia of a functioning state, in the fall of 1918 the peoples of the Dual Monarchy chose nationalism over a discredited dynasty as the organizing principle around which to build their states. They did so because they lacked a feeling of community and a common civic identity binding them to one another and to the multiethnic state they had shared. The ideas of Bloch, had the Habsburg government chosen to fully embrace them, could perhaps have provided that common identity.

Steven Beller has recently countered the revisionist school by arguing that Austria-Hungary's absolute reliance on the dynasty as its legitimating *Staatsidee*, a policy dictated from above by the Habsburgs, was in itself a fundamental weakness because it prevented the formation of a common supraethnic identity and civic patriotism.[24] In a similar vein,

---

[24] Beller, *Francis Joseph*. For a more sympathetic portrayal of Franz Joseph, see Jean-Paul Bled, *Franz Joseph* (Cambridge, MA: Blackwell Publishers, 1992). See also Bled, "Les Allemandes d'Autriche et la Question Nationale (1850–1918)," *Revue d'Allemagne et des pays de langue allemande*, 28 (1996), pp. 71–86. For an analysis that focused specifically on Franz Joseph's relationship with Hungary, see András Gerő, *Emperor Francis Joseph, King of the Hungarians* (Boulder, CO: Social Science Monographs, 2001). Most recently, Mark Cornwall reviewed Beller's and Sked's interpretations of the Monarchy's fall and endorsed the Beller view as the most persuasive. Cornwall, "Disintegration and Defeat: The Austro-Hungarian Revolution" in *The Last Years of Austria-Hungary* 2nd (revised) ed., Cornwall, ed. (Exeter: University of Exeter Press, 2002), pp. 167–96, see pp. 168–9. This essay offered a broad analysis of the political situation in the last months of Austria-Hungary and documented the breakdown of Habsburg authority.

Solomon Wank declared, "apart from support for imperial ambitions and maintaining the military capacity needed to survive in the international arena, there was no coherent *Staatsidee* that bound together the diverse domains of the Habsburgs."[25] Bloch's strident calls to create such bonds, and his growing pessimism by the turn of the century over Austria's failure to do so provide evidence in support of Beller's and Wank's assessment of the ill-health of political and civic life in the Monarchy. Bloch becomes the exception that proves the rule, in that while he desperately believed in the need for Austria to develop a common civic identity, he found himself unable to garner much support outside the Austrian Jewish community.

The Habsburgs consistently sought to nourish dynastic loyalty and feared the spread of state patriotism and the development of a common Austrian identity. For example, the following apocryphal allegory demonstrates this mindset: Emperor Franz I, when told that one of his subjects was an Austrian patriot, asked "but is he a patriot for me?"[26] Franz, just like his grandson, Emperor Franz Joseph, seemed to prefer that citizens express a personal loyalty to him as an individual rather than a state patriotism and identification with the Austrian state as an institution.

During the neo-absolutist period that followed Franz Joseph's accession and the defeat of the revolution in 1849, the government enacted some educational reforms with an eye towards developing a greater loyalty to the state. Led by the energetic efforts of Josef Alexander Helfert, one of the chief assistants to Minister for Education Count Leo Thun-Hohenstein, the government created the *Institut für Österreichische Geschichtsforschung*, which Helfert envisioned would train scholars as historians for the study of the history of the Austrian Monarchy.[27] He hoped to inculcate in these young scholars a sense of

---

25 Solomon Wank, "Some Reflections on the Habsburg Empire and Its Legacy in the Nationalities Question," *Austrian History Yearbook*, 28 (1997), pp. 131–46, quotation on p. 137.

26 Quoted in Taylor, *The Habsburg Monarchy*, p. 22.

27 Walter Leitsch, "East Europeans Studying History in Vienna (1855–1918), in Dennis Deletant & Harry Hanak, eds. *Historians as Nation-Builders: Central and South-East Europe* (London: Macmillan, 1988), pp. 139–156. See p. 141. For more on the Institute itself, see Alphons Lhotsky, *Geschichte des Instituts für Österreicische Geschichtsforschung, 1854–1954* (Graz: H. Böhlaus Nachf, 1954).

Austrian patriotism, but this was to be a purely dynastic patriotism.[28] While the Institute's faculty did teach with this mission in mind at the outset, it began relatively quickly to focus on the professional training of scholars of history and related disciplines, and did not contribute in a meaningful way to an increased loyalty to the Monarchy.[29]

The Institute represented an effort by the state to inculcate Austrian patriotism, at least among potential scholars of history; however, the kind of patriotism Helfert envisioned differed sharply from that of Bloch. Whereas the latter envisioned an Austrian civic nationalism based on equality and civil rights guaranteed by a constitutional and democratic system of government, Helfert, a conservative, believed that the peoples should celebrate the benefits they passively received as Habsburg subjects. He hoped to build a common identity that would strengthen the centralized, German-dominated, neo-absolutist system he served.[30] Helfert's concept of Austrian patriotism was based on that form of government, and thus could not have provided the basis for a state patriotism and a common feeling of being Austrian when an overwhelming majority of Austrians rejected that system.

Education in post-1867 Austria continued to concentrate on strengthening the devotion of the subject to the dynasty, as demonstrated by the title of the history textbook commonly used in Austrian schools, *What the Emperor Francis Joseph Did for his Peoples*, and failed to inculcate a sense of civic identity based on common citizenship and active participation in the state and society in which the peoples lived.[31]

---

[28] Joseph Alexander Helfert, *Über Nationalgeschichte und den gegenwärtigen Stand ihrer Pflege in Oesterreich* (Prague: Calve, 1854).

[29] Leitsch, p. 142.

[30] See Joseph Alexander Helfert, *Oesterreich und die Nationalitäten: Ein offenes Wort an Herrn Franz Palacky* (Vienna: C. Gerold, 1850). In this criticism of Palacký's federalization plan, Helfert extolled the benefits centralized government brought to the Monarchy. For more on Palacký, see Chapter 5.

[31] Beller, *Francis Joseph*, p. 227. For a more broader discussion of education in Austria and its emphasis on strengthening dynastic fealty, see Jászi, pp. 435–9. For an alternate view of Austrian education, see Shedel, p. 103. He asserted that Austrian teachers highlighted the concept of the Monarchy as a *Rechtsstaat*, and cited a guide for Austrian teachers written by Ludwig Fleischer, *Österreichischer Bürgerkund: Ein Lehr- und Hilfsbuch für Bürgerschulen und die mit denselben verbundenen Einjährigen Lehrkurse*, 4th ed. (Vienna, 1908), in note 29 of p. 103.

In 1913 Otto Bauer decried the fact that the schools continued to present Austrian history such that "the fate of the state and the peoples appears dependent on the talents, good will and luck of the individual rulers."[32] Although such a presentation of events had a certain basis in reality, it did not serve to cultivate a supraethnic Austrian consciousness among students.

Increasingly throughout Franz Joseph's reign, his government promoted a specifically dynastic loyalty through public religious ceremonies, official visits by the monarch to the outlying regions of the Monarchy, and commemorations such as those for the 25th anniversary of the Emperor's ascension to the Habsburg throne (1873), the 25th anniversary of his wedding to Empress Elizabeth (1879), and the 1898 and especially the 1908 Jubilees marking the 50th and 60th anniversaries respectively of his ascension.[33] Most conspicuously, the 1908 Jubilee parade, coming only one year after the introduction of universal male suffrage in Cisleithania, contained no celebration whatsoever of the constitution, democratic institutions, or of Austria as a state in any sense apart from the Habsburg dynasty. Rather than try to raise a civic Austrian consciousness, the parade focused solely on personal fealty to Franz Joseph and his family.[34]

In the summer of 1918, just months before its collapse, the Monarchy belatedly realized the need to create a state patriotism based on something in addition to feelings of allegiance to the House of Habsburg. The government tried to build morale among soldiers (it attempted nothing similar with the civilian population) by initiating a campaign of what it referred to as 'patriotic education.' The campaign emphasized the advantages of living in a large state that protected the

---

[32] Otto Bauer, *Geschichte Oesterreichs*, 2nd ed. (Vienna: Verlag von Robert Danneberg, 1913), p. 4.

[33] Daniel Unowsky, "Creating Patriotism: Imperial Celebrations and the Cult of Franz Joseph," *Österreichische Zeitschrift für Geschichtswissenschaften*, 9 (1998) No. 2, pp. 280–93.

[34] Steven Beller, "Kraus's Firework: State Consciousness Raising in the 1908 Jubilee Parade in Vienna and the Problem of Austrian Identity," in Maria Bucur and Nancy Wingfield, eds. *Staging the Past: The Politics of Commemoration in Habsburg Central Europe, 1848 to the Present* (West Lafayette, IN: Purdue University Press, 2001), pp. 46–71. See p. 69.

equality and freedom of each of its nationalities.[35] That campaign, however, proved unable to hold the Monarchy together after the defeat of the Central Powers in the fall of 1918.

Austria-Hungary was not an unfortunate and inevitable victim of the rising tide of nationalism. In fact, its political system actively encouraged rivalry and distrust among the ethnic groups by placing them in a zero sum game in which they battled each other for slices of the pie.[36] This system sought to maintain "a more-or-less balanced and equitable distribution of dissatisfaction among the more important nationalities."[37] An enduring solution to the nationalities question would have required the comprehensive restructuring of the political system along democratic and federalist lines such that dynastic power would have been drastically reduced.[38] Moreover, such a solution would have necessitated political compromise and cooperation among the Habsburg nationalities, the very thing Franz Joseph had worked so hard to prevent because he recognized that it would have threatened his personal political authority and the entire monarchic system on which it rested.[39] Franz Joseph and his predecessors, because they acted to protect their dynastic power at the expense of the interests of the state, must be held responsible for the inability of the multiethnic polity to survive the fall of its dynasty.[40] The peoples of Austria-Hungary never

---

35 Mark Cornwall, "The Dissolution of Austria-Hungary," in Mark Cornwall, ed., *The Last Years of Austria-Hungary* (Exeter: University of Exeter Press, 1990), pp. 117–42. See p. 137.

36 Wank, "Some Reflections on the Habsburg Empire and Its Legacy in the Nationalities Question," p. 146. See also Jászi, *The Dissolution of the Habsburg Monarchy.*

37 Rusinow, p. 254.

38 Wank, "Some Reflections on the Habsburg Empire and Its Legacy in the Nationalities Question," p. 138.

39 Beller, *Francis Joseph*, pp. 227–30.

40 In a perfect example of his placing dynastic interests over those of the state, Franz Joseph, during the Austro-Prussian War of 1866, sent his best general, his cousin Archduke Albrecht, south to the Italian theater, which had been rendered meaningless by the Emperor's agreement to cede Venetia to Italy via Napoleon III in case of a victory. Franz Joseph assigned an inferior general, Benedek, to fight the main Prussian enemy in the north, because he feared that the defeat of a Habsburg commander on a particular battlefield would damage Habsburg honor, irrespective of the interest of the state in defeating Prussia and maintaining its leadership of Germany. See Sked, p. 181, and Taylor, p. 127.

developed the common civic consciousness envisioned by Bloch in large part because Franz Joseph himself worked to keep them divided so as to preserve as much authority as possible in his own hands.

While the lack of a common identity among its peoples did not directly cause the Habsburgs to lose their throne in November 1918 (defeat in war did that), this failing did prevent the continuation of that state under another form of government without them. Oskar Jászi made this argument in his seminal work, one that comprehensively analyzed the political system of Austria-Hungary, as did Kann in his analysis of the Monarchy's disintegration. Furthermore, Beller and Wank among others have offered variations on this theme more recently. This book neither examines the political and social institutions of Austria-Hungary, nor seeks to prove that the Monarchy was not a 'true' democracy, after all what pre-1914 state was? Rather my work builds on the analyses of those mentioned above by offering a history of the ideas put forth by thinkers, Bloch in particular, who recognized the lack of a supraethnic identity binding together that diverse society and sought to develop one.

Bloch was not the only Habsburg citizen, however, to seek an answer to the Austrian nationalities question. Austro-Marxists such as Renner and Bauer also wanted to preserve Austria-Hungary. They saw it as a large, unified economy that could be more easily made socialist than an indeterminate number of successor states. Unlike Bloch, they were not overly concerned with creating an Austrian identity *per se* because they hoped that class-consciousness would unify the workers of a socialist Austria-Hungary into a single proletariat, albeit one organized into cultural-linguistic groups (a Germanic cultural bias was nonetheless implicit in their writings and the policies they advanced, particularly regarding the organization of the multiethnic Austrian Social Democratic Party). The state would ensure cultural and linguistic rights for each nationality by, for example, educating students in their mother tongue, and thus defuse ethnic nationalism's disruptive potential. Renner built his reform plans for Austria around the idea of individual cultural rights or 'personal autonomy.' This idea reflected his belief that taking care of the cultural and linguistic needs of individuals and, in particular, improving the material lot of the workers would satisfy the collective interests of the peoples and defuse the destructive power of nationalism.

Most other reformers, despite their very real differences of opinion on specific issues, were moderate nationalists who endorsed the decentralization of Austria along the borders of either the historic province-kingdoms, as did Palacký (for most of his career) and Eötvös, or those of ethnically defined territories, as did Popovici and Holovatskyj. Their different approaches derived from the political position of the ethnic group with which its author identified.

Overall, these moderate nationalist reformers were less concerned than Bloch with the creation of a specifically Austrian identity that could transcend ethnic ties, although most of them endorsed such a development either implicitly or explicitly. These leaders were first and foremost concerned with the interests of their individual nationalities, which, in their view, were consistent with a reformed Austria-Hungary. To them, Austria remained necessary mostly because it protected the small Central European nations from Germany and Russia, an argument that implies that the peoples of Central Europe would seek to form nation-states, rather than remain bound together as multiethnic Austria-Hungary, were they not surrounded by more powerful neighbors. The various reform proposals presented by the moderate nationalists thus conditioned their support for Austria's existence on geo-political circumstances.

Unlike other reformers of his period, Bloch argued that Austria-Hungary should exist not as a means to a political end, but as an end in itself—not in spite of its diversity, but because of it. He saw the creation of a supraethnic Austrian nation in the hearts and minds of its citizens as much more than a potential by-product of a set of constitutional reforms whose primary purpose was to save the Monarchy. Bloch considered the development of a sense of nationhood among its diverse peoples to be the most important reason that the Austrian state existed in the first place. Rather than apologize for multiethnic Austria's existence in an era of nationalism, Bloch aggressively promoted its potential to serve as a model for the accommodation of ethnic consciousness within the framework of an overarching civic unity. He asserted that a tolerant, liberal, multiethnic state could provide a counterweight to ethnic nationalism and the desire for homogeneous nation-states that was to prove so destructive to Central Europe in the 1930s and 40s.

Chapter 1 briefly reviews various explanations offered by scholars for how national consciousness, i.e. the feeling that an individual belongs to a nation, has developed in general as well as in specific cases. It also examines whether one can accurately distinguish between such concepts as civic and ethnic national identities, a distinction at the heart of Bloch's vision of an Austrian identity. Chapter 2 analyzes the vision of a reformed Austria put forth by Fischhof, in order to examine it in its own right and also to compare it to that of Bloch. Chapter 3 looks at Bloch's analysis of racial nationalism and, in particular, the effects racial antisemitism had on Jewish attempts to assimilate into the dominant culture(s) surrounding them in the various regions of Austria-Hungary. Chapter 4 explores Bloch's response to ethnic hatred and antisemitism: the cultivation of a common civic Austrian identity. Chapter 5 discusses the views of the six selected political thinkers previously mentioned on the Austrian nationalities question between 1846 and 1918 both in terms of the reform plans they proposed and what form of Austrian consciousness they envisioned.

Chapter 1

'WHAT IS A NATION?': THEORETICAL ISSUES RELATING TO THE FORMATION OF NATIONAL IDENTITIES

This book presents a history of ideas. It examines how selected political thinkers envisioned a common identity for the multiethnic society in which they lived. They sought to create a consciousness, to build a nation. An analysis of such ideas requires a discussion of the meaning and nature of national identities and nationalism in the abstract before it can examine a specific case of one society. Nationalism is a slippery concept. This book will define it here in the broadest of terms, simply as a political, ideological, or cultural movement organized around a group's shared identity. Nationalisms that emerged in the nineteenth and twentieth centuries often drew on previously existing historical ties among a given people. Nevertheless, scholars and students of nationalism cannot ignore the role of nationalistically-minded thinkers and politicians who sought to inculcate a common consciousness among individuals who share or, equally importantly, believe that they share certain characteristics, including but not limited to: language, religion, culture, and/or descent (i.e. tribal or so-called racial ties). Nationalism can take various forms depending on how the group under discussion defines itself. It can be inclusive or exclusionary, peaceful or aggressive, political or non-political, and in fact the same group's nationalism can differ from one era to the next.[41]

---

[41] For a comprehensive analysis of theories of nationalism over the past three decades, see Anthony Smith, *Nationalism and Modernism: A Critical Survey of Recent Theories of Nations and Nationalism* (London: Routledge, 1998). Unless otherwise noted all the authors referred to in this chapter are social scientists who have studied the phenomenon of nationalism.

In a lecture at the Sorbonne on March 11, 1882, Ernest Renan asked the question "What is a nation?"[42] His well-known answer provides an appropriate starting point for our discussion here, as it represented the beginning of the modern debate on the nature of nations and national identities. Renan explained that a nation exists as a feeling, a consciousness, a state of mind. He defined a nation as a

> a grand solidarity constituted by the sentiment of sacrifices which one has made and those one is disposed to make again. It supposes a past, it renews itself especially in the present by a tangible deed: the approval, the desire, clearly expressed, to continue the communal life. The existence of a nation (pardon this metaphor!) is an everyday plebiscite.[43]

By this Renan meant that a nation exists if and when a broad majority of the people defined as members say that it does. Renan's definition directly challenged the concept of the nation as a natural outgrowth of a pre-existing entity, simply a modern form of a particular ethnos or tribe. He acknowledged that a nation "supposes a past," but his use of the word supposes demonstrated his contention that a conscious, intellectual process forms a nation.

In a book that appeared approximately one century later, Benedict Anderson coined his own phrase, one that has become even more widely quoted among scholars than Renan's "everyday plebiscite." Anderson described nations as "imagined communities." He did not mean that because nations are imagined that they are not real, but rather that, echoing Renan, a nation exists primarily in the consciousness of its people, that it is consciously created and neither primordial nor biological. People within a national community imagine or believe that they are connected in some meaningful way with their fellow co-nationals, even if they have never met and have no personal or tangible connection. Anderson explained national identity formation as a

---

42 E.J. Hobsbawm, *Nations and Nationalism since 1780* (Cambridge: Cambridge University Press, 1990), p. 2.

43 Ernest Renan, "What is a Nation?," in *The Dynamics of Nationalism, L.L. Snyder* (D. Van Nostrand: Princeton, 1964), pp. 9–10.

cultural and intellectual phenomenon. The growth of literacy and print capitalism created a common sense of belonging among the members of a population in a contiguous territory that shared a common literary language.[44] Ernest Gellner agreed with Anderson that nations were "imagined," although he claimed that industrialization and the concomitant need to have an economy in which the actors could communicate efficiently created national communities built around a common language and cultural points of reference.[45]

Whereas Gellner and Anderson viewed nations to a large degree as entities constructed by their environments, Anthony Smith emphasized the pre-modern roots of modern nations. He rejected the approaches of Gellner and Anderson, which he characterized as the modernist theory of nationalism, and claimed that such analyses "fail to account for the historical depth and spatial reach of the ties that underpin modern nations because they have no theory of ethnicity and its relationship to modern nationalism."[46] Smith argued that nations are not solely the products of the modern age, the Industrial Revolution, print capitalism, the bureaucratic state, and/or other relatively recent phenomena.[47] Instead, he pointed to the centuries-old roots of contemporary nations in older communities, and their reliance in large part on pre-existing myths, symbols, cultures and traditions. "Put simply, modern nations are not as 'modern' as modernists would have us believe...nations require ethnic cores if they are to survive. If they lack one, they must 're-invent' one."[48]

Scholars of nationalism such as Anderson, Gellner, and Smith have largely agreed that the consciousness of a common identity among the members is central to the creation of a nation, although they disagree on whether or not that consciousness must derive from a set of pre-modern, kinship-based ties. After the tide of theoretical works in the early and mid-1980s, a series of case studies including the influential

---

44 Anderson, *Imagined Communities.*

45 Ernest Gellner, *Nations and Nationalism* (Oxford: Blackwell, 1983).

46 Smith, *Nationalism and Modernism*, p. 46.

47 Anthony Smith, *The Ethnic Origins of Nationalism* (New York: Basil Blackwell, 1986).

48 Ibid., p. 212.

works of Rogers Brubaker and Liah Greenfeld demonstrated how different the process of forming a nation can be from one case to another. Greenfeld analyzed how the English, French, German, Russian and American national communities have developed their respective identities.[49] She rejected the notion, exemplified by Gellner and Anderson, that the appearance of national communities can be explained by a single unifying theory. According to Greenfeld, national identities and feelings of nationalism have resulted from the desire to create a fulfilling self-image; they were psychologically motivated and molded by political frameworks rather than economic forces.[50] She contended that national identities arose differently in these five cases because of different historical circumstances and contingencies, and summarized, "nationalism is not a uniform phenomenon."[51]

In his work, Brubaker juxtaposed the formation of standards of citizenship in France and Germany over the past two centuries.[52] Because both of these are nation-states, countries that serve as the political expression of a particular nation, the way each has defined its standards of citizenship says much about the way it has defined membership in the national community. Brubaker explained that in France, a sense of nationhood was political and civic, built around a centuries-old state. French nationhood, at least in its ideal form, derived from the Roman model. According to this formula, anyone can become French as long as he or she identifies as a member of the nation by actively participating in its civic and political process and adopting high French (i.e. Parisian) culture, part of which requires the abandonment of other cultural and linguistic traditions. Openness combined with a demand for total cultural assimilation defines French nationhood. In addition, the French state had existed for centuries before the development of French national consciousness, and by the end of seventeenth century it had gained its basic territorial shape. Thus, French society possessed

---

49 Liah Greenfeld, *Nationalism: Five Roads to Modernity* (Cambridge: Harvard University Press, 1992).

50 Ibid., pp. 487–91.

51 Ibid., p. 490.

52 Rogers Brubaker, *Citizenship and Nationhood in France and Germany* (Cambridge: Harvard University Press, 1992).

a common political experience upon which to base its unity as a nation. The French defined themselves as a nation of citizens who lived within a single set of borders and shared a culture. After 1792, when France wanted to spread its model of nationalism throughout Europe, its universalist pretensions ruled out an exclusionary conception of French nationhood.

In Germany, on the other hand, the circumstances were radically different. Germans lacked a similarly powerful common state in their post-medieval history. Their shared identity derived from a particularistic and non-political sense of Germanness based on language, culture, and historical traditions through the mid-nineteenth century, and increasingly on perceived racial ties after that.[53] Furthermore, while Frenchness emanated out from Paris, the center, German national feeling emanated most powerfully from the experiences of the German-Slav borderland, in which Germans who had migrated east during the previous centuries did not assimilate into the region's Slavic cultures, but fought to maintain a separate identity, especially in the cities they helped found. A German national identity had to encompass these borderland Germans. Thus, even after the founding of the German Empire in 1871, the definition of Germanness could not be based on common citizenship in a German state because millions of Germans who lived outside the borders of Imperial Germany were not citizens of that state. Nationhood for Germans therefore remained divorced from the concept of citizenship, one that could have potentially included Jews and other non-ethnic Germans (Danes in Schleswig, French in Alsace-Lorraine, Poles in Posen) within the German national community. Thus there existed German citizens who were not accepted by the majority as 'real' Germans. Such a situation reinforced a non-political definition of membership in the German nation. Increasingly by 1900 Germans did not accept the idea of assimilation as plausible because nationhood was

---

[53] One scholar has argued that the Holy Roman Empire did provide Germans with a civic and political basis for a common identity, but the destruction of that polity in 1806 at the hands of Napoleon fundamentally altered the nature of German identity and severed it from its civic foundation. See John Gagliardo, *Reich and Nation: The Holy Roman Empire as Idea and Reality, 1763–1806* (Bloomington, IN: Indiana University Press, 1980).

based on membership in the German Volk, a term that defined the German people as a racial group linked by blood as well as by a quasi-mystical bond, an inherited experience and consciousness one cannot possess unless he or she is born with it. Furthermore, even after 1871 many self-defined Germans in Central Europe lived outside Germany, which increased the need for an identity that could include them. Such an acute desire existed especially among many Germans in the Habsburg Monarchy, men such as Georg von Schönerer and Adolf Hitler, who could not stomach the idea of defining the German national community based on German citizenship, a definition that would exclude them but include Yiddish-speaking *Ostjuden* living in a *shtetl* in Posen.

Brubaker's analysis provides a historical explanation for why individuals who are raised in another national community can become French through an act of will, but have had a much harder time becoming German. Like Greenfeld, Brubaker emphasized the impact of circumstances and contingencies on the formation of a national consciousness. While incidents such as the Dreyfus Affair and the collaboration of some of the French with the Nazi extermination of Jews, Gypsies, and others during the Second World War caution against seeing the French as having been consistently inclusive, the basic distinction between how the two national communities have defined themselves over the last two centuries stands as generally accurate.

Both Brubaker and Greenfeld distinguished between ethnic and civic forms of national identity and nationalism. This dichotomy goes back to the work of Hans Kohn, one of "the twin founding fathers" (along with Carleton Hayes) of the academic study of nationalism.[54] Kohn himself did not use the words 'civic' and 'ethnic' in his analysis, but rather referred to the kind of nationalism found in the West and typified by the United States among others as "liberal nationalism."[55] He contrasted this "liberal nationalism," which was based on a definition of the national community that included all citizens, with what he referred to as Eastern nationalism (referring to Eastern Europe), based

---

54 Aira Kemiläinen, *Nationalism: Problems Concerning the Word, Concept and Classification* (Jyväskylä: Kustantajat, 1964), cited in Anderson, p. 4 and Hobsbawm, *Nations and Nationalism since 1780*, p. 3.

55 Hans Kohn, *The Idea of Nationalism: A Study in Its Origins and Background* (New York: Macmillan, 1946), p. 321.

on closed ethnic groups.[56] Although the Western democracies have obviously not always lived up to the standard of inclusion implied by the term liberal nationalism, Kohn used these as comparative terms rather than as absolutes.

More polemical works have continued to emphasize the distinction between ethnic and civic nations. For example, in his 1994 study of Yugoslavia Bogdan Denitch condemned without any qualification national identity based on ethnic origin, and declared, "the only possible kind of decent, modern democratic state is one that is, at the very least, defined as the state of all of its citizens, irrespective of national origin or religion."[57] Michael Ignatieff differentiated between an ethnic nation based on "inherited" ties and a civic nation that promoted a "rational attachment" based on political ideals.[58] However, not all scholars have accepted this type of normative distinction between ethnic and civic forms of national consciousness.

In a recent edited collection, *Theorizing Nationalism*, the contributors debated whether one can really differentiate between these two forms of nationalism and whether such a thing as civic nationalism really exists.[59] Bernard Yack took direct aim at Ignatieff in particular, not for his criticism of ethnic nationalism but rather for his characterization of civic nationalism as rational and apolitical in practice.[60] Canadian nationalism, for example, so often described as civic in contrast to ethnic *Québécois* nationalism also contains a powerful Anglo-Canadian cultural element alongside its political ideals.[61] Will Kymlicka similarly criticized Ignatieff's civic/ethnic distinction because it conflated ethnic with inclusive cultural national identities and denied the cultural aspects of civic nationalisms.[62] Kai Nielsen proclaimed "all nationalisms are

---

56 For a further discussion, see Smith, *Nationalism and Modernism*, pp. 126, 146.

57 Bogdan Denitch, *Ethnic Nationalism: The Tragic Death of Yugoslavia* (Minneapolis: University of Minnesota Press, 1994), p. 141.

58 Michael Ignatieff, *Blood and Belonging: Journeys into the New Nationalism* (New York: Farrar, Straus & Giroux, 1994), pp. 7–8.

59 Ronald Beiner, ed., *Theorizing Nationalism* (Albany: State University of New York Press, 1999).

60 Bernard Yack, "The Myth of the Civic Nation," pp. 103–118, in ibid.

61 Yack, p. 105.

62 Will Kymlicka, "Misunderstanding Nationalism," pp. 132–3, in Beiner, *Theorizing Nationalism*.

cultural nationalisms of one kind or another. There is no purely political conception of the nation, liberal or otherwise."[63]

These arguments made important points that guard against a rose-colored view of national identity in western democracies. Yack correctly recognized as an oversimplification a dichotomy that views civic nationalism as 'rational' and ethnic as 'emotional.' Perhaps a more useful distinction among the national identities of countries such as the U.S., Canada, Britain, and post-apartheid South Africa, as opposed to those of, for example, Japan, Germany, and South Korea, is that the former are, both in theory and largely in practice, inclusive—they do not exclude people based on inherited characteristics—while the latter, even though democratic, are exclusive in that those defined as outsiders find it virtually impossible to find acceptance as members of the nation, even if they actually receive citizenship (also a difficult hurdle for outsiders to overcome in those countries). One cannot move to Seoul and 'become Korean' in as complete a manner as an immigrant can become an American or a Canadian simply because the latter accepts a greater degree of heterogeneity within its ranks than does the former. The distinction becomes clearer when one adds to the second group the example of the Serbia, at least under Milosevic. As one scholar put it, "it is not possible to join an ethnic group as an act of will."[64] One must be born into it.

Thus, one can identify important differences between the two types of national consciousness. Civic nations, in theory and largely in practice, have to accept individuals who wish to join the group from the outside and allow them to become equal participants in the politi-

63 Kai Nielsen, "Cultural Nationalism, Neither Ethnic nor Civic," p. 127, in Beiner, *Theorizing Nationalism.*

64 Brian Barry, "Self-Government Revisited," p. 257, in Beiner, *Theorizing Nationalism.* The question of the Jews (and perhaps also the Armenians) serves as somewhat of an exception to Barry's statement because they form both an ethnic group and a religious community open to voluntary conversion (although some Jews define Jewishness differently than others). Such groups occupy a separate and unique position among the larger body of peoples. However, most established ethnic groups do not have a religion that encompasses its entire membership and is also unique to that group, even if a particular religion may be associated with an ethnicity. For example, even though the overwhelming majority of Poles are Catholic one can be Catholic without being Polish and vice versa, and becoming Catholic does not make one a Pole.

cal and governing process, whereas ethnic nations define which types of individuals are in or out based on inherited characteristics. American, Canadian, and British (although less than perhaps English, Scottish, or Welsh) are cultural identities as well as civic identities, but one can be a civic American, Canadian, or Briton without participating in the predominant culture. Almost all immigrants fit this description for at least a few years or even decades after they become members of the civic nation. This is less simple in France, which is inclusive in terms of civic nationality, but which demands a greater level of cultural assimilation than the aforementioned civic national communities. Rather than seeing civic nationalism as rational and ethnic nationalism as emotional, it makes more sense to distinguish between civic and ethnic national identities based on whom they include. Civic national identities fully and equally include of all citizens within a given territory (such territory can be a state or a region within a state) irrespective of their background, while ethnic nations only recognize as members residents of a given area if they possess a certain, unacquirable pedigree.

Civic nationalism simply means a form of nationalism, a feeling of solidarity, based on the bonds created among all the citizens in a state, territory or region. Civic nationalism explicitly rejects the concept of ethnic nationalism. Although most civic nations are democracies and participation in the political process strengthens the identification of the citizens with their nation, absolute inclusiveness is the defining characteristic of civic nationalism, even more than political participation. Civic nationalism is, at its core, simply any form of nationalism that does not recognize ethnicity, culture, language, religion, gender, sexual orientation, or any characteristic other than citizenship (which of course cannot be restricted according to any of the above characteristics) as criteria for membership. As long as the whole body of citizens see themselves and accept one another as members of one nation, they express a form of civic nationalism even if they live in a dictatorship or a monarchy, albeit a more limited one than do citizens in a democracy. Civic nationalism differs from patriotism in that it requires something in addition to mere loyalty to the state or ruler, namely the existence of a sense of community that unifies the citizens into a single nation.

A recent study by Nicholas Miller relied on the distinction between ethnic and civic nationalism to examine a case within the late Habsburg period.[65] Miller studied the political strategy of Serbs in Croatia between 1903 and 1914, during which time Croat and Serb political leaders created an electoral and governing coalition between the two major ethnic communities in the area. This coalition called for a civic concept of Croatian nationhood based on individual political rights according to which Serbs could maintain a separate ethnic identity and culture from that of the Croats while pledging their loyalty to a civic and territorial concept of Croatia. Among Serbs, this concept competed with another vision of Serbdom that sought only to remain isolated from the Croats until such time as they could become part of a Serbian nation-state that would protect their collective national existence. The two rival Serb parties in Croatia, the Independents, who endorsed a civic national identity, and the Radicals, who defended an ethnic national identity, made real the theoretical debate over the validity of making such a distinction between the two visions of nationhood. Although it did not survive the outbreak of the First World War, the coalition between the Serbian Independent Party and their Croatian partners tried to develop an ideology that protected the individual rights and shared interests of both ethnic groups as well as the collective needs of each one to preserve its culture and heritage. The coalition was founded on the idea of a multiethnic and civic Croatian nation.

More recently, political scientists have developed theoretical models for a type of national consciousness that would allow people to identify themselves both as individual citizens and members of ethnic groups. Ronald Beiner described two opposite theoretical poles of citizenship, and characterized them as the two sides of a "universalism/ particularism conundrum."[66] The universalist or "liberal" conception of citizenship focuses solely on the individual, and leads to "rootlessness" because it deprives individuals of any sense of community.[67] The particularist conception, also known as "communitarian," emphasizes group solidarity and the collective needs of a people to defend its identity.[68]

---

65 Nicholas J. Miller, *Between Nation and State: Serbian Politics in Croatia Before the First World War* (Pittsburgh: University of Pittsburgh Press, 1997).

66 Ronald Beiner, "Introduction: Why Citizenship Constitutes a Theoretical Problem in the Last Decade of the Twentieth Century," in Beiner, ed., *Theorizing Citizenship* (Albany: State University of New York Press, 1995), p. 12.

67 Ibid., pp. 12–13.

68 Ibid., p. 13.

The particularist pole itself breaks down into two options according to Beiner:

The first option is nationalism. In Beiner's view, nationalists generally define a nation as a network of social identities and shared cultural meanings. He explained that most nationalists reject the concept of a pluralistic nation, defined as one in which two or more peoples, each with a separate collective consciousness, can form a cohesive societal unit. For example, Roger Scruton contended that a worthwhile feeling of community requires "sanctity, intolerance, exclusion, and a sense that life's meaning depends on obedience, and also on vigilance against the enemy."[69] Multiculturalism is the second option. As Beiner described it, this vision argues that the state exists to serve the particularistic needs of the collective groups living within its borders, but not vice versa. Furthermore, he explained that multiculturalism rejects any more than the most limited identification of the various cultural groups with the state in which they reside and the larger population (outside their own ethnic group) among whom they live. These two poles, while different in practice, are similar in theory and multiculturalism can be seen as the nationalism of ethnic groups not powerful enough to break free of the state in which they live.

Beiner rejected universalism and both kinds of particularism as threats to the concept of a healthy citizenship, defined as "a political community that is reducible neither to an aggregation of individuals nor to a conjunction of identity-constituting groups." He offered a third alternative, called "republican" that emphasized "civic" ties, according to which citizens must adopt a larger set of norms and values based on political participation and rights rather than a common culture, religion, or any other characteristic that defines an ethnic group. Unlike, for example, French civic nationalism, such a concept divorces equal participation in the political community and membership in the nation from adoption of the majority culture. Beiner cites Habermas' term "constitutional patriotism" as encapsulating the meaning of his theoretical concept of a middle ground between ethnic and cultural forms

---

69 Roger Scruton, "In Defense of the Nation," in Scruton, *The Philosopher on Dover Beach* (Manchester, U.K.: Carcanet, 1990), pp. 299–337, quotation on p. 310, cited in Beiner, p. 22, n. 19.

of nationalism on the one hand and multiculturalism on the other.[70]

In a similar vein, Yael Tamir has endorsed a concept she termed "liberal nationalism" which seeks to balance the principles of democratic liberalism and its emphasis on universally applied individual rights with the rights of peoples as collective entities to preserve and develop their cultures.[71] She explained that national consciousness based on ethnicity, culture, language, and/or religion cannot be reduced to an irrational need that can be overcome, a mistake some cosmopolitan liberals and socialists have made.[72] Instead Tamir described such nationalism as part of a legitimate and healthy desire for bonds based on cultural familiarity. However, Tamir differentiated between national consciousness in general, which she saw as benign, and more extreme forms of nationalism that exhibited prejudice and advocated violence against outsiders. She supported the existence of non-racist national consciousness.

Furthermore, Tamir sought to moderate national prejudice and improve the climate in multiethnic societies by combining support for the rights and interests of groups with a strong emphasis on individual democratic rights. She discussed how, in practical terms, constitutional structures built around such a balance might operate. Tamir analyzed as one possibility the ideas of Arend Ljiphardt, a political scientist who developed a structural model for pluralistic democracies known as 'consociational democracy.' According to this model, units (normally organized around ethnic, cultural, and/or religious groups) acquire control over their own institutions such as schools, cultural and community centers, etc. These groups also receive proportionate representation in a common legislative body that deals with larger issues. Such a model helps to moderate ethnic tensions by acknowledging group identities, giving each group autonomous institutions in areas of particular importance, but then forcing the groups to cooperate in a broader arena through which they see first-hand their shared interests.[73] Tamir noted

---

70 Beiner, "Introduction," in *Theorizing Citizenship*, p. 14, see also pp. 7–8. See the introduction for Habermas' definition of constitutional patriotism.

71 Tamir, *Liberal Nationalism.*

72 See also Isaiah Berlin, "The Bent Twig: On the Rise of Nationalism," p. 248, in Berlin, *The Crooked Timber of Humanity* (London: John Murray, 1990).

73 Arend Ljiphardt, *Democracy in Plural Societies* (New Haven: Yale University Press, 1977), esp. pp. 10–11.

two potential obstacles that this model would have to overcome: the problem of minorities within territories assigned to one nationality, and the problem of immigration (both internal and external) that might alter the ethnic composition within a region.[74] As she noted, no perfect constitutional model exists for multiethnic societies, each country's system must be flexible enough to deal with its own unique set of cultural, social, political, and demographic circumstances.

Some scholars, like Scruton, have argued that nations can only exist in societies that display a high degree of cultural homogeneity. They reject the possibility of creating an inclusive civic national identity in a culturally pluralistic society. Gellner, for example, whose family lived through the failures of such an experiment both in Habsburg Austria and interwar Czechoslovakia, stated flatly that "genuine cultural pluralism" can no longer exist in industrial societies.[75]

However, civic nationalism and the related concept of constitutional patriotism can provide the ideological foundation for a nation that is both pluralistic and unified. Tamir contended that multiethnic states can exist and have cohesive unity as long as they allow for wide cultural autonomy for their peoples. National consciousness need not necessarily lead to the destruction of every multiethnic state.[76] Habermas eloquently made a similar point.

> Examples of multicultural societies like Switzerland and the United States demonstrate that a political culture in the seedbed of which constitutional principles are rooted by no means has to be based on all citizens sharing the same language or the same ethnic and cultural origins. Rather, the political culture must serve as the common denominator for a constitutional patriotism which simultaneously sharpens an awareness of the multiplicity and integrity of the different forms of life which coexist in a multicultural society.[77]

---

74 Tamir, pp. 156–58.

75 Gellner, *Nations and Nationalism*, p. 55.

76 Tamir, pp. 69–72.

77 Jürgen Habermas, "Citizenship and National Identity: Some Reflections on the Future of Europe," p. 264, in Beiner, *Theorizing Citizenship*.

Alfred Stepan claimed that by providing "a roof of rights over their heads," a multiethnic society can cultivate among its ethnic groups an identification with the state and a sense of civic national identity. He argued that civic and ethnic national identities can complement one another, and need not be mutually exclusive.[78]

This book relies on the distinction between ethnic and civic forms of nationhood, and characterizes Bloch's ideas as a form of civic nationalism. Bloch, however, did not himself use the term civic nationalism, which did not come into use until the middle of the twentieth century and is, strictly speaking, anachronistic in a discussion of Habsburg Austria. Nevertheless, such a term serves as a useful shorthand to describe the sense of nationhood he hoped to develop among Austrians. Bloch, building on the ideas of Fischhof, believed in the need to create an Austrian consciousness based on the shared rights of all citizens and the need to work together to support and protect the state that guaranteed those rights. This consciousness exemplified what would later become known as civic nationhood. Furthermore, Bloch condemned ethnic and racial prejudice as well as nationalism based solely on ethnic origin. He contrasted his concept of a political or civic nationalism to this form of ethnic nationalism.

This book focuses on the ideas of a particular individual who sought to forge a civic national identity where none had previously existed. Politicians and intellectuals have had a profound impact in shaping the consciousness of virtually every national community.[79] Previous studies, such as those of Greenfeld, Brubaker, and also Linda Colley, who studied the formation of a British identity in the eighteenth century, have looked backward to discover the roots of national identities that came into being at some point in history.[80] Unlike these, my work is not a comprehensive study of the creation of a supraethnic Austrian nation because no such nation ever emerged. Rather, it analyzes how Bloch as well as other reformers of the late Habsburg peri-

---

78 Alfred Stepan, "Modern Multinational Democracies: Transcending a Gellnerian Oxymoron," pp. 232–36, in John Hall, *The State and the Nation: Ernest Gellner and the Theory of Nationalism* (Cambridge: Cambridge University Press, 1998).

79 Greenfeld, p. 22.

80 Linda Colley, *Britons: Forging the Nation, 1707–1837* (New Haven: Yale University Press, 1992).

od envisioned such an identity. For him, the distinction between a civic and ethnic conception of nationhood was real. Bloch acknowledged and incorporated both forms of consciousness into his formulation of an Austrian identity in an attempt to prove that a population of different ethnic groups could preserve their differences and yet still become a nation. The following chapters offer an analysis of his ideas, beginning by examining those of his mentor, Adolf Fischhof.

Chapter 2

'BLOCH'S MENTOR': ADOLF FISCHHOF AND HIS PLAN FOR REFORM IN AUSTRIA

Adolf Fischhof (1816–1893) argued throughout his career that the survival of the multiethnic Habsburg polity required the strengthening of each nationality's separate consciousness as an ethno-cultural unit. In terms of the reform plan he espoused, he was perhaps more supportive of the rights of the non-German peoples of Austria than any other German liberal politician of the post-1848 era. Nevertheless, Fischhof's rationale for proposing such reforms, namely that they would lead the Monarchy's Slavs to reject the notion of ethnic kinship with Russia and instead join the 'civilized' European (read: German) side in its inevitable clash with 'Muscovite barbarism,' revealed a clear belief in the supremacy of German *Kultur* and in a German-centered *raison d'etre* for the Austrian state. Fischhof was an Austrian patriot, a progressive liberal democrat, a Jew, a supporter of cultural pluralism and the federalization of Austria. Yet, unlike Bloch, he also identified himself as a member of the German people (which he defined culturally), believed in the superiority of German culture, and envisioned a profoundly German mission for the Austrian state. The differences in the way each of them defined his identity shaped the differences between their visions for Austria.

Bloch revered Fischhof for his commitment to bringing about reconciliation among the Austrian nationalities. On numerous occasions he praised Fischhof in his newspaper and invoked his mentor's name in defense of his own ideas or political actions.[81] In his memoirs, Bloch

[81] See, for example, the following articles from the *Oesterreichische Wochenschrift*: "Adolf Fischhof," Nr. 48, Year 3, December 10, 1886, pp. 569–570; "Dr. Adolf Fischhof," Nr. 27, Year 5, July 4, 1888, pp. 419–420; "Adolf Fischhof als Jude," Nr. 13, Year 10, March 31, 1893, pp. 236–8; "Der Lehrertag und die Judenhetze," Nr. 30, Year 14, July 23, 1897, pp. 609–10; "Zur Reichsratswahl im fünften Wahlkreis. Ein Wort der Abwehr, von Dr. Josef S. Bloch" Nr. 13, Year 24, March 29, 1907, pp. 213–17.

commended his mentor's attempts to "transform Austria into a liberal state of nations, so as to make it a real home for all its various peoples."[82] He considered Fischhof a true leader, one who was "free from national intoxication."[83] Fischhof also counseled Bloch personally. For example, in the summer of 1885 Bloch sent Fischhof the draft of a lecture, "Workers in the Time of Jesus," he was planning to deliver later that year, and expressed pride at the enthusiastic response he received.[84] In addition, Fischhof encouraged Bloch to run for the *Reichsrat* in 1884,[85] and Bloch sought his mentor's advice before every important *Reichsrat* debate.[86]

Bloch did not put forth his own specific plan for reforming the institutions of government in Austria. Rather, he simply endorsed the reform proposals put forth by Fischhof, a plan well known to anyone in Austrian politics in the late nineteenth century. Fischhof had called for a comprehensive decentralization of government authority in Austria with power devolving to the crownlands and localities, the borders of which were to be drawn according to ethnicity as much as possible. He also wanted to place each nationality in control of its own cultural and educational institutions so that each would be able to develop its culture and language to the fullest possible degree. Bloch viewed Fischhof's blueprint as the institutional solution to the strife among the peoples of Austria.[87] The two men took different approaches to building support for constitutional reform. Fischhof concentrated his ener-

82 Joseph Samuel Bloch, *My Reminiscences*, Vol. I (Vienna: R. Lowit, 1923), p. 55.

83 Ibid., p. 80.

84 Ibid., p. 55, and Werner J. Cahnmann, "Adolf Fischhof als Verfechter der Nationalität und seine Auswirkung auf das jüdisch-politische Denken in Österreich," in Wolfgang Häusler, ed., *Studia Judaica Austriaca*, Bd. I (Vienna: Verlag Herold, 1974), 78–91, see. p. 84.

85 Bloch, *My Reminiscences*, Vol. I, p. 79.

86 Cahnmann, "Adolf Fischhof als Verfechter der Nationalität und seine Auswirkung auf das jüdisch-politische Denken in Österreich," p. 84. Their communications resulted in a collection of over twenty letters from Fischhof to Bloch, a handful of which Bloch cited in his memoirs. However, the collection, which had come into the possession of his brother, Rabbi Chaim Bloch, was burned in 1938 while the latter was under arrest by the SS. Chaim Bloch eventually emigrated to New York. (Ibid., p. 84, n. 29).

87 Cahnmann, "Adolf Fischhof als Verfechter der Nationalität und seine Auswirkung auf das jüdisch-politische Denken in Österreich," p. 80.

gies in two areas. In addition to developing his reform plan, throughout his career he sought to organize an alliance of democrats and liberals of all nationalities to support it. Bloch, on the other hand, was neither a political organizer nor an architect of institutional reforms. He focused more on cultivating the common civic consciousness Fischhof had called for in his own writings, and placed that task at the center of his efforts. Both wanted a reformed, federalized Austria. They simply had different styles and points of emphasis.

Fischhof had a distinguished political career that spanned five decades from 1848 into the 1890s. Although he was Jewish, he became one of the most well known German left-liberal politicians of his era thanks to his role in the 1848–49 revolution. Fischhof was born in Pest, on December 8, 1816, into a German-speaking environment.[88] Most Jews living in Pest in the early nineteenth century spoke German and experienced varying degrees of German acculturation. In the first half of the century the Jews of Pest fell under the influence of the *Haskalah*, the Jewish Enlightenment, as did the Jewish communities in the cities and towns of Bohemia and Moravia, the area where Fischhof's father was born. In fact, the frequent contact that Pest Jews had with Bohemian and Moravian Jewry helped spread the Reform movement into Hungary.[89] Religious reformers had begun to win followers in Pest as early as 1810, and introduced German language sermons and other reforms that helped draw that community's Jews more tightly into the German cultural realm.[90]

It was not until after 1848 and especially 1867 that Hungarian Jewry became Magyarized.[91] Hungarian Jewish writers in the first half

---

[88] For a detailed biographical discussion of Fischhof before 1848, see Richard Charmatz, *Adolf Fischhof: Ein politisches Lebensbild* (Stuttgart: Cotta, 1910), pp. 1–16. Interestingly, Charmatz did not discuss Fischhof's Jewish background, and indeed barely mentioned that he was Jewish. See also Werner J. Cahnmann, "Adolf Fischhof and his Jewish Followers," *Leo Baeck Institute Yearbook* 4 (1959), pp. 111–39. Cahnmann called attention to Charmatz's omission on this point (see Ibid., p. 117, n. 9), but himself offered few details about Fischhof's Jewish background in either of his articles.

[89] Michael Silber, "The Historical Experience of German Jewry and Its Impact on Haskalah and Reform in Hungary," in Jacob Katz, ed., *Toward Modernity: The European Jewish Model* (New Brunswick, NJ: Transaction Books, 1986), pp. 107–58, see p. 107.

[90] Ibid., p. 121.

[91] McCagg, *A History of Habsburg Jews*, pp. 133–5.

of the nineteenth century wrote either in Hebrew, Yiddish or German, but almost never Hungarian. In fact the first work in Hungarian by a Jew appeared only in 1840.[92] Unlike Bloch, who grew up in East Galicia two generations later, Fischhof came of age in a place and time where educated Jews felt an almost irresistible attraction to German culture as the bearer of Enlightenment values. Many of these Jews, including Fischhof, came to see themselves as members of the German *Kulturnation*.

As a young man Fischhof left Hungary to study medicine at the University of Vienna, and earned an appointment in 1846 as an assistant doctor at the University.[93] He still held this position on March 13, 1848, the day on which he served as the catalyst that sparked the 1848 revolution in Vienna.[94] On that date a crowd gathered outside the Lower Austrian *Landhaus* while inside the provincial diet met and discussed the contents of a petition to be submitted to Emperor Ferdinand I (known as 'the Good') that would describe their humble request for reforms. The crowd waited for some time and finally grew restless.[95] Fischhof, a political unknown, called out for the attention of the hitherto unfocused crowd and delivered an impromptu speech that arguably started a revolution. He proclaimed that they, the people, should make their demands known to the deputies and to the Crown. He listed freedom of the press and of education as two reforms that were necessary to satisfy the people. Fischhof also discussed the nationalities' issue, which was then emerging as a major potential barrier to the unity and strength of Austria. This issue became his life's

---

92 Raphael Patai, *The Jews of Hungary: History, Culture, Psychology* (Detroit: Wayne State University Press, 1996), p. 250. Of course Magyars mostly published in German themselves before the 1830s.

93 R. John Rath, *The Viennese Revolution of 1848* (New York: Greenwood Press, 1957), p. 394.

94 Charmatz, pp. 19–21. Before 1848 Jews did not possess the right to live in Vienna, although individual Jews could get a special dispensation to take up residence in the Habsburg capital. See McCagg, pp. 48–51. Fischhof's status as a medical student and then as a doctor on the faculty of the University presumably earned him permission to reside in the city.

95 For a broader discussion of the revolutions of 1848 throughout the German states, see Hans Joachim Hahn, *The 1848 Revolutions in German-Speaking Europe* (Harlow: Longman, 2001).

passion. In his speech, Fischhof encapsulated the desire for reconciliation and cooperation among the Austrian peoples that provided the motivation for all his later work.

> Ill-advised statesmanship has kept the peoples of Austria opposed to one another; they must now come together in brotherhood and increase their power through unity. The weaknesses of one nationality will be balanced by the virtues of the other, and all of their merits will be enhanced through their combination, which, if employed for the good of the state, will raise Austria to an unforeseen height of welfare and power. If we, the ambitious Germans filled with ideas, the tenacious, diligent, unflagging Slavs, the gallant and spirited Magyars, the ingenious and sharp-eyed Italians think of the common problems of the state with united and thus more potent power, there can be no doubt that the position of Austria among the states of Europe must become an imposing one...Hail Austria and its glorious future! Hail the united peoples of Austria! Hail freedom![96]

In these remarks, Fischhof evinced a potent Austrian patriotism combined with a recognition that only through the cooperation and political unity of its nationalities could it remain a powerful state. He acknowledged differences among the peoples, but recognized this diversity as a boon to the overall strength of Austria. Fischhof made clear his belief that Austria did not have to fight nationalism and the national awakening of its peoples in order to survive; it could, by encouraging their cultural development and treating each one equally, earn their gratitude and thus co-opt ethnic consciousness, making it a force that increased the stability of the state. Although simplistic in this early formulation, in the following decades Fischhof's pluralistic vision provided the backbone for what came to be known as 'the Austrian idea.'

In order to achieve a solution to the nationalities question, Fischhof called for radical constitutional and institutional changes in Austria, an

---

96 Quoted in Charmatz, p. 20.

end to the "ill-advised statesmanship" he referred to in his speech. Following his remarks and those of a few other subsequent speakers, representatives of the crowd made their way into the *Landhaus*, and eventually forced the deputies to incorporate their demands, including their demand for a constitutional government, into the petition to the Emperor. The 1848 revolution was underway.[97]

Fischhof remained active throughout the revolutionary period. The Vienna Security Committee chose him as its chairman on June 1, 1848.[98] In mid-June he won election to the Austrian *Reichstag*, which opened in Vienna on July 22, 1848, and later relocated to Kremsier, where it drafted a new constitution.[99] The *Reichstag* almost immediately faced the dilemma of what language it should use to conduct its business, a question that encapsulated the problem of how to administer a multilinguistic state. On the basis of practicality, Fischhof called for German to be the language of communication in the *Reichstag*, and asked the non-German members not to feel insulted by his suggestion. He asked them to look to the world of diplomacy, where representatives of all states accepted French as the language of communication.[100] By making this analogy, Fischhof acknowledged that the *Reichstag* was more akin to an international body than a national parliament. Thus, even though it must conduct its business in one language, it must also respect the cultural sensitivities of its members.

As he did on the issue of language, Fischhof consistently sought to keep ethnic interests separate from political decisions. He urged the representatives not to let their quarrels about cultural and linguistic issues distract them from securing political freedom for all their constituents. At Kremsier, he demanded that on political issues they become "no longer Czechs, no longer Germans, no longer Poles, but rather the representatives of the Austrian peoples...So long as we hold our ground will we not allow our independence, our honor to be weak-

---

97 Rath, pp. 62ff. For more on Fischhof's activities during the 1848 Revolution, see also Stefan Walz, *Staat, Nationalität, und Jüdische Identität in Österreich vom 18. Jahrhundert bis 1914* (Frankfurt am Main: Peter Lang, 1996), pp. 49–54.

98 Rath., p. 219.

99 For a detailed discussion of Fischhof's activities at the *Reichstag* in Vienna, see Charmatz, pp. 66–75; for his activities at Kremsier, see pp. 93–110, and also Walz, p. 65.

100 Charmatz., p. 68.

ened, that which is one with the independence and the honor of the peoples of Austria."[101]

One can characterize Fischhof in 1848 as a left-liberal who possessed strong democratic leanings. He supported only a suspensive veto power for the monarch.[102] Furthermore, he argued for universal male suffrage[103] as well as for the abolition of the death penalty.[104] On the nationalities question, the left-liberal democrats as a group called for a democratic, decentralized federal Austrian state that guaranteed the equal rights of all peoples.[105] Such a formula paralleled the plan offered by Fischhof during the 1860s in his major works, which will be discussed below. The left-liberal position opposed that of the mainstream German liberals who, although they supported equal rights for the nationalities, demanded a highly centralized state.[106]

In the first week of March 1849, after two months of hard negotiations, the constitutional committee unanimously approved the final draft version of a new constitution.[107] Fischhof represented the German left-liberals on the committee and played an important role in the creation of the draft.[108] All the parties of the *Reichstag* agreed to the committee's proposed constitution, including Fischhof and his left-liberal

101 Ibid., p. 105.

102 Ibid., p. 100.

103 Ibid., p. 99. This was rejected in favor of a broad, but not universal male suffrage.

104 Ibid., pp. 106-9. Fischhof was on the winning side in this case, as the *Reichstag* abolished the death penalty by a vote of 197 to 106.

105 Rath, p. 276.

106 Ibid., and Kann, *The Multinational Empire*, Vol. II, p. 32.

107 Ibid., p. 35. For a detailed discussion of the Kremsier constitution as a whole, see Ibid., pp. 35–9, and Okey, pp. 154–6. Selected excerpts of the document appear in Reinhart Koselleck and Rudof Vierhaus, eds. *Das Nationalitätenproblem in Österreich 1848–1918* (Göttingen: Vandenhoeck & Ruprecht, 1973), pp. 30–32. This highly useful collection contains a number of important documents, including (either in part or in whole) the Stadion Constitution of March 1849 (p.35), the unimplemented Bohemian nationality compromise of 1871 (pp. 55–58), the Badeni language ordinances of 1897 (pp. 64–67), the Social Democrats' Brünn nationality program of 1899 (pp. 73–74), the Moravian compromise of 1905 (pp. 81–85), and Emperor Karl's ill-fated federalization plan of October 1918 (pp. 121–22), all of which will be discussed further.

108 Kann, *The Multinational Empire*, Vol. II, p. 144. The committee consisted of thirty members, with three representatives from each Austrian crownland. See Judson, p. 64, n. 100.

allies.[109] The draft solved the nationalities question with a compromise between centralism and federalism, and was thus more centralized than Fischhof would have preferred.[110]

This document, historically known as the Kremsier Constitution, was the most important achievement of the *Reichstag*, in particular because of its proposed solution to the Austrian nationalities problem. The Constitution did not cover Hungary or Lombardy-Venetia, then both in revolt. The area it did cover thus corresponds to Cisleithanian Austria as defined by the 1867 *Ausgleich*. Section I of the draft version declared the indivisibility of the Austrian state. Article 21 declared the equal rights of each of the peoples, including "an inviolable right to the preservation and cultivation of its nationality in general and its language in particular. Legal equality of all languages spoken in school, government agencies, and public life will be guaranteed by the state."[111] It then distributed various powers to the federal, crownland, and district or *Kreis* levels. It redrew the existing districts within each crownland into *Kreise* divided as much as possible along ethnic lines. The devolution of power to the *Kreise*, and within counties, the implementation of municipal autonomy, were central elements of the Kremsier draft's solution to the nationalities question. The *Kreise* were to determine educational policy, specifically the language of instruction and any additional languages to be taught in schools. The various nationalities would thus have control over their own schools and could feel secure in their ability to develop and protect their language and culture. For elections to the crownland legislatures, each crownland was divided as much as possible into ethnically homogeneous districts so that each deputy would represent one nationality.

The Kremsier Constitution represented the only occasion when elected representatives of the peoples of the Monarchy (outside of Hungary and Lombardy-Venetia) were called together to work on comprehensive constitutional reforms. The compromise agreement they

---

109 Ibid., p. 35. For the a detailed record of the committee's debates, see Anton Springer, *Stenographisches Protokolle des Verfassungsauschusses im österreichischen Reichstage 1848–9* (Leipzig: n.p., 1885).

110 Kann, *The Multinational Empire*, Vol. II, p. 32.

111 Quoted in Ibid., p. 35–6. This clause, with minor changes, also appeared in the 1867 constitution.

produced stood as a symbol of a possible solution to the nationalities question. However, by the time it had been achieved, the forces of counter-revolution in Austria had already gained the upper hand. Ferdinand had been convinced to abdicate in favor of Franz Joseph, his eighteen year old nephew, who became the new Emperor on December 2, 1848, and who had been educated to believe that a sovereign should rule as an absolute monarch.[112]

On March 6, 1849, the young Emperor tore up the Constitution he had previously promised to accept, much to the detriment of subsequent generations of Central Europeans. This action was the most fateful and tragic choice of Franz Joseph's reign, even more so than the decision to declare war on Serbia in 1914, because the achievement of a long-term solution to the Habsburg nationalities question implemented in the middle of the nineteenth century could well have altered the way nationalism(s) developed in Central and Eastern Europe in that century's last decades, perhaps preventing the tensions and hatreds among the region's peoples that later played a major role in the outbreak of war in the Balkans in the summer of 1914, and the unspeakable carnage that followed in the subsequent three decades of conflict. While one can argue that the failure of the major attempts at compromise made in the late nineteenth century, as seen in the Badeni crisis for example (see Chapter 4), makes clear the difficulty of finding a solution, it is equally true that Franz Joseph's decision to ignore the solution worked out at Kremsier in 1848–49 helped give rise over time to the more radical nationalists who sabotaged those later attempts at compromise.

Having gotten rid of the constitution created by his peoples, Franz Joseph instead introduced a plan drawn up by Count Franz Stadion.[113] Although it had the disadvantage of not being chosen by the people, Stadion had produced an impressive document. It covered the whole of the Monarchy, including Hungary and Lombardy-Venetia, organizing the entire Habsburg patrimony as a unitary, centralized state with a single

---

112 For more on Franz Joseph's 'education' as a future monarch, see Beller, *Francis Joseph*, pp. 31–34.

113 For the specifics of the Stadion constitution, see Kann, *The Multinational Empire*, Vol. II, pp. 59–65.

Parliament, elected directly by the voters, and a Prime Minster and cabinet that were responsible to the legislature. Yet the Emperor never implemented even his own constitution, and ruled as an absolute monarch for the subsequent decade.[114] He governed personally through a completely centralized, German-speaking administration that extended to every corner of the Monarchy, including Hungary. He relied on the prestige of the dynasty, the efficiency of his administration and, if necessary, the power of his army to guarantee support for or at least acquiescence to his absolute rule.[115] Contemporary observers joked that Franz Joseph's government consisted of four armies: a standing army of soldiers, a sitting army of administrators, a kneeling army of clergymen, and a crawling army of informers.[116] However, this system proved unable to survive for long.

The internal dissension that followed the Austrian military defeats at the hands of France and Piedmont-Sardinia in 1859 led Franz Joseph to realize that absolutism had become politically untenable. It clearly lacked the support of all but a small section of the population. The early 1860s saw a number of half-hearted attempts at reform, but only in 1866, with his defeat by Prussia at Königgrätz and the expulsion of his state from the German Confederation in the Treaty of Prague, did Franz Joseph accept that Austria needed fundamental change.[117]

After the Emperor dissolved the *Reichstag* in 1849, the government arrested many of its members. Fischhof refused to go into exile to avoid prosecution.[118] He was arrested and tried for high treason, and although acquitted, the government still considered him a threat and prevented him from playing a public role for the next ten years.[119] During that decade Fischhof returned to his pre-revolutionary career as a physician.[120] Following the end of absolutist rule, he received a spe-

---

114 On the 'neo-absolutist' period in general, see Okey, pp. 158–65.

115 Beller, *Francis Joseph*, p. 59.

116 Ibid.

117 On the various constitutional schemes of the 1860s leading up to the *Ausgleich*, see Ibid., pp. 80–99, and Okey, pp. 158–65.

118 See his letter to the *Ostdeutsche Post*, quoted in Charmatz, p. 111.

119 Kann, *The Multinational Empire*, Vol. II, p. 144.

120 Charmatz, p. 127.

cial amnesty that allowed him to become politically active once again.[121] Fischhof reemerged as a public figure in the mid-1860s. He attempted to influence the constitutional reform process with his pen, publishing articles on various aspects of the nationalities issue in such major newspapers as the *Pester Lloyd* and the *Neue Freie Presse*, as well as a number of book-length treatises that gathered together the ideas previously expressed in article form.[122] Fischhof aimed his message particularly at the leadership of the German liberal party in order to convince them that their support for centralized government was misguided. Between the years 1866 and 1869, Fischhof published a number of pieces, culminating in 1869 with *Österreich und die Bürgschaften seines Bestandes*,[123] in which he laid out his reform plan for Austria, the mission he envisioned for the Austrian state, and the relationship between the two.

In his writings Fischhof criticized the various systems of government that had existed in Austria since 1849. He dismissed the centralized neo-absolutism of the 1850s as an utter failure, noting that it only necessitated two setbacks: the battles of Solferino and Magenta, to destroy it.[124] As far back as Joseph II (whom Fischhof otherwise admired for his enlightened thinking and attempt to end class privileges) Austria had tried to emulate the models of its powerful neighbors, Prussia in particular, and create a unitary German-speaking state. Fischhof considered the entire idea flawed in its conception because centralized government conflicted with the very nature of a multiethnic state.[125]

Fischhof also believed that the constitutional systems of the early to mid-1860's were disasters that differed little from neo-absolutism in their handling of the nationalities question. He cared for neither the

---

121 Ibid., p. 130.

122 For example, he published a series in the *Pester Lloyd* in January, 1866, see nrs 18, 19, 22, 26, cited in Charmatz, p. 161, and a two-part series in the *Neue Freie Presse* on November 12, and 20, 1867 (nrs. 1150, 1158), cited in ibid., pp. 185–6.

123 Adolf Fischhof, *Österreich und die Bürgschaften seines Bestandes* (Vienna: Wallishauser, 1869).

124 Ibid., p. 172.

125 Ibid., p. 171–2, 204–5. In this argument Fischhof anticipated by 125 years the criticism offered by the historian T.C.W. Blanning in *Joseph II* (London: Longman, 1994).

October Diploma, which lasted only few months in 1860-1, nor the February Patent, a more democratic system run by the German liberal Anton von Schmerling. The Schmerling plan demonstrated to Fischhof only that "centralization in Austria could obtain no more through fake constitutionalism than it was able to extort through absolutism."[126]

Although disappointed by Austria's defeat in the Seven Weeks' War of 1866, Fischhof was optimistic about the chances for lasting and successful reform because Hungary and Venetia (ceded to Italy) were no longer to be organized politically as one with the rest of the Monarchy. He believed that Hungary's administrative and legislative systems had to be separated from those of the rest of the Habsburg patrimony. In a pamphlet Fischhof co-wrote with Joseph Unger in 1861, "Lösung der ungarischen Frage," he had called for complete autonomy for Hungary, combined with full cooperation between the Hungarian and Austrian (i.e. non-Hungarian) legislatures on such common affairs as the military budget, international trade, etc. Common bills would have to be adopted by both houses in order to take effect.[127]

The defeat of his armies by Prussia forced Franz Joseph to compromise with the Magyar leaders and accept their demand for the autonomy of Hungary from the rest of the Monarchy.[128] In the fall of 1866, Fischhof declared that the current moment offered Austria the best opportunity since 1848 to create a new system of government that would satisfy the needs of its peoples and guarantee its stability and survival. He also believed that he had an important role to play in that process.[129]

The *Ausgleich* and the subsequent constitution Franz Joseph proclaimed for Austria on December 21, 1867, greatly disappointed Fischhof. He felt that it drove even deeper the wedge between the German and non-German peoples of Cisleithania.[130] Incorrectly predicting that it could not last in its current form, he declared "the Bach

126 Fischhof, *Österreich und die Bürgschaften seines Bestandes*, p. 176.

127 See also Kann, *The Multinational Empire*, Vol. II., p. 145, and Charmatz, p. 147ff. The pamphlet was published anonymously, see Ibid., p. 455.

128 Sked, p. 182.

129 Adolf Fischhof, *Ein Blick auf Oesterreichs Lage* (Vienna: Wallishauser, 1866), p. 6.

130 Fischhof, *Österreich und die Bürgschaften seines Bestandes*, p. 177.

regime lasted a decade, the February patent had only four years of life, and doubtlessly the days of existence for the December Constitution will be measured in even smaller numbers."[131] Fischhof criticized the constitution for maintaining the voting system created in the February Patent, a scheme that through electoral gerrymandering produced a German majority in the *Reichsrat* despite an almost two to one Slavic majority among the population of Cisleithania.

> Whereas the clever Schmerling never doubted for a second that only through a fake constitution could the rule of fake majority be preserved, our current statesmen are under an illusion that threatens the state, namely that a genuine constitution and a fictitious majority, that freedom and injustice, that the December fundamental laws and the February voting system can coexist.[132]

Fischhof warned that the current system would turn the Slavs of Cisleithania against Austria, and urged immediate electoral reform. The underrepresentation of the Slavs in the *Reichsrat*, he feared, gravely endangered the state. Not only was the system undemocratic, it continued the major flaw of neo-absolutism, namely that the Slavs felt themselves ruled by a German state.[133] Fischhof asked, "has hegemony not devolved on to the Germans through their possession of a parliamentary majority?...German domination appears to the peoples as tyranny."[134] He recognized that on issues such as culture, language, and education, issues that stood at the core of their development as peoples, the non-German ethnic groups could not simply accept defeat and move on to the next debate.

> One cannot expect that, like a political minority, a national minority will subordinate itself to the majority without coercion....The political party defends ideas or interests, which, if neglected today, might be acted on tomorrow. It can thus lose without perishing. The national party defends the national

[131] Ibid., pp. 180–1.

[132] Ibid., p. 181.

[133] Ibid., p. 1.

[134] Ibid., pp. 101–2.

> existence, which cannot develop if it is perpetually menaced, and can rarely be rejuvenated once atrophied.[135]

Austria could not expect one or more of the peoples among its population to sacrifice their national existence for the greater good, because, Fischhof argued, a more tenuous, conditional bond holds together the citizens of a multiethnic state than that which exists in a national state.

> How different is this in a complex of lands and nationalities. There exists no deep physical relationship, no relation of the blood, no community of military and literary glory....No internal connection, none of the mutual attraction of a homogeneous people holds such a state together. Only a commonality of interests is the binding material of such heterogeneous elements. Here there exists no unified people, but rather a union of peoples.[136]

Fischhof hoped to convince the various nationalities that it was in their interest to accept a multiethnic state even though they each wanted a state of their own. An ethnic group would support the continued existence of a state like Austria only if it believed that it could develop its national treasures, its culture, literature, and particularly its language, to their fullest potential.[137] Fischhof saw language, "which grows out of the spirit and soul of a people,"[138] as the defining characteristic of a nationality, and thus the one thing each would fight to the death to preserve. He contended that, for this reason, "a constitutionally governed state of nationalities...must...avoid conflicts with the national life interests of its peoples, and must create institutions under whose protection the individ-

---

135 Ibid., p. 70.

136 Ibid., p. 68.

137 Ibid., pp. 68–9.

138 Adolf Fischhof, *Die Sprachenrechte in den Staaten gemischter Nationalität* (Vienna: Manz, 1885), p. 5. This publication was a collection of articles that had appeared in the *Wiener Allgemeine Zeitung* in February, March and April, 1884 (Charmatz, p. 351). Although this particular quotation appeared in the 1880s, it is consistent with views Fischhof expressed throughout his entire career on the importance a people places on its language.

ual existence of the nationalities remains safe."[139] Thus, each nationality had to receive not only its just representation in the *Reichsrat*, but also the ability to administer its own cultural and educational institutions.

The non-German nationalities feared that they would be oppressed in a centralized Austria. Fischhof sympathized with their concerns and attempted to make his target audience, German liberal centralists, at least understand the reason why the non-Germans could not accept centralization. "Not blind opposition, not German-hatred, rather the most powerful of all driving forces for individuals and peoples, the drive for self-preservation, drives the peoples to fight against centralization, which for them means death."[140] Fischhof feared that if the political discord over this issue grew too serious the rule of law might be threatened. The government would have "no choice other than to either remain idle spectators while the freedom of the state is undermined, or to take measures so that the state corrupts freedom."[141]

Fischhof described a political system seething with ethnic enmity and distrust. He believed that the nationalities question divided the Austrian bourgeoisie, which otherwise shared both ideology and material interests. Fischhof condemned "the permanence of unnatural party alliances and rivalries, the fact that all are placed in false positions whereby a friend fires a wounding arrow into the breast of a friend, and political enemies stand shoulder to shoulder and fight in the same ranks."[142] He feared that feelings of pride in one's *Stamm*

> will be used from the one side by the ultra-nationalists in order to destroy the Empire, and from the other side by the feudalists in order to drive language and race, like a wedge, between the democratic elements that belong together and to separate those whose interests lie in working together.[143]

Without ethnic rivalry and distrust to separate them, Fischhof trusted

---

139 Fischhof, *Österreich und die Bürgschaften seines Bestandes*, p. 69.

140 Ibid., p. 110.

141 Ibid., p. 179.

142 Ibid., p. 197.

143 Ibid., p. 225.

that the broad middle-classes would stand together in a multiethnic political coalition in support of democratic and liberal principles.

The 1867 Constitution created a system that Fischhof characterized as unworkable, despite its protection of individual civil rights, because it preserved a centralized administrative system within Cisleithania. Such an organization might be consistent with freedom and equality in a national state, but not in Austria.[144] Fischhof contended that, because of its diverse population, and, in particular, its lack of a powerful majority nationality, Austria required a different form of government. "The Austrian Monarchy is the first Empire of nationalities, which would be reorganized according to modern principles into a representative state. Such a creation lacks a model of a great common polity."[145]

Fischhof asserted that, in a multiethnic polity, democratic government and the guarantee of individual rights through a liberal constitution would not earn the loyalty of all the nationalities to the state because these measures alone could not ensure the survival of the peoples as collective entities. If Austria could not protect the cultural development and provide for the equal treatment of its peoples, then they would surely attempt to break free at the first opportunity. He believed that only by nurturing all of its peoples could the Austrian state hope to strengthen the loyalty of its nationalities, and thus ensure its stability.

> The consolidation of a state of nationalities requires that no race is neglected or feels totally subordinated to another, because nothing is more injurious to a people than foreign rule, even if that rule offers the most liberal institutions....No wish is greater than that for a national government. It is in the interest of survival for the state of nationalities to respect the feelings of its peoples, avoid all that smacks of foreign rule, and fulfill their wishes [for a national government] as much as its security allows.[146]

Centralization, rather than diversity in and of itself, fostered political instability in Austria, according to Fischhof. Thus, he offered a

144 Ibid., p. 178.

145 Ibid., pp. 65–6.

146 Ibid., p. 70.

reform plan based on a decentralized system of government.[147] He maintained that Austria differed from national states because of its ethnic composition, and thus required a different form of government. Decentralization would strengthen the state by increasing the identification of all its peoples with the common polity.

> Austria is not a state body, but a system of state bodies, each of which rotates on its own axis. It is the mission of Austria not to destroy these particular motions, rather to work with them so that all these state bodies find their common political centers of gravity in the *Reich*...Only centralization makes the peoples centrifugal! Decentralize Austria, and they will become centripetal![148]

Fischhof urged his fellow German liberals to reconsider their position on centralization before it was too late to save Austria.

> If the Germans consider not the fleeting and problematic advantage of the moment, but rather their true and long-term interests for the future, they must see centralization as their most dangerous enemy. And it would be an act of political foresight to graciously offer a federative structure, which they perhaps tomorrow might have to claim as a concession.[149]

---

147 Fischhof placed himself in the pantheon of earlier reformers who had discussed decentralization, such as Anton Springer, who wrote *Geschichte Oesterreichs seit dem Wiener Frieden 1809*, and "Oesterreich nach der Revolution," an 1850 brochure; Josef Eötvös, the author of *Die Garantien der Macht und Einheit Oesterreichs* (1859); and Victor von Andrian, who authored *Oesterreich und dessen Zukunft* (1850). See Ibid., pp. 73–83. This section offered proof of Fischhof's familiarity with Eötvös.

148 Ibid., p. 111. Fischhof and Bloch both used the terms 'centripetal' and 'centrifugal' to characterize various forces within Austrian politics and society. Oskar Jászi later employed these terms in his analysis of the Monarchy, which suggests that they were in common usage at least among reform-minded Austrian political thinkers as far back as the 1860s.

149 Ibid., p. 186. The German liberal centralists hated the federalization plan Fischhof called for in *Österreich und die Bürgschaften seines Bestandes*. Dr. W. Lustkandl, a professor at the University of Vienna, wrote "Föderation oder Realunion?," a response that appeared the following year (1870). He rejected the applicability of the Swiss model to Austria and condemned the Fischhof plan as fatally flawed. (Charmatz, p. 246).

Fischhof also hoped the non-German nationalities would see that their ability to survive as independent states, i.e. without the Austrian union, was limited at best. In any case, he knew that Austria's ability to survive as an independent state without the support, or at least acquiescence, of a majority of its people was equally limited. Thus, Fischhof called on all those throughout Austria-Hungary who wanted to preserve the common state to work together to find a political solution that would satisfy all the peoples. He warned that

> each [nationality], through its resistance, is able to endanger the Empire all on its own...but something constructive can only be achieved by all united. Only if the government, the representatives of the peoples and the press on both sides of the Leitha [i.e. in both the Austrian and Hungarian halves of the Monarchy] keep this truth before their eyes...will Austria be consolidated.[150]

The centerpiece of Fischhof's reform plan was his proposal for a new 'Nationalities' Law' that would guarantee the equal development of all the peoples. The first draft of this proposal appeared in *Politik*, a Prague publication, on October 2, 1867.[151] It was thus available before the proclamation of the Austrian Constitution on December 21, 1867, although it is unlikely that Franz Joseph, who promulgated the document without consulting any political leaders in Austria, knew anything about it.

For Fischhof, a constitutional statement guaranteeing the equality of the peoples had to be combined with a fundamental commitment on the part of the government to ensure that all the nationalities had the institutional tools to develop their culture and language to the highest possible degree. He declared that only a complete decentralization of governmental authority on all domestic issues could satisfy the desire for equality on the part of the peoples in a multiethnic state such as Austria.

---

150 Fischhof, *Österreich und die Bürgschaften seines Bestandes*, p. 1.

151 Charmatz, p. 201. In his appendix (see pp. 447–454), Charmatz included a later version of this document that was more precise yet virtually identical in content to that found in the Nachlass of the Czech leader Frantisek L. Rieger. According to Charmatz, Rieger mentioned that this version appeared in an early 1868 publication.

> [Austria] must institute such a large measure of autonomy that each people is placed in a position of full sovereignty both legislatively and administratively...In a state of nationalities constituted in this way, the peoples feel on the one hand that their cultural progress, their national and linguistic development is secured through the self-government afforded them as much as if they had formed their own fully independent polity, while, on the other hand, in their political union and in the dynamic pooling of the power of all of them, each finds protection from the outside. None of these peoples, if isolated, would be able to confront the great neighboring states.[152]

Fischhof proposed a decentralization of the bureaucracy and the legislative process, envisioning autonomous bodies at both the crownland and local levels.[153] Furthermore, each *Stamm* within each locality would receive control over the decision-making process for educational and cultural issues. He called for a decentralized court system on the American model in which judges would answer to the individual crownlands rather than the center, with a *Reich* supreme court empowered to deal with disputes among the crownlands or nationalities as well as the prosecution of offenses against the security of the *Reich*.[154] For conflicts among nationalities, there would be a court of arbitration, in which two judges of each nationality in the conflict would assemble under the leadership of a chief judge from a "neutral nationality," who would have the deciding vote in a tie.[155] The question remained whether, for example, Germans would accept Czechs as a neutral group in a German-Slovene dispute. Nevertheless, the plan was at least a starting point in the search for a fair compromise.

American and Swiss examples provided models for Fischhof in dealing with how states with diverse populations should be represent-

---

152 Fischhof, *Österreich und die Bürgschaften seines Bestandes*, pp. 71–2. Although Fischhof was a German, this statement strongly resembles the Austro-Slavist justification for supporting the multiethnic state.

153 Ibid., pp. 99–170.

154 Ibid., pp. 162–3.

155 Ibid., p. 194.

ed in a central legislature.[156] He explained every detail of how his system would function, down to how the government would collect taxes, both direct and indirect, according to the principles of a decentralized, federal system.[157] Fischhof also made clear that a federalized Austria would remain a monarchy, and would not in any way reduce the rights of the monarch from those described in the 1867 Constitution. He did recommend that Franz Joseph be crowned King of Bohemia in Prague as a symbolic act, although he did not want the Bohemian lands to have any special status compared to the other provinces of Cisleithania.[158] He simply redesignated to the crownland legislatures some powers the previous Constitution had already assigned to the *Reichsrat*, while those of the Emperor remained untouched.[159] These rights even included the absolute veto, which Fischhof had not supported in 1848.

In addition to autonomy at the crownland level, Fischhof also argued for the importance of municipal autonomy, which had actually survived to some degree through the neo-absolutist period.[160] He believed that self-rule for towns and cities provided for a closer identification between the populace and government officials, whom the townspeople were more likely to know personally on the local level, than that which existed in a top-down system.[161] Furthermore, Fischhof recognized that it would be easier to create ethnically homogeneous administrative districts at the municipal, and, if necessary, sub-municipal level than at the level of crownland. Such ethnically-based districts could, even within mixed cities, administer potentially divisive issues such as those relating to language and education with less of a chance of imposing the will of one *Stamm* on another, thus increasing the legitimacy and acceptance of the larger Austrian state by its nationalities.[162]

---

156 Ibid., p. 111.

157 Ibid., pp. 165–9.

158 Ibid., pp. 221–2.

159 Ibid., p. 199.

160 Kann, *The Multinational Empire*, Vol. II, p. 38. Fischhof hoped to build on what already existed, as demonstrated by the title of his 1868 work, *Zur Erweiterung der Municipal-Autonomie* (Vienna: Wallishauser, 1868).

161 Fischhof, *Zur Erweiterung der Municipal-Autonomie*, p. 9.

162 Ibid., pp. 9–10.

Fischhof rejected the idea that his proposals for decentralization would weaken the central government and the ability of the *Reichsrat* to serve as a unifying body for Austria. The central *Reichsrat* would deal with all issues common to the whole Austrian state, and its members would be elected according to a democratic franchise that would, unlike the system created after the *Ausgleich*, ensure the proportional representation of each *Stamm*. He did not specify what these issues were, but presumably they would have included those specified in the *Ausgleich* as common to the whole Monarchy, namely military, trade, financial, and budgetary matters. Fischhof explained that wide-ranging local and crownland autonomy would complement the parliamentary system, and together provide a stronger foundation for the state.[163] He contended that freedom required not only a democratically elected central parliament, but also strong local autonomy of the type that existed in North America, England, and Switzerland.[164] According to Fischhof, "parliamentarism without self-government is like a fortress that only has one wall around it."[165] In fact, Fischhof looked to Switzerland as the primary model for his federalized system of government. He saw many similarities between Switzerland and Austria, such as the historical traditions of sovereignty in many of its states, their agglomeration by largely voluntary actions rather than by pure conquest or national consolidation, and the ethnic variety of their populations.[166] Fischhof maintained that the success and stability of Switzerland demonstrated the efficacy of a federal system of government for a multiethnic state.

In addition to decentralizing the administrative and legislative processes, Fischhof's proposal emphasized the need to protect the rights of the various nationalities, in particular those who formed a minority in a given crownland. He discussed in greater detail his proposed Nationalities' Law, which went much further than its counterpart, Article 19, of the 1867 Constitution. Article 19 read simply: "All peoples in the state are equal, and each people has an inalienable right to preserve and foster its nationality and language." Fischhof main-

163 Ibid., p. 12.

164 Ibid., p. 5.

165 Ibid.

166 Fischhof, *Österreich und die Bürgschaften seines Bestandes*, pp. 89–99.

tained that the constitution did little to ensure what Article 19 had promised. "[The article] must stand as the guiding principle grouped in a series of special supplementary laws....As long as these supplements are not enacted, Article 19 will always represent only a small step of little worth within the complex of the rest of the fundamental laws."[167]

Fischhof proposed a series of measures to be placed in the fundamental laws that would guarantee the equality of the various languages in the schools and churches, as well as the administrative, judicial, and legislative bodies in each crownland and at the federal level. Each citizen would have the right to communicate either in written or spoken form with the local government in any language used in that area.[168] Each district would determine its own internal language of administration, as would the crownlands. Communication between the top level of the crownland administrations and the central government would be in German, but this was the only breach of the principle of equality of languages, and would require literally only a few bureaucrats in each province to be bilingual. Schools would offer instruction in the language(s) of the people(s) within any district, and, in order to improve communication between the peoples, offer all students the opportunity to learn any other language(s) spoken within the crownland.

These measures would reassure minority nationalities within a province that felt threatened by the superior numbers of the majority. Fischhof also called for the legislatures of each province with a significant population of more than one ethnic group to have a chamber for each nationality, and reminded his readers that such an idea was no stranger than that of separate chambers for nobles. Laws in the crownlands that dealt with language and education would need the assent of all the chambers.[169] He declared that his system of nationality chambers, elected by separate curiae defined by *Stamm*, was central to protecting the rights of minority peoples on issues sensitive to their cultural development as a *Stamm*.

---

[167] Fischhof, *Die Sprachenrechte in den Staaten gemischter Nationalität*, p. 51.

[168] See Kann, *The Multinational Empire*, Vol. II, pp. 145–6.

[169] Fischhof, *Österreich und die Bürgschaften seines Bestandes*, pp. 186–91.

> The curia voting system removes the fate of the nationalities from the vagaries of political parties, and it places the majority and the minority in the *Landtage* on equal footings relative to one another regarding decisions about national questions. It is the protection of the weak, the strong shield with which each nationality defends itself.[170]

Fischhof trusted that institutional changes would lead to changes of the heart. His whole plan rested on the notion that fair treatment would lead the nationalities to identify their interests with those of the Austrian state.

> Dissolve through institutions...national hatred from the land, and our public life would rapidly become healthy. If the national interests are made independent from a parliamentary majority, voting will not be as it is now, by race and language, rather political principles will be the standard, nationality will no longer serve as a wedge between a partisan and his political party.[171]

Austria had to end its practice of divide and rule with regard to the nationalities, Fischhof believed, if it wanted to ensure its survival. Previously, the Monarchy had enacted only the minimum amount of reforms it thought were necessary to avoid open revolt, rather than seeing reform as a tool to improve and strengthen the position of the state. Oskar Jászi, who shared much ideologically with Fischhof, eloquently echoed this criticism in his 1929 analysis of Austria-Hungary. "The chief political task never was how, out of the decaying feudal castle a comfortable, modern house could be created for all the peoples of Austria but rather how this unhygienic slum could be further rented with the help of superficial and cheap alterations."[172]

Fischhof also saw the shortsightedness of such a strategy, and challenged the government to give the nationalities a positive reason to stay with Austria and develop a feeling of deeper loyalty. He declared that

---

170 Ibid., p. 191. Fischhof's system resembles to a good degree Ljiphardt's concept of consociational democracy discussed in Chapter 1.

171 Ibid., p. 196–7.

172 Jászi, *The Dissolution of the Habsburg Monarchy*, pp. 291–2.

his reforms would do so by creating a true measure of equality among all the Austrian peoples.

> Austria--if it wants to secure its survival--must from now on be the standard-bearer of a high ethical notion...that justice is the highest moral idea...As soon as this idea is given clear and certain expression in the Constitution of Austria, all its races will advance their cultures undisturbed and be better able to preserve their spiritual, moral and physical properties... through this also the...stability of Austria is secured without doubt. Once these peoples have acquired the consciousness that only in their harmonic coexistence will they be able to secure their most precious lifeblood, then they will stand...solidly for the state that protects these things, and develop also a recognition of the common good and the feeling of fellowship that will bind these heterogeneous parts into an organic whole and slowly, but surely call forth this Austrian consciousness that some have tried in vain to impose by force.[173]

Much like Bloch, Fischhof proclaimed the importance of creating an Austrian civic consciousness based on participation and common citizenship.

> A constitutional state of nationalities, such as Austria, must, if it wants to achieve the compactness and cohesion of a national state, carefully work to strengthen the political-national common consciousness of its peoples alongside their individual genetic-national (*genetisch-national*) consciousnesses, as has been done so excellently in Switzerland.[174]

In this statement, Fischhof described the hyphenated, ethnic-civic identity for Austrians that Bloch made central to his ideological worldview.

173 Fischhof, *Österreich und die Bürgschaften seines Bestandes*, p. 6.

174 Adolf Fischhof, *Der österreichische Sprachenzwist* (Vienna: Manz, 1888), pp. 33–4. These articles first appeared in the *Neues Wiener Tagblatt* (Nr. 45, 58, 72, 86) in February and March 1888 (Charmatz, p. 361).

Fischhof called for the development of symbols to inspire this sense of civic nationhood among the peoples and give a new identity to the Austrian state. For example, he proposed a design for a new tricolor flag, which would be white, red, and gold, a combination of the red and white of Lower Austria (presumably representing the crownlands) with gold, one of the Habsburg dynastic colors.[175] Furthermore, Fischhof argued that the state needed to play an active role in creating a spirit of comity and cooperation across ethnic lines. First, it had to create a constitutional and political system in which the peoples could develop equally, but such reforms alone would not suffice. He maintained that the Austrian government had to help with the construction of the Austrian civic nation, although he did not describe the specific steps the government should take in this regard.

> The crafting of this Austrian consciousness...requires more than the ending of the national struggles. The state must also work to ensure that the peoples of its crownlands do more than co-exist indifferently to one another, rather it must encourage them to cooperate in a friendly manner and ever so slowly to develop a sense of brotherhood.[176]

After issuing his comprehensive reform plan in 1869, Fischhof continued his political activities into the 1870s and 80s. He took great interest and played a background role in the negotiations that led to the nationality compromise adopted by the Bohemian *Landtag* in 1871.[177] In accordance with Fischhofian ideals, the plan organized the province into districts to be drawn according to nationality lines and applied the principle of vote by nationality curiae for any decision relating to language. Fischhof praised the agreement and argued that it merited the attention of anyone interested in solving the nationality question in

---

175 Fischhof, *Ein Blick auf Oesterreichs Lage*, p. 45.

176 Fischhof, *Österreich und die Bürgschaften seines Bestandes*, p. 34.

177 See Charmatz, pp. 265–277, for letters from Fischhof on the Bohemian *Landtag* compromise and the Hohenwart reforms (see below), including his many missives to Rieger, his compatriot as far back as the 1848–9 *Reichstag*. See also pp. 319–24 for more letters between Rieger and Fischhof that discuss the latter's continuing mission and a plea to Rieger to cooperate and work out differences with the Germans.

Bohemia, the province with the most intractable national problems of any in Austria.[178] The Bohemian language compromise was part of a larger plan supported by Count Karl Hohenwart, appointed Minister President (the Austrian equivalent of Prime Minister) in February 1871, that recognized the right of Bohemia to govern its own internal affairs.[179] The Hohenwart plan, including the Bohemian language compromise, would have opened the door towards a comprehensive decentralization of Austria by giving autonomy to the crownlands while offering protection for minorities within them through the ethnic curiae.[180] Even with the support of the Emperor at the outset, Hohenwart failed to turn his plan into law. Faced with the strong opposition of the German liberals and, more importantly, the Magyar elites who would brook no fundamental constitutional changes, Franz Joseph backed down from the fight and withdrew his support for Hohenwart's federalization plan. To Fischhof's lament, Bohemia did not receive autonomy and the language compromise did not become law. The Emperor chose to continue the state's support for and reliance upon the superior political position of a narrow German-Magyar plurality rather than risk a battle that might have led to an enduring solution to Austria's problems.[181]

Although he did write on other issues occasionally, Fischhof remained largely focused on the nationality question, particularly in Bohemia, throughout the next two decades.[182] On October 31, 1878, Fischhof, Rieger, and Michael Etienne, then editor-in-chief of the *Neue Freie Presse*, the leading Austrian paper and a staunch proponent of German liberalism, issued the Emmersdorf Memorandum, which called for nationality compromise in Bohemia and throughout Austria, as well as autonomy for the provinces combined with equal rights for each nationality within a province. It was not a systematic plan for such a compromise, but a statement of principles and common purpose between leading Czech and German liberals, and reflected Fischhofian

---

[178] Fischhof, *Die Sprachenrechte in den Staaten gemischter Nationalität*, p. 46. He included a copy of the text in Appendix C, I., pp. 74–78.

[179] For more on the details of this affair, see Okey, pp. 222–3.

[180] Jászi, p. 113.

[181] Beller, *Francis Joseph*, p. 83.

[182] See, for example, Adolf Fischhof, *On the Reduction of Continental Armies*, translated by Humphry William Freeland (London: Williams and Norgate, 1875).

principles.[183] Despite this initiative, a solution to the language question in Bohemia remained elusive.

One conflict in 1870–71 (and again later during the Badeni affair) had been the question of the language of communication between citizens and the bureaucracy. During the mid-1880s Fischhof proposed a compromise solution to this difficult issue.[184] He criticized the Czech proposal that any citizen be able to deal with the administration in the language of his choice at any location in the province because it would have effectively required all bureaucrats in Bohemia to be bilingual. Most Czechs already spoke German, but the Germans would have to learn Czech, a seemingly one-sided burden. In addition, the Germans chauvinistically refused to be forced to learn a language they considered inferior. Although he rejected the aforementioned Czech position, Fischhof realized that the German stance, which rejected any adjustment to the status quo according to which German was the sole language of provincial administration, also stood in the way of a solution. He suggested what he considered a compromise. Bureaucrats would be required to be bilingual only in districts of mixed nationalities, which, if drawn properly, would be few.[185] According to this scheme, Czechs and Germans would both be able to converse with government officials in their native tongue, which was the goal of the original Czech proposal, without forcing the Germans who wanted a government job to learn Czech, which was the chief German complaint against the Czech proposal. Fischhof's suggestion fell on deaf ears.

Later in this same publication, Fischhof pleaded with his fellow citizens to moderate their demands and come to a compromise. He proclaimed that the time had come for Austria to solve its nationality problems before class added another layer to the divisions within society. "There has been no moment...like the present, in which the specter of the social problem also brings forth uncomfortable noise in Austria."[186]

---

183 Charmatz, pp. 326–7.

184 This proposal did not deal with the language of communication between offices or between the province and the center. Fischhof had already made his stance on those questions clear in his Nationalities Law proposal. In the 1870s, all communication within the Bohemian bureaucracy and between itself and Vienna was in German, and had been as long as anything like a modern bureaucracy had existed in the Monarchy.

185 Fischhof, *Die Sprachenrechte in den Staaten gemischter Nationalität*, pp. 47–8.

186 Ibid., pp. 62–3.

Unlike his writings from the 1860s, he did not primarily address the German liberals and ask them to compromise with the Slavs, but rather vice versa. He called on the Slavs to include the Germans in their reconstruction of Austria because without the Germans, who remained the foundation of the Monarchy, any newly formed state organization would not last. Likely, Fischhof addressed the Slavs rather than the German liberals because in 1885 Taaffe's Slav-Conservative coalition held power, and the liberals formed the opposition.

In his last major publication, which appeared in 1888, Fischhof again returned to the Bohemian question, and this time called for strict protection for minorities, i.e. the German-speakers sprinkled in Czech majority districts, without which he claimed they would likely become Czechified.[187] He urged the Czechs to support such a proposal because they had their own minorities in majority-German districts. Fischhof hoped that the reality that each nationality had minority populations in districts of the other would lead both to recognize the need for fairness and compromise.[188] However, his optimism had begun to wane. He asked longingly "Where are the peacemakers?"[189] Fischhof wistfully remarked that, although he had unsuccessfully been urging the same solutions for twenty years, his patriotism would force him to continue trying.[190]

On only one occasion during these years did Fischhof put down his pen and make a public appearance in a political setting. He had always hoped to unite liberals from all the Habsburg peoples into a supraethnic alliance of liberal parties, each one organized along ethnic lines. To this end, he attempted to found a new organization, the *Deutsche Volkspartei*, which was to serve as the German party in this multiethnic coalition. Fischhof presented the program for this new party on July 16, 1882, to an audience gathered at the *Musikvereinsaal* in Vienna that included Bloch as well as Karl Lueger.[191]

---

187 Fischhof, *Der österreichische Sprachenzwist*, pp. 31–2.

188 Ibid., pp. 32–3.

189 IIbid., p. 3.

190 Ibid., pp. 4–5.

191 For a more complete discussion of the details of this event, including the full text of Fischhof's statement at the *Musikvereinsaal*, see Charmatz, pp. 389–97. Fischhof's written text was actually delivered by Dr. Edmund Singer, although Fischhof greeted the crowd and thanked them for attending before turning the floor over to Singer. (Ibid., p. 389.)

The new party's program centered on Fischhof's by then familiar constitutional reform plan that called for compromise between the nationalities and the transformation of Austria into a federal state based on the Swiss model. The party's motto would be: "No nationality may be privileged, and none disadvantaged."[192] Fischhof's audience on this occasion was his fellow Austro-German liberals, and he demonstrated his identification with them by discussing what "we eight million Germans" had to do.[193]

Fischhof had long tried to convince the Austro-Germans to abandon the idea of a centralized, German-speaking Austrian state that they could dominate politically. He urged them to see that only a system in which each of the nationalities shared political power equally could create peace among the peoples, and only such a system would convince the non-Germans to truly accept Austria as their state. Fischhof reminded his German audience that Austria would then be in a position to fulfill what they all saw as its larger mission of spreading German culture and German *Bildung* to the non-German peoples of the Monarchy.[194] He further argued that their commitment to a centralized, German-dominated state structure had marginalized and splintered the German liberal movement in Austria, with the result of subjugating liberal principles to those of German nationalism. Fischhof called on all Germans who wished to solve the national question and create a stable, unified Austria to join his party. He urged his German liberal colleagues to work towards a compromise solution because, for the sake of Austria, they had no other choice.

> The only possibility that remains is a league with the non-German liberals. The *Deutsche Volkspartei* will stand up for this alliance because this alliance alone offers a secure majority behind the freedom of the country. Certainly this alliance requires the peaceful solution of the language question, but if King Henry IV was able to say: 'Paris is worth a mass,' then we may with a greater right say that the securing of progress,

192 Ibid., p. 391.

193 Ibid., p. 392.

194 Ibid., pp. 396–7.

> the elimination of the national troubles, and the consolidation of the *Reich* with a few concessions over language is not too dearly bought.[195]

Unfortunately, Fischhof and his allies, mostly the ever-shrinking contingent of democratic left-liberals, failed to convince their audience to join this new political organization and support federalist reforms. After Fischhof and two allies, Theodor Hertzka and Baron von Walterskirchen had spoken, a group German of nationalists, ironically consisting largely of Jews and led by Heinrich Friedjung, disrupted the discussion and violently dispersed the gathering. As Austro-German liberals became more openly nationalistic, they had little desire for a compromise position that would, from their perspective, strengthen the Austrian Slavs at German expense.[196] The *Neue Freie Presse* condemned the new party, and mocked the gathering's inauspicious conclusion in the paper's lead article on July 18, 1882. Other pro-centralist German liberal institutions and leaders dismissed it as "a party of Count Taaffe."[197] When the new party failed, most of the older leaders of the Viennese democratic movement retired from politics.[198]

Ironically, one of the movement's younger members, Karl Lueger, went on to become the leader of the antisemitic Christian Social Party.[199] Lueger, however, maintained his personal esteem for Fischhof even after the former abandoned liberal politics. On December 3, 1886, Lueger admonished a gathering of his political colleagues by proclaiming, "no one in this room can hold a candle to Fischhof, and no one has lived who can match himself against him in terms of his political career, service to the city of Vienna, and integrity of character."[200] Later that

---

195 Ibid., p. 396.

196 Cahnmann, "Adolf Fischhof als Verfechter der Nationalität und seine Auswirkung auf das jüdisch-politische Denken in Österreich," p. 90, n. 16.

197 Charmatz, pp. 397–8.

198 Bloch, *My Reminiscences*, Vol. I, pp. 58–9.

199 Richard S. Geehr, *Karl Lueger, Mayor of Fin de Siècle Vienna* (Detroit: Wayne State University Press, 1990), p. 62. John Boyer is less certain about the sincerity of Lueger's support for Fischhof's party than is Geehr. See Boyer, *Political Radicalism in Late Imperial Vienna: Origins of the Christian Social Movement, 1848–1897*.

200 As quoted in Charmatz, p. 296.

month, Lueger even claimed that when making a decision he often asked himself, "What will the man in Emmersdorf [Fischhof] think of you?"[201]

In a publication that appeared in 1885, only three years after his presentation at the *Musikvereinsaal*, Fischhof again returned to the same themes. If the nationalities could come to a political compromise, he predicted that there would arise "a political party drawn from the coming together of different national elements, whose majority has its broad, strong, and secure support in the majority of the whole of the Austrian population."[202] The Germans, Fischhof claimed, would be the natural leaders of such a coalition, if only they refrained from trying to force their leadership on their Slavic compatriots. German leadership would be obvious, in that "in regards to intellectual, cultural, economic, and other definitions, [the German-Austrians] stand above all our nationalities...If the German places himself at the head of our peoples not roughly but benevolently he will become the leader in Austria for all time."[203]

Fischhof asserted that the Germans did not need the kind of political hegemony that was built into the centralized, post-*Ausgleich* Austrian system. "[The German's] moral superiority offers him a more lasting guarantee than an artfully won parliamentary preponderance; because raw violence can easily push him from the pedestal of privilege, but no power can bring him down from the height of his culture."[204] He also noted, "a constitution cannot give the Germans numerical preponderance in Austria, but neither can it take away their moral superiority."[205] Fischhof's belief in the "moral superiority" of the German-Austrians, as well as the ultimately German-centered mission he prescribed for the Austrian state were central to his worldview, and constituted a crucial and irreconcilable difference between his ideas and those of Bloch.

Not only in this speech, but also in virtually all his major publications, Fischhof carefully detailed the larger role Austria and its Germans were to play in the present and future of European civilization. In 1866 he published *Ein Blick auf Oesterreichs Lage*, an assessment of Austria's

201 Ibid., p. 298. Cited from *Die Zeit* (Vienna), March 23, 1903. Lueger made the remark on December 15, 1886.

202 Fischhof, *Der österreichische Sprachenzwist*, p. 44.

203 Ibid., pp. 45–6.

204 Fischhof, *Österreich und die Bürgschaften seines Bestandes*, p. 106.

205 Ibid., p. 220.

position after its defeat at the battle of Königgrätz by Prussia and its removal, in political terms, from Germany itself as a result of its expulsion from the German Confederation. In this work Fischhof asserted that the mission of the Austrian state was intimately connected to the overall mission of the greater German people.

The end of his country's four centuries of political leadership of Germany evoked a great sadness in Fischhof. Holy Roman Emperor Maximilian, grandfather of the famous Charles V (on whose empire the sun literally never set), had laid the groundwork for Habsburg leadership of Germany, and for the Habsburg bid for mastery of all of Europe with his incredibly complex and fortuitous marriage alliances. Although the Habsburgs lost control of Spain and its overseas empire at end of the War of the Spanish Succession in 1714, Maximilian's work had led to the union of the ancient Habsburg lands, the so-called *Erblande* (roughly corresponding to present-day Austria) with the crowns of Bohemia and Hungary. These three units formed the core of an Austrian state strong enough to allow the Habsburgs, as Holy Roman Emperors, to be the leaders of Germandom and of Central Europe. However, the emergence of Prussia in the mid-late seventeenth century as a regional power in North Germany, followed by their bold annexation of Habsburg Silesia in the War of the Austrian Succession (1740–48) under Frederick the Great paved the way for a century of rivalry between Austria and Prussia that ultimately led to Königgrätz.[206]

In addition to his sadness, Fischhof also hoped that Austria's exclusion from Germany would clarify the relationship between the Habsburg Germans and their brethren in the other German states. Fischhof related that after their great defeat, a feeling of despair reigned among Austro-Germans. They felt collectively like a helpless infant thrown out into the world. He contended, however, that such emotions were misguided. "The German-Austrian is no orphaned child, he is a man who, over the course of time, has built a great household and has drawn such a numerous family of peoples around himself that there is no longer room for him in his father's house."[207] Patriarchal and famil-

---

[206] For an excellent survey of early modern Austrian history, see Charles Ingrao, *The Habsburg Monarchy, 1618–1815* (Cambridge: Cambridge University Press, 1994).

[207] Fischhof, *Ein Blick auf Oesterreichs Lage*, p. 20.

ial images abounded in this statement. The German-Austrian is a man who has gone out into the world and started a new household of which he is the head, but he still retains a connection to his "father's house," the greater German people. Fischhof's designation of the Germans as the leader of this new Austrian-Habsburg family of peoples, like the father who according to nineteenth century patriarchal views possessed the unquestioned leadership in his family, reflected his view that the Germans occupied a leadership position in Austrian politics and society almost by birthright.

Fischhof explained how the Austro-German would define his German identity. Although Austria was no longer politically tied to Germany, Fischhof never imagined that Austro-Germans would cease feeling German, speaking German, or participating in and creating German culture. "The spiritual bonds, which join us to the alma mater, will always continue to be a deep and powerful inner tie for us...the pulse of German life will henceforth flow more powerfully than ever through our veins."[208] It is ironic that Fischhof described the essence of Germanness as flowing through the veins of German-Austrians. He, a Jew, did not mean to suggest the primacy of racial or blood ties between the Germans in Austria and the new Prussian-led German *Reich*, but of course others did just that within a short time; he simply meant to emphasize that their Germanness was very important to the Germans of the Monarchy.

Defining the relationship between being German and being Austrian was the key question in terms of their identity for all Austro-Germans after 1866. Fischhof wanted German-Austrians to be Austrians first (although Austria itself had a German connotation in his eyes) and Germans second. In his July 16, 1882, speech at the *Musikvereinsaal*, he declared that German-Austrians had to fulfill their duties according to the following hierarchy: "First as a loyal son of Austria, second as a deserving son of the great German people (*Volk*)."[209] Other more nationalistically minded German-Austrians, such as Schönerer and Hitler, considered themselves to be Germans first and Austrians second, if at all. How an Austro-German defined his or her Germanness in relation

208 Ibid., p. 21.

209 As quoted in Charmatz, p. 390.

to the Austrian state was the central point from which flowed that person's definition of the German nation and nationalism.

Fischhof felt his Germannness deeply, and did not merely employ it as a rhetorical tool in his public writings to win a greater influence with his German target audience. This is evident in a private letter of August 23, 1870, in which Fischhof, reacting to the victories of German forces in the Franco-Prussian war, proclaimed "I can only say that the heart of anyone who speaks, thinks and feels German must beat faster as a result of the great feats of the German army. However, not merely as a German but also as a good Austrian I am pleased by the Prussian success."[210]

Although disappointed by the exclusion of Austro-Germans from the newly united Germany, Fischhof, at least in his public statements, considered their exile to be a cultural and intellectual trial by fire that could only strengthen the German people in Austria and increase the reach of Germandom as a whole. Now separate from Germany, the Austro-Germans would have to struggle on their own to spread their culture to the non-Germans of the Monarchy. He argued that such a task would "increase our power, and all nations of world-historical importance acquire such power in a fight against a resisting foe. Only peoples with expansionary power are peoples on the rise."[211] One could see these remarks as Fischhof simply trying to make the best of Austria's exclusion from the soon to be unified German Empire. His positive attitude, however, does correspond with his vision of Austria as a German-led, yet basically pluralistic state. Furthermore, despite their political separation, Fischhof contended that the Austro-Germans would have the whole of the German nation on their side in this "spiritual and moral struggle."[212]

Fischhof envisioned a cultural struggle between the Germans and non-Germans in Austria, and viewed this contest in what might be called cultural Darwinist terms. Like those who before 1914 viewed war as a means of spiritually purifying the nation, Fischhof saw this cultural clash as beneficial to the Germans of Austria. He believed that the difficult task of being a minority spreading its intellectual values to

---

210 As quoted in ibid., p. 254. Charmatz reprinted this as well as numerous other letters.

211 Fischhof, *Österreich und die Bürgschaften seines Bestandes*, p. 26.

212 Ibid., p. 28–9.

a reluctant if not hostile majority would, through force of necessity, sharpen the cultural acumen of the German people in Austria.

> Our isolation will nevertheless be advantageous for the development of our character, because, we must admit to ourselves, that the comfortable reliance on our non-Austrian co-nationals (*Stammesgenossen*) has made the character of the German-Austrian somewhat slack and flabby. The clashes with numerically superior peoples, based solely on our intellectual superiority, will require us to devote ourselves to the intellectual work of the nation. Through the work will our fibers become tighter, our power will become greater, and the increased consciousness will bestow on us the very moral superiority that every man yields to without the protection of the government on high[213]

In addition, Fischhof hoped that Austria's separation from Germany would help define the Monarchy's identity as a state, as well as its place in Europe. He believed that with the question of who would lead Germany decided the Austro-Prussian rivalry would become a moot point. More importantly, no longer distracted by having enemies on all its fronts, Austria could concentrate its efforts on what Fischhof deemed the "one great vital question: the eastern one, and...only one rival, Russia."[214] As Austria had once defended European Christendom against the Muslim Turks, it must now defend civilization against "Muscovite barbarism."[215] He maintained that when Austria began treating all its peoples equally, it would not only strengthen its position for the coming war with Russia, but would also be able to take over the protection of the Romanians and South Slavs of Turkey with the consent both of European opinion and those peoples. In 1869 Fischhof made clear whose cause Austria would serve when it brought these peoples under the wings of the Habsburg eagle by proclaiming "we will win [Romania and Serbia] for Germandom through just and reasoned

---

213 Fischhof, *Ein Blick auf Oesterreichs Lage*, p. 21.

214 Ibid., pp. 23–4.

215 Ibid., p. 24.

action."[216] Such statements make clear that, although he wanted equality for all the Habsburg peoples, Fischhof considered that equality to be simply a means to an end, namely the expansion of the German sphere of influence in Central and Eastern Europe.

As early as 1866, Fischhof predicted that Germany and what he hoped would become a newly stable and expanded Austria, the two states on the eastern border of European civilization, would conclude an offensive and defensive alliance against Russia. He declared that once the Austrian and German Empires (the latter not yet even created) had consolidated their internal structures, and the peoples of Austria felt secure that the individuality of each *Stamm* was protected, "the idea of a Central European federation can be brought to fruition."[217] Fischhof later described the *Mitteleuropa* he had in mind, which, in addition to the military alliance, would also include an economic union of Austria and Germany, a customs and trade union, a currency, weights and measures union, and conformity in the areas of mail, telegraphs, and railroads.[218] As long as laws were passed that would secure the separate existence and cultural development of the peoples, their mistrust would be overcome and a great Central European federation, linked by strong economic and political ties, could come into being with the consent of all involved.[219]

Fischhof did ignore certain practical concerns regarding the legal and constitutional structure of his proposed federation, namely the question of minorities within the German Empire. Could these minorities in Germany find protection without the kind of autonomy and decentralization that would exist in a reformed Austria? If they could not, would Germany be willing give up what Fischhof saw as its right as a nation-state to centralized government and national unity, and pass laws he had prescribed as appropriate for a state of nationalities? It would have been hard enough to convince Austro-Germans in Styria to allow Slovenes control over educational and cultural issues in a multiethnic state such as Austria, but to convince the Germans in Posen and

216 Fischhof, *Österreich und die Bürgschaften seines Bestandes*, p. 33.
217 Fischhof, *Ein Blick auf Oesterreichs Lage*, p. 25.
218 Fischhof, *Österreich und die Bürgschaften seines Bestandes*, p. 36.
219 Ibid., pp. 36–7.

East Prussia, regions within the German nation-state with significant non-German populations, to do the same for their Polish neighbors would have been even more difficult.

Even after the battle of Königgrätz, Fischhof apparently still dreamed of a *Grossdeutschland*, albeit a kinder and gentler version with administrative autonomy and cultural equality for the non-German peoples in the Habsburg Monarchy. Like his fellow German liberals, he envisioned a united Central Europe led by what he saw as its most civilized and culturally advanced people, the Germans. This vision is central to understanding why Fischhof was willing to compromise on direct German control over Austria, and why he was less concerned than radical nationalists with winning battles over, for example, individual schools in towns on the German-Czech or German-Slovene linguistic borders. There was a much larger battle at stake.

Fischhof assigned to the Austrian state the central role in this coming war between what he saw as civilization and backwardness. If the state encouraged the cultural and literary development of its nationalities, it would strengthen each one's consciousness as a separate people. Such a policy would not only increase the support for Austria of those oppressed under the current system, mostly Slavs, but it would also counter the growing strength of Pan-Slavism, which Fischhof feared as a stalking horse for Russian control of all the Slavs, and thus Russian domination of Eastern and Central Europe.[220] For Fischhof, Austria's ultimate mission was to ensure the victory of German culture and civilization over barbaric Russia by winning the Monarchy's Slavs over to the German side.

> This...is the mission of Austria; it is the cultural task of the German Austrians. 'Racial unity' is the Muscovite watchword, 'separateness of the peoples' is the Austrian. Our statesmen must call forth the particularistic senses of the Slavic races...The Germans will not fulfill their cultural mission through attempts at Germanization, rather these will awaken the hatred of the nationalities and advance the cause

220 Ibid., p. 142. Ironically, he compared such a development to the tragedy that befell Europe when German barbarians overran the Roman Empire.

> of Russia. [The Austro-Germans] serve the cause of Germany and the interests of Europe by smoothing the path of the western and southern Slavs towards self-development, which will ever increasingly widen the gap between them and the Russians.[221]

It is worth noting that Fischhof called on the Austro-Germans to serve Germany in this task. Austria thus became little more than a medium through which the Germans could help win the western and southern Slavs over to the side of European civilization, represented of course by German culture. He described this task using religious overtones, viewing it as an echo of the historical mission of the medieval Germans who had Christianized their Slavic neighbors.[222]

Fischhof linked the prospects of winning this clash of civilizations to the ability and willingness of the Austrian state to earn the loyalty of its Slavs. "If the politics of our statesmen leaves them no other choice than to allow themselves to be absorbed by either the Russians or the Germans, who are fully foreign to them in language and blood, they will choose the former."[223] Yet he also predicted that the Austrian Slavs, if given the opportunity to develop their cultures within the Habsburg union, would recognize their stake in the survival and strengthening of multiethnic Austria.

> The non-German nationalities have a powerful interest in [Austria's] preservation because they know that if it falls, then they will fall as booty to one or the other of the neighboring states, and that their individuality as peoples will disappear...Austria will appeal both to their natural instincts and to the commands of reason, but only if it makes the development of nationality the goal of the state's activities, because the particularism of its peoples-in particular that of the Slavs-is the guarantee of its existence; if it is weakened, there could

221 Ibid., pp. 142–3.

222 Ibid., p. 143.

223 Ibid., p. 141.

> be a self-mutilation, a great pulling of Pan-Slavism, a power grab to the benefit of Russia.[224]

Fischhof emphasized that only by decentralizing state authority would the Monarchy be able to nurture the individuality of its Slavic peoples. "Only the mature, the self-conscious Slav will be a fully-conscious Austrian. In a centralized Austria, national consciousness and patriotism must remain contradictory for Slavs that have been treated like children and oppressed."[225] He applied this argument to the issue of education, rejecting the notion that only through centralized control could the state ensure that its children were educated to be "good Austrians," as well as the belief that decentralized education would lead to schools that inculcated "anti-Austrian agitation."[226] Fischhof contended that an education that strengthened a student's knowledge of the particular culture and literature of his *Stamm* would also produce a loyal Austrian, while a lack of identification with their individual nationalities would lead Slavs to fall back on a more amorphous racial kinship and identify with pan-Slavism and Russia.[227] Thus *Stamm* consciousness and perceived racial ties existed in inverse proportions to one another. "Racial feeling *(Racegefühl)* is the pathological product of deep injury to the national feeling...Peoples who are oppressed, lack national possessions and lack culture hear well the call of a distant but powerful relative who poses as a liberator."[228] Fischhof predicted that the success of Austria in its role as the vanguard of Germany and Europe would depend on its ability to educate, not win wars.[229]

According to Fischhof, a curriculum that sought to suppress the non-German cultures in the name of creating good Austrians would fail miserably. "Unlike the ABC's, patriotism cannot be learned from a primer; the holy flame of love of fatherland will be kindled in the hearth of the home. If the school sets itself in opposition to the house of the

224 Ibid., p. 61.

225 Ibid., p. 143.

226 IIbid., p. 137.

227 Ibid., pp. 138–9.

228 Fischhof, *Der österreichische Sprachenzwist*, p. 12.

229 Fischhof, *Österreich und die Bürgschaften seines Bestandes*, p. 33.

father, it will only damage its authority without bringing any prizes to the state."[230] In a similar vein he cited Franz Smolka, a Galician Pole and President of the *Reichstag* from October 1848 until its dissolution in March 1849, who criticized centralization as an attempt to enforce loyalty through direct control. Smolka had exclaimed "let us be Poles and Czechs and we will become good Austrians, but you want to violently make us into good Austrians, and we remain Poles and Czechs."[231]

Fischhof imagined that education would serve as the central conduit for the spread of European civilization, of course via German culture and the fruits of German learning. He contended that as long as a centralized government did not force German culture on the non-German nationalities of Austria, they would naturally gravitate towards German institutions and ideas because of their own ambition to reach the highest levels of politics, business, academia, etc. "Our nations will look for their model in Germany if we do not through obtrusiveness make German ways and German science oppositional to the will of resistance. German culture has no more dangerous enemy in Austria than its forceful protection!"[232]

Fischhof called for the Monarchy to develop institutions of higher education in all its provinces, and to support any organization that sought to increase scientific learning. Furthermore, Vienna was to become the center of education for all Central Europeans so that bright young minds of every Habsburg nationality would receive a first rate German education at the state's expense, and then return to the provinces to enlighten their ethnic brethren in their own native tongue. Thus, Austria would become the vessel that brought European/German civilization to the peoples of Eastern Europe.

> The German *Geist* will stream out from Vienna over the whole *Reich*, not in order to inundate and suffocate the national cultures of its peoples, rather to pollinate them. And the German language, as in ancient times, will become the idiom of educated peoples who do not lie in chains, but rather

---

230 Ibid., p. 143.

231 As quoted in Ibid.

232 Ibid., p. 148.

> who soar. The German-Austrian should be neither the task-master of subjugated peoples, nor the nurse of peoples who are wasting away, but the leader of powerful and free peoples. That is his cultural mission, his civilizing call![233]

This statement reflects the difficulty of Fischhof's attempt to balance his belief in pluralism with his desire to spread German culture to the South and East. On the one hand, he hoped that the Germans could 'civilize' the non-Germans in Austria, yet he wanted each one to preserve its culture and sense of peoplehood. Fischhof did argue that pluralism in and of itself brought benefits to Austria. "The diversity of the peoples and the rich segmentation of the provinces creates the appeal of Austria, and makes it one of the most attractive and instructive polities in Europe."[234] Furthermore, he drew attention to the benefits of pluralism in general, arguing "the high level of national and spiritual culture is a result of diversity, not uniformity."[235] In this vein Fischhof dismissed those who supported the idea of a planet with only one language as "intellectually sterile utilitarians."[236]

Nevertheless, Fischhof's statements in support of pluralism cannot be separated from the Germanizing mission he prescribed for the Austrian state. In his conception, Austria had always served as the staging ground for the German people to civilize their inferior colonial subjects. Fischhof praised what he saw as the historical role of the Habsburgs, whose rule had spread "the German language and German power far beyond the Eastern Marches of the old Holy Empire, [the Habsburgs] project the energy of the German people into a great arena and offer the civilizing power of the German language a wide field of activity."[237] He called the German-Austrians "missionaries of German thinking," referred to the non-German provinces as "colonies," and finally asked, "Are Galicia and Hungary not the best markets for the products of German work?"[238]

233 Ibid., pp. 148–9.
234 Ibid., p. 63.
235 Ibid., p. 60.
236 Ibid.
237 IIbid., pp. 26–7.
238 Ibid., p. 28.

His German-centric view of Austria is difficult to reconcile with Fischhof's comparatively passionate calls for the equality of the Austrian peoples until one considers that he wanted Austria to provide equal treatment for the Slavs in order to win them over to the German side in a war against Russia. His belief in an intimate relationship between multiethnic Austria and the German people on both sides of its border with Bismarck's *Reich* marked a clear dividing point between the roles Bloch and Fischhof envisioned for the Austrian state, and between their conceptions of Austrian identity.

Central to Fischhof's understanding of Austrian identity was his paternalistic, almost missionary-like view of the relationship between Germans and non-Germans in Central and Southeast Europe. He seemed to consider non-Germans almost as children who must first be taught in their mother tongue before the more advanced Germans could introduce them to a higher level of *Kultur*. However, the ultimate goal remained the spreading of the superior German culture to their backward neighbors. Fischhof explained

> We seek not to devour the peoples...but to assimilate them spiritually...by invigorating their national spirit and their national language. Instead of, as before, violently driving the peoples through the German language to culture, we will lead them through an education won in their own idiom softly towards the German language.[239]

Fischhof believed that by allowing the peoples to preserve their native language in their schools, Austria could later bring them into the German/European sphere while preserving their loyalty to the state. He applied this logic most specifically to the case of the Czechs, one of the most numerous and important ethnic groups in the Monarchy.

> No people in Austria have a stronger Austrian consciousness than the Czechs, because only in this state are they a not unimportant factor in public life. The destruction of Austria would mean their own destruction. They would be lost no matter who

239 Ibid., p. 30.

> was to win the inheritance of the provinces in which they live....In Germany, they would go under in time, as have all the Slavs who live and have lived on German territory. In Russia they would save their race, but only at the cost of their unity as a *Stamm*. An Austria that allows them the development of their individuality will find in them devoted citizens.[240]

These statements clearly reveal the difference between Fischhof's and Bloch's idea of the Austrian mission. For Fischhof, the mission of Austria was to thwart pan-Slavism by providing a home for the small nations between Germany and Russia who, if Austria did not exist, would find themselves absorbed by one or the other. He recognized quite realistically that if the Czechs, to take one example, no longer needed Austria to protect them, they would have no reason to remain in a multiethnic state as opposed to creating a Czech nation-state, which remained the ideal if circumstances would only allow it. Thus, Fischhof tried to motivate the Czechs to support Austria's existence based on geopolitical considerations, and in this respect resembled moderate nationalists such as Palacký and other Austro-Slavists. In fact, when discussing Austria as "the most secure guarantee of the European balance," Fischhof paraphrased Palacký's famous statement on this same theme.[241]

Fischhof's justification for the existence of multiethnic Austria on geopolitical grounds does not address the criticism of Austria on the grounds of what would later be called the principle of national self-determination. He thus accepted the nation-state as the highest form of political expression but excused the violation of this principle in the case of Austria because of its international role in protecting the balance of power and extending the reach of German culture.

Nation-states appeared to Fischhof as somehow more organic, the natural outcome of the existence of a people.

> The national state is the family of a people, the nationalities state is a union of peoples. All citizens of a national state are

[240] Ibid., p. 43.

[241] Ibid., p. 4. This statement provides confirmation that Fischhof knew of Palacký's ideas, which are discussed further in Chapter 5.

> related through the physical bond of blood, through the spiritual bond of language, as through their common fate, and literary as well as military glory. A thousand relationships of the soul bind all citizens to one another; the great family of the people brings each individual to happily sacrifice his rights, because the power and luster of the state exerts its full force on the head of an individual. There exists the unity of sensibility, unity in the national tendencies; there the unity of the state is self-generated.[242]

This statement expressed an almost romantic notion of the national state according to which he accepted that individuals would place the nation above their "rights." Although it is not clear exactly what type of rights Fischhof meant in this case, he nevertheless praised this "sacrifice" for the nation-state. He asserted,

> In a unified nation-state the national idea is primary. The unity and power of the nation will itself subjugate all others mercilessly, and here in Europe not a single great state is without mixture with some foreign nationalities, thus this *Staatsidee* finds its satisfaction only at the cost of justice as regards those people that find themselves in the minority.[243]

Fischhof did not criticize this phenomenon, but rather he accepted it part and parcel of the creation of a national state. Apropos he rhetorically posed the question: if the French are assimilating their Germans (in pre-1870 Alsace-Lorraine), and the Prussians and Russians their Poles, why should the German Austrians not do the same to the non-Germans of the Monarchy? Fischhof answered that the difference was one of numbers, that while 50 million Russians could perhaps absorb 5

---

[242] Ibid., pp. 67–8. In describing the citizens of a national state as related by blood, Fischhof seems to making a case for a racial definition of nationhood that would have excluded him, as well as all Jews, from the German *Volk*. This statement is odd, to say the least, in light of his Jewish faith and self-identification as a German. He did not explain where his Judaism fit into his identification as a German or Austrian, or how it fit into his identity at all in his public political writings.

[243] Ibid., p. 6.

million Poles (although even this proved impossible in the end), 8 million Austro-Germans could certainly not absorb their 27 million non-German fellow Habsburg citizens, and noted "the appetite must not be stronger than the digestion."[244] Fischhof did not condemn what can only be called an attempt at forced assimilation in the cases of France, Prussia and Russia, but merely placed such an achievement beyond the practical capability of the German minority in Austria. He accepted that it was necessary for Austria, "where no people is powerful enough to subjugate the others," to operate along different lines.[245] These statements strongly imply that had Austria been more heavily German, Fischhof would have supported a more active Germanization policy.

In his view of nation-states, Fischhof clearly differed from Bloch. The latter hoped to build a multiethnic civic nation to fight against nationalist hatred *sui generis*. For him, the great battle was not a coming war between two civilizations, as it was for Fischhof, but rather a moral struggle between ideologies that opposed each other within European civilization. It was a clash between the concept of the multiethnic society and that of the nation-state, between civic unity and racial hatred, between his ideas and those of Schönerer and, two generations later, Hitler. The profound differences between Bloch's and Fischhof's views of the ultimate mission of Austria reflect fundamental differences in their identities.

Whereas Bloch saw himself politically as an Austrian *sans phrase*, Fischhof's political identity was that of the German-Austrian.[246] Bloch never publicly criticized Fischhof for his identification as a German or his rhetoric on the German mission for Austria. Perhaps because Bloch so strongly supported the substance of Fischhof's federalization plan, he did not want to speak ill of its author. Instead, Bloch constantly emphasized Fischhof's Jewishness, perhaps in an attempt to erase the memory of his mentor's statements regarding the superiority of German culture.[247] In an 1893 article "Adolf Fischhof als Jude" (Adolf

---

244 Ibid., p. 30.

245 Ibid.

246 See also Walz, who refers to Fischhof as a "German-Austrian Liberal" (p. 206).

247 See for example, "Adolf Fischhof," *Oesterreichische Wochenschrift*, Nr. 48, Year 3, December 10, 1886, pp. 569–570.

Fischhof as a Jew) published just after Fischhof's death, Bloch acknowledged his mentor's love of things German, but then emphasized his commitment to equality, a Jewish idea.[248]

Although both Fischhof and Bloch were Jewish, each one had a very different way of incorporating his Jewishness into his overall identity. Bloch saw himself as a Jew not only by religion, but also by *Stamm*. Fischhof never discussed being Jewish as part of his ethno-cultural identity or even mentioned Jews in any of his published essays, although he apparently remained a religious Jew throughout his life.[249] When Fischhof called for the preservation of each ethnic group's separate consciousness and culture, he never included Jews as one of those groups.[250] He only referred to Jews once in his writings, a letter in which he offered to help create "agricultural colonies" to encourage Galician Jews to work the soil.[251] Such an offer demonstrated his desire that Jews integrate themselves socio-economically into the larger society around them, which in Galicia meant involvement in agriculture.

Fischhof saw himself as a member of the German *Kulturvolk*, albeit a German of the Jewish faith. Enlightenment thinkers, even early German nationalists such as Fichte, had defined the German *Volk* as a cultural-linguistic group. Fischhof and other Jews who were acculturated and who identified as Germans also subscribed to this definition, and could not accept a racial conception of the nation that would have defined them out of the circle. Thus, before the racial definition of the

---

248 "Adolf Fischhof als Jude," *Oesterreichische Wochenschrift*, Nr. 13, Year 10, March 31, 1893, pp. 236–8.

249 Sigmund Singer (Fischhof's nephew), "Erinnerungen an Adolph Fischhof zu seinem 10. Todestage," *Neue Freie Presse*, March 22, 1903, cited in Cahnmann, "Adolf Fischhof and his Jewish Followers," p. 121, n. 18.

250 For an alternate interpretation, see Cahnmann, "Adolf Fischhof als Verfechter der Nationalität und seine Auswirkung auf das jüdisch-politische Denken in Österreich," p. 82. Cahnmann argued that Fischhof "implied" that he considered Jews one of the nationalities that should be recognized and given autonomy. Cahnmann stated that Fischhof only mentioned Jews directly one time, and quoted a passage from p. 38 of *Österreich und die Bürgschaften seines Bestandes*, in which Fischhof compared the plight of Jews and Slavs. However, I was unable to find the quotation Cahnmann cited, and I found no statement by Fischhof that either implicitly or explicitly recognized Jews as one of the Austrian nationalities in his writings.

251 Charmatz, pp. 279–81.

Volk conquered the idea of an inclusive German *Kulturvolk* in the late nineteenth and early twentieth centuries, Jews such as Fischhof could see themselves as part of the German people because they defined membership in that people culturally. In fact, many liberal Austrian Jews continued to see themselves as German in this sense down to the end of the Monarchy, as statements by Arthur Schnitzler and even Sigmund Freud in the early months the First World War make clear.[252]

Unlike Bloch, Fischhof did not discuss being Jewish as part of his ethno-cultural identity in any of his published essays. For example, although he emphasized perceived bonds of race as one reason why forced Germanization would drive the Slavs into the arms of Moscow, Fischhof never talked about Jews in this context.[253] He never offered an intellectual explanation of why he seemed to define Germandom culturally when it came to Jews (as seen in the example of himself and his family's adoption of German culture and German *Stamm* identity), but racially when it came to Slavs. Perhaps it was simply not relevant to his discussion of constitutional reform and nationality policy. Relevance aside, such a topic simply might have been too threatening to Fischhof's own identity as a German, which was under attack by racial nationalists who rejected the notion that anyone of Jewish origins could be a German.

Although Fischhof did not explain his understanding of Jewish ethnicity or 'blood,' by the 1870s he recognized the growing prevalence of racial definitions of nationhood. He could see that, in terms of descent, Ukrainians were more closely related to Russians than they were to Germans. Fischhof acknowledged this reality and saw that an attempt to impose Germanization on, for example, Ukrainians, would cause them to place greater emphasis on their 'blood' ties to Russians. Although he could see the importance people placed on these 'racial' ties, he hoped that a policy of equality would enable Austria to overcome them and bind together its peoples despite their different tribal origins. Furthermore, Fischhof condemned racism and racial nationalism as destructive to liberal ideas and, in more practical terms, to

---

252 Steven Beller, "Patriotism and the National Identity of Habsburg Jewry," *Leo Baeck Institute Year Book* XLI (1996), pp. 215–238, see p. 237.

253 Fischhof, *Österreich und die Bürgschaften seines Bestandes*, p. 141.

Austria's ability to bring its non-Germans into the German/European cultural sphere. He feared that racism would transform nationalism from a force for liberation and cultural development into a justification for terrible oppression. Fischhof urged his fellow liberals to reject racial conceptions of nationalism in favor of the concept of the *Kulturnation*, which he praised as "pure from racial hatred."[254]

Fischhof further argued that, in a practical sense, it was impossible to accurately define a people in terms of racial homogeneity. He cited multiethnic regions that had seen such a high degree of intermixing between ethnic groups as to make absurd the idea of racial purity. Bohemia, for example, was a place where "no German who disparages the nationality of a Czech, and no Czech who does so to a German can know whether he has not insulted his forefathers or his uncle."[255] Fischhof emphasized his point by listing some of the more Germanic names of Czech leaders, such as Rieger, Brauner, and Zeithammer, and the Czech names of German ones: Schmeykal, Chlumecky and Tomaszczuk.[256]

****

Bloch adopted Fischhof's plans for a federal reform of Austria, shared his liberal democratic political ideology, and agreed with his arguments on the benefits of pluralism and the preservation of *Stamm* identities. However, Bloch held these views free from a chauvinistic belief in the superiority of German or any individual culture, including that of the Jews. Fischhof, on the other hand, viewed Austria through the prism of his German identity in both a cultural and political sense because he was raised in a liberal tradition that was profoundly German as well as liberal. This explains to a large degree why he imagined that Austria, even as it protected the equality of all its peoples, would act as an arm of the greater German cause. In addition, the great task Fischhof assigned to the multiethnic Austrian state, the reason why its reform

254 Fischhof, *Die Sprachenrechte in den Staaten gemischter Nationalität*, p. 5.

255 Ibid., p. 59.

256 Ibid.

was so crucial had a decidedly German tinge to it. Fischhof's mission for Austria was a German mission, and reflected his self-identification as a German.

On the nationalities question, Fischhof was perhaps the most pro-Slav German liberal politician in Austria. Virtually alone among them he supported a decentralized system of government and full cultural autonomy for each nationality. Yet even he displayed a profound German national egoism in his writings. Thus, a comparison between the views of Bloch and other German liberals on the nationalities question becomes superfluous because virtually all of them viewed the Austrian question through German eyes to a greater degree even than Fischhof.

Fischhof's German national egoism confirms Judson's analysis of German liberalism in Austria by demonstrating that even the most 'liberal' of German politicians still displayed strong nationalist feelings.[257] Judson contended that national chauvinism existed within German liberalism from its very start. On this point, Judson echoed Lewis Namier, who five decades earlier had condemned the German liberal revolutionaries of 1848 for their blatant chauvinism towards non-Germans.[258] In fact, Namier traced Germany's twentieth century barbarity to German liberalism rather than Bismarck's Prussian militarism, referring to the German liberals as "forerunners of Hitler."[259]

Liberalism, Judson explained, centered on a hierarchical vision in which the educated and economically successful, due to their demonstrably superior intellect, earned the right to govern on behalf of all citizens. All citizens possessed equal civil rights, but the liberal hierarchy separated them into those with active and passive rights, the rulers and the ruled. From the 1840s into the 1870s, Austro-German liberalism's

---

257 See Judson, *Exclusive Revolutionaries.*

258 Lewis B. Namier, *1848: The Revolution of the Intellectuals* (London: Geoffrey Cumberlege, 1944). For a more recent analysis of the members of the Frankfurt Parliament and their ideas on German nationalism, see Brian E. Vick., *Defining Germany: The 1848 Frankfurt Parliamentarians and National Identity* (Cambridge: Harvard University Press, 2001). Lewis B. Namier, *1848: The Revolution of the Intellectuals* (London: Geoffrey Cumberlege, 1944). For a more recent analysis of the members of the Frankfurt Parliament and their ideas on German nationalism, see Brian E. Vick., *Defining Germany: The 1848 Frankfurt Parliamentarians and National Identity* (Cambridge: Harvard University Press, 2001).

259 Namier, p. 33.

early decades, this division remained fluid. The new elite was, in theory, open to members of any ethnic group and was solely based on merit and achievement. This inclusiveness, however, contained a powerful assumption that those joining the educated elite would adopt its values, namely German values. Judson contended that in the last two decades of the nineteenth century, when the position of both Germans and liberals came under attack in Austria, this fluid division between Germans and non-Germans was transformed in the minds of many Germans into a biologically defined chasm that could no longer be overcome by education and acculturation.

Judson maintained that when the liberals denied the lower classes, who were disproportionately non-German, full voting rights in 1848 and again in 1867 based on a lack of 'merit,' this exclusion left hidden its racist implications. By demanding that non-Germans adopt German *Kultur* in order to be considered worthy of active political rights, Austro-German liberals, even those as otherwise sympathetic as Fischhof, demonstrated that they considered German culture superior to the other cultures of the Monarchy. By the turn of the twentieth century, Austro-German nationalists had divided Austrian society into categories previously developed by liberals, and merely made explicit the implicit racism of Austro-German liberalism. Thus, according to Judson, the seeds of exclusivist and even racist German nationalism grew out of the hierarchical worldview of early German liberalism.[260] Fischhof, along with some other Austro-German (albeit mostly Jewish) liberals, steadfastly rejected the idea of German racial superiority. Nevertheless, even they did accept the cultural chauvinism and hierarchical vision of Austrian society that Judson contended was central to liberal thought from the outset. German racial nationalism simply took the implicit assumptions of German liberalism to their fullest conclusions.

Bloch inherited much of Fischhof's liberal political ideology. Thus, one can also discuss his ideology in the context of Judson's analysis of liberalism in Austria. In light of Judson's argument that nationalism and liberalism were intrinsically linked in Austria among Germans, Bloch's non-German liberalism becomes more distinctive. Clearly, Bloch does not fit into Judson's definition of who was a German liberal because he

---

260 Judson, p. 260–1.

did not identify himself as a German. Thus, Bloch's consistent support for legal equality among the peoples and his lack of cultural chauvinism does not somehow prove wrong Judson's paradigm.

One could argue that Bloch was not a liberal at all, but was instead a democrat. However, such a distinction ignores the fact that in broad ideological terms non-Marxist democrats are a subset of liberals. Democrats express a more egalitarian version of liberalism, but they are liberals nonetheless. Although Bloch did not join the Liberal Party or any liberal associations, he was an ideological liberal based on his support for constitutional government, the rule of law, and equal civil rights for all. However, he rejected a German identity and diluted the Germanness of Austro-German liberalism with a universalism derived in part from Jewish thought to the point where it became Austrian liberalism.

Unlike the German liberals described by Judson, Bloch's liberalism did not contain within it a hidden racism or a cultural egoism of any kind. However, his liberalism did reflect Jewish ideals to an important degree. These ideals, although they derived partly from Jewish tradition and reflected the particular needs and interests of European Jews, had a potentially universalistic appeal because they preached tolerance, pluralism, and the unity of mankind. Bloch's ideas thus represent a particularistic universalism.

One may be tempted to dismiss Bloch's ideology as Austrian Jewish liberalism, a characterization that does reflect to a good degree its audience. However, Bloch's vision for Austrian society was ethnically and culturally neutral in a way Austro-German liberalism, as Judson pointed out, was not. Bloch sought to impose equality, not Jewish dominance, on the peoples of the Habsburg Monarchy. Thus, his ideas were not inherently restricted to Jews, and can be seen from an ideological perspective as a non-ethnic or transethnic Austrian liberalism. Had it received the backing of the state, such a vision could perhaps have provided the Habsburg peoples with a unifying political ideology and laid the foundation for the creation of a civic Austrian nation.

Chapter 3

JOSEPH SAMUEL BLOCH: THE PROBLEM OF RACIAL NATIONALISM AND ANTISEMITISM IN AUSTRIA

Throughout the nineteenth century, the so-called 'Jewish question,' namely the changing legal, social, and economic status of Jews in European states, was intimately linked with the issue of Jewish assimilation.[261] Both Jews and Gentiles grappled with the question of whether and to what degree Jews should assimilate, as well as what the term itself meant. According to Bloch, assimilation occurred when a Jew no longer acknowledged his or her Jewish ethnic identity (this did not require religious conversion) and proclaimed membership in another nationality.[262] Thus, according to his definition, assimilation depended on how Jews identified themselves rather than the level of observance to religious or even cultural practices they maintained.

When he emerged as a public figure in the early 1880s, Bloch challenged the views of the Jewish establishment in Vienna on the proper response to antisemitism, as well as on questions of assimilation and identity. The 'establishment' included most of the bourgeois Viennese Jews, the wealthy financiers and industrialists, as well as the religious leadership. In the early 1880s, the 'establishment' dominated the city's *Israelitische Kultusgemeinde*, the state-sanctioned body that governed the religious affairs of the Jewish community in each municipality or

---

261 See Jacob Katz, *Out of the Ghetto: The Social Background of Jewish Emancipation, 1770–1870* (Cambridge: Harvard University Press, 1973). Katz remains the preeminent synthetic work on Jewish emancipation and social change in the eighteenth and nineteenth centuries.

262 Joseph Samuel Bloch, *Der Nationale Zwist und die Juden in Österreich* (Vienna: M. Gottlieb, 1886), p. 27.

town. Bloch rejected the establishment's position that Viennese Jews needed to integrate into Austro-German society (a long-held goal), remain politically passive, at least regarding issues such as antisemitism that could be seen as 'Jewish issues,' and refrain from recognizing a Jewish *Stamm* identity.

The Jews of Habsburg Austria did not all agree on how best to protect themselves against antisemitism and preserve their hard-won freedom and equality. Until relatively recently, however, the historiography of the Jews of Vienna largely reflected the experiences of that community's elite because it examined only how they experienced the attempt at assimilation, and offered their views as representative of all Austrian Jewry. Before the 1980s most historians portrayed the Jews of the western Austrian lands[263] as having fully acculturated as Germans. These historians argued that Austro-German society had gradually but successfully absorbed even the immigrant *Ostjuden* who had immigrated to Vienna from Galicia.[264] To an extent, this older view accurately

---

263 These refer to the Alpine German provinces of Upper and Lower Austria, Styria, Carinthia, Salzburg, Tyrol, and Vorarlberg, the lands of the Bohemian Crown (Bohemia, Moravia and Silesia), and the Istrian peninsula. More simply, they refer to all of Cisleithanian Austria minus Galicia and Bukovina in the East and Dalmatia in the South along the Adriatic coastline. Jews in these lands concentrated largely in either Vienna and its environs or the Bohemian provinces.

264 The earliest historians were themselves members of the Viennese Jewish bourgeoisie, such as Sigmund Mayer, *Die Wiener Juden, 1700–1900: Kommerz, Kultur, Politik* (Vienna: R. Lowit, 1917) and Max Grunwald, *Vienna* (Philadelphia: The Jewish Publication Society of America, 1936). Other early influential works include Hans Tietze, *Die Juden Wiens: Geschichte-Wirtschaft-Kultur* (Leipzig: E.P. Tal & Co., 1933); Ludwig Bato, *Die Juden im alten Wien* (Vienna: Phaidon-Verlag, 1928). Among later works, Peter Pulzer argued that in East Central Europe Jews traditionally identified with the historic nations, especially the German nation. Peter Pulzer, *The Rise of Political Antisemitism in Germany and Austria* (New York: Wiley, 1964; rev. ed., Harvard University Press, 1988). See also Wolfgang Häusler, "Toleranz, Emanzipation und Antisemitismus: Das österreichische Judentum des bürgerlichen Zeitalters (1782–1918)," pp. 83–134, in Anna Drabek, et. al., ed., *Das Österreichische Judentum: Voraussetzungen und Geschichte* (Vienna: Jugend und Volk, 1974). Häusler contended that Jewish "national peculiarities" had disappeared as a result of their absorption by Austro-German society, but qualified this statement by noting that it represented only the elites. See Ibid., p. 108. This qualification demonstrated that by the 1970s historians were beginning to acknowledge the differences between the situation of the bourgeois elites and the rest of Viennese Jewry.

described the Jewish elites of western Austria; however, it ignored the middle and especially the lower strata of Jewish society. Historians now debate such issues as the extent and form of assimilation, as well as the impact of social class on the process.

Three of the most important works of the 1980s argue, albeit in very different ways, that the Jewish community in Vienna was far more Jewish than previously imagined. Marsha Rozenblit, Robert Wistrich, and Steven Beller have radically transformed the traditional picture of Viennese Jewish assimilation.[265] Oxaal recognized the similarity between Rozenblit and Beller in that they both emphasize Jewish differences from Viennese Christians. Rozenblit wrote a social and quantitative history of the Jews of Vienna in which she explained how they created patterns of economic and social behavior that marked them as Jews both to themselves and the outside world. Ordinary Viennese Jews who absorbed German culture did so "in the company of other Jews."[266] Wistrich examined the ideology of the Viennese Jewish community, focusing largely on Jewish political and intellectual leaders. He found that even those most supportive of Jewish assimilation into German society expressed a strong sense of belonging to a Jewish people.[267]

Beller, on the other hand, focused on those Viennese Jews, specifically the liberal bourgeoisie, who integrated into the German cultural sphere and provided much of that city's cultural elite.[268] He maintained that even the most acculturated bourgeois Viennese Jews maintained an identity separate from the non-Jewish bourgeoisie. They absorbed an Enlightenment German culture that differed from the *Gefühlskultur*, an aesthetic culture based on beauty and emotion rather than rationalism, that dominated Austro-German society. By accepting the Enlightenment-based liberal ideology and cultural traditions of Protestant North Germany, these Jews remained distinct from their neighbors in Vienna, who were Catholic, South Germans. Beller demonstrated that, by the

---

265 See also Ivar Oxaal, "The Jews of Young Hitler's Vienna," in Ivar Oxaal, et. al. ed, *Jews, Antisemitism and Culture in Vienna* (London: Routledge, Kegan-Paul, 1987), p. 25.

266 Rozenblit, *The Jews of Vienna*, p. 195.

267 Wistrich, *The Jews of Vienna in the Age of Franz Joseph.*

268 Steven Beller, *Vienna and the Jews, 1867–1938: A Cultural History* (Cambridge: Cambridge University Press, 1989).

late nineteenth century, Viennese Jews who joined the liberal cultural elite entered into a world of already acculturated Jews.[269] Rozenblit, Wistrich, and Beller have not ended the debate on Jewish assimilation and identity, but they certainly have put to rest the traditional historiographical picture of a fully acculturated Viennese Jewry that was culturally indistinguishable from its non-Jewish neighbors.

Beller also analyzed the intellectual foundations of assimilation among bourgeois Viennese Jews. The German Enlightenment and the ideas of liberalism played an important role in shaping these Jews' sense of Austrian and Jewish identity. The Enlightenment had offered an attractive path out of the ghetto, not only because it promised emancipation and civic equality, but also because it professed a worldview many Jews were able to reconcile with Jewish tradition. Acculturated Jews saw in both the Enlightenment and Jewish tradition an emphasis on education and a shared belief in the "ethical autonomy of the individual."[270] This is not to say that the acculturated Jews' association of these Enlightenment values with Jewish tradition concurred with the traditional interpretation of Judaism. Nevertheless, they were able to reconcile for themselves the tenets of the Enlightenment with their desire to remain Jewish by seeing in the Enlightenment the application of what they saw as traditional Judaism's core spirit of ethical rationality as well as its worship of knowledge. Since they believed that the Enlightenment reflected the core beliefs of the Jewish religion, acculturated Jews had allowed themselves to abandon some or all traditional Jewish rituals without feeling that they had abandoned the substance of Judaism. Enlightenment philosophy, expressed politically as liberalism in the nineteenth century, became the foundation of acculturated Austrian Jews' identity. Thus, many Jews in Austria wholeheartedly supported the liberal cause.[271]

The Enlightenment envisioned one cosmopolitan humanity, in which rational thought and tolerant behavior would provide the foundation for a society open to anyone through education and assimilation. The idea that even a Jew could enter the *Menschenadel* (the nobility of human-

---

269 Ibid., p. 216.

270 Ibid., pp. 129–30, 137–43.

271 Ibid., p. 122.

ity) was central to this philosophy. Such optimism attracted Jews who sought to throw off their ancient practices for the freedom of the modern world. In Austria, these Jews were supposed to be 'humanized' through a secular education and integration into Enlightenment German society. Enlightenment and assimilation were inseparable for liberal Viennese Jews. Assimilationist Jews did not lament the loss of their old identity. As Beller put it, "The values of humanity which Jews had cherished in their religion thus came to be safeguarded in the new forms which the Enlightenment had offered. In this way assimilation came to be the continuation of Judaism by other means beyond the Jewish identity."[272]

In the late nineteenth century, increasing numbers of Austro-German antisemites opposed the Jewish assimilation called for by the Enlightenment. This repudiation caused a problem for liberal Jews. How could they call for assimilation and Enlightenment humanism when an increasing number of those around them rejected the Enlightenment? Beller contended that liberal Jews paradoxically attempted to reconcile this contradiction by making the Enlightenment the triumph of Jewish, rather than German or European ideals.[273] Liberal acculturated Jews began to see themselves as the true bearers of Enlightenment rationalism, as the teachers who would have to enlighten the benighted masses. Such a paternalistic self-conception served to further separate the acculturated Jews from the rest of Austro-German society in Vienna.

Solomon Ehrmann provided an example of this view in a 1902 speech to the *B'nai B'rith* in which he predicted that humanity would someday adopt Enlightenment values, characterized by him as Jewish, as the basis for human relations. At that point, rather than assimilate into a society based on Enlightenment principles, "Judaism will have fulfilled its task. They [Jews] will disappear as a self-contained community, because all of mankind will have been judaized."[274] 'Judaized' meant not that the Jewish people and religion would absorb the world's population, rather, that the spread of Enlightenment principles would reflect the triumph of Jewish rational and humanist values. Even

---

272 Ibid., p. 143.

273 Ibid.

274 As quoted in Ibid.

according to this view, Jews would still 'disappear' inside of the larger society, even if the roles of assimilators and assimilees had been reversed.

Bloch rejected the idea that Jews should disappear as a collective entity, although he did display some ideological similarities with his liberal, German-acculturated Jewish counterparts. Like these Jews, he envisioned an Austrian state founded on Enlightenment principles. However, although Bloch's ideal state guaranteed individual freedom and civic equality, it did not require Jews or any other people to assimilate, only to support the equality of all the Austrian peoples. Furthermore, Bloch differed from the assimilationists on the question of identity. He could not accept even Ehrmann's views because he maintained a strong Jewish *Stamm* consciousness, according to which he valued the continued existence of a separate Jewish people as one member of a confederated, yet heterogeneous human family.

Some other *Stamm*-conscious Austrian Jews turned to Zionism, a movement founded by Theodor Herzl[275] that called for the creation of a national homeland for Jews.[276] However, most ethnically conscious Jews in Habsburg Austria were not Zionists.[277] Because he identified

---

[275] See also Ian Reifowitz, "An Austrianist and a Zionist: The Ideas of Joseph Samuel Bloch and Theodor Herzl on National Identity and the Multinational State," in *Zerfall und Rekonstruktion. Identitäten und ihre Representation in der österreichischen Moderne (Studien zur Moderne*, Band 5, Hildegard Kernmayer, ed., Moritz Csáky, series ed., Passagen Verlag, forthcoming); and Chaim Bloch, "Theodor Herzl and Joseph S. Bloch," *Herzl Yearbook* 1 (1958), pp. 154–64. For a biography of Herzl, see Jacques Kornberg, *Theodor Herzl* (Bloomington: Indiana University Press, 1993).

[276] For a general history of Zionism, see Walter Laqueur, *A History of Zionism* (London: Weidenfeld and Nicolson, 1972). On Zionism as a vehicle for assimilation of Jews see Stephen Poppel, *Zionism in Germany: the Shaping of a Jewish Identity* (Philadelphia: The Jewish Publication Society of America, 1976); Steven Aschheim, *Brothers and Strangers: the East European Jews in German and German-Jewish Consciousness* (Madison: University of Wisconsin Press, 1982).

[277] See McCagg, *A History of Habsburg Jewry*. He argues that after the emergence of Herzl in the late 1890s, Zionism remained "conspicuously low" in Vienna and Austria as a whole with the exception of Galicia (pp. 198–99). Even in that province, however, so-called 'autonomists' (with whom Bloch was sympathetic despite their difference on the desire for Jewish political autonomy within Austria) found much more success than did Zionists. In 1907 four autonomists, Adolf Stand, Benno Straucher, Heinrich Gabel, and Arthur Mahler, won election to the *Reichsrat* and founded a Jewish Club (pp. 185–6). Bloch greeted this development with great satisfaction.

Austria as his homeland, Bloch rejected Zionism and any particularistic form of Jewish nationalism, in addition to assimilation and/or support for German (or Czech, etc.) nationalism, as options for Jews. The existence of a multiethnic Austrian state allowed Jews like Bloch to oppose Zionism, yet still preserve a sense of peoplehood distinct from that of their non-Jewish neighbors, while also identifying as members of an Austrian civic nation. He wanted to encourage a separate Jewish consciousness, but not a separatistic Jewish politics.[278] Zionists, while also loyal Austrians, would rather by definition have been citizens of a Jewish homeland. Bloch, on the other hand, had a deeper identification with Austria that went beyond mere loyalty. He was able to feel identify completely with Austria because it demanded not assimilation into any one nationality, but rather individual loyalty to the Monarchy.

A Jew in Prague, for example, could have legitimately claimed, "I am neither German nor Czech. I am a Jew and also an Austrian," because the state did not represent any of the ethnic nationalities; it was the patrimony of a dynasty, not the legatee of an ancient tribal kingdom in Central Europe to which a majority of Austrians (but not Jews) could trace their roots. Bloch could feel both Austrian and Jewish because his civic identification with the Austrian polity did not conflict with his *Stamm* identification with the Jewish people. Unlike the governments of Russia or even Hungary, the post-*Ausgleich* Austrian government made little effort to absorb 'minorities' into the most populous nationality, the Germans in this case. Germanization would have been unworkable, as German-speakers, including Jews who identified as such, were only 35.6% of Austria's population in 1910, down from 36.8% in 1880.[279] An ethnically conscious Jew in Austria could have chosen to identify as a member of the Jewish political nation, as did the Zionists, or as a member of the Austrian political nation, as did Bloch.

In her recent work on Habsburg Jewry, Rozenblit explained that these Jews adopted a "tripartite identity" that was, in fact, politically Austrian and ethnically Jewish, and also allowed them to affiliate with

---

278 Many Jews who opposed Zionism, including Bloch, supported the idea of small-scale emigration to Palestine, but not the creation of a Jewish polity there. See "Die 'Oesterreichische Wochenschrift' und der Zionismus," *Oesterreichische Wochenschrift*, Nr. 33, Year 13, August 14, 1896, pp. 649–50.

279 Sked, *The Decline and Fall of the Habsburg Empire*, p. 278.

one of the cultures of the area, mostly German in the regions on which she focused.[280] Bloch, who called for the embracing of Jewish ethnicity and an Austrian political or civic consciousness while leaving the question of cultural affinity to each individual, not only provided the basic framework of the tripartite identity Rozenblit described, but helped make it predominant among his fellow Austrian Jews. He believed that this formula was the best way to combat the racial nationalism and antisemitism that threatened to destroy his world, and spent his entire public career spreading that message.

Joseph Samuel Bloch was born in the year 1850, in an East Galician town called Dukla. He first became a public figure in 1883 as a result of his confrontation with and ultimate victory over August Rohling, an antisemitic professor of ancient Hebrew at Charles University in Prague. Rohling had testified under oath earlier that year at the Tiszaeszlár blood-libel proceedings that Jews murdered Christian children and consumed their blood as part of a religious ritual.[281] Bloch, then an unknown orthodox rabbi of a synagogue in Floridsdorf, an industrial suburb of Vienna, publicly condemned Rohling as an antisemite and an academic fraud who had not only testified falsely about sections of the Talmud at Tiszaeszlár, but could not even read Hebrew. Bloch challenged Rohling to translate a randomly selected page of the Talmud, and offered 3,000 florins as incentive.[282] Rohling filed suit against Bloch for libel, but, after a two-year investigation, admitted defeat and dropped his suit two weeks before the trial was set to begin. A coal baron named von Gutmann had confiden-

280 Marsha Rozenblit, *Reconstructing a National Identity: The Jews of Habsburg Austria during World War I* (Oxford: Oxford University Press, 2001), pp. 3–4. She centers her analysis of Austro-German Jewish identity on this concept.

281 The charge of ritual murder, or blood-libel, was a medieval myth that never completely disappeared from European antisemitism. In the late nineteenth century, a number of blood-libel trials took place in Eastern and Central Europe, including Austria-Hungary. The Tiszaeszlar trial received great publicity, as did Rohling's indictment of Jewish laws and practices as brutal and barbaric. For more on the trial and surrounding events, see Andrew Handler, *Blood Libel at Tiszaeszlár* (New York: Columbia University Press, 1980).

282 For the details of this affair, see Bloch, *My Reminiscences*, Vol. I, pp. 61–76. Bloch was ready to go to trial, having prepared a document that contained 319 quotations in Hebrew from the Talmud and other Halachic sources, as well as German translations thereof to be submitted as evidence. Josef Kopp, his attorney, had written a companion document that discussed how the quotations could be used at trial. See Central Archives for the History of the Jewish People, Jerusalem, File no. P/150/5, Papers of Joseph Samuel Bloch.

tially offered to pay Bloch's legal expenses in contesting the suit, which provides evidence of immediate Jewish support for Bloch even among some of the elite leadership, the majority of whom preferred to ignore antisemites such as Rohling rather than publicly contradict their claims.[283]

The *Wiener Allgemeine Zeitung* published a special edition containing the collection of Bloch's attacks on Rohling and sold three hundred thousand copies in one day. There existed a huge audience in Vienna and especially among the *Ostjuden* of Galicia and Bukovina that wanted Jews to fight back against antisemitic agitation.[284] Almost overnight, Bloch became "the foremost public defender of Jewish constitutional rights in Austria."[285] After the Rohling affair, the fight against antisemitism remained a central theme in Bloch's public ideology.

In 1884 Bloch won election to the *Reichsrat* as a representative of the Kolomea-Buczacz-Sniatyn electoral district in Galicia, and served for eleven years. Also in 1884 he called for the creation of a civic organization to fight antisemitism and defend the rights of Jews, and, two years later, co-founded the *Österreichisch-Israelitische Union*, an association charged with that mission.[286] Although the *Union* gradually grew less vociferous in its opposition to assimilation than Bloch would have liked, it continued to reflect his overall ideology to a good degree.[287] This was true especially regarding the need to solve the nationalities question through equality for all the Austrian peoples. On February 20, 1897, the Union declared its support for "the return to the program of the reconciliation of peoples, nationalities, denominations, estates, and

283 See Jacob Toury, "Troubled Beginnings: The Emergence of the Österreichisch-Israelitische Union," *Leo Baeck Institute Year Book* 30 (1985), pp. 457–75, see p. 460, n. 12.

284 Wistrich, *Vienna and the Jews in the Age of Franz Joseph*, p. 283.

285 Ibid., p. 289.

286 For more on Bloch's involvement in this Jewish self-defense organization, see Lander, "Joseph Samuel Bloch und die Österreichisch-Israelitische Union," pp. 183–222; Rozenblit, *The Jews of Vienna*, pp. 153–59, 180–84, 189–91, Toury, "Troubled Beginnings: The Emergence of the Österreichisch-Israelitische Union," Toury, "Years of Strife: The Contest of the Österreichisch-Israelitische Union for the Leadership of Austrian Jewry," *Leo Baeck Institute Year Book* 33 (1988): 179–99, and Wistrich, *Vienna and the Jews in the Age of Franz Joseph*, pp. 289–92. Toury detailed the debates between Bloch and other founders, a result of which was the moderation of Bloch's original vision for the OIU.

287 Rozenblit, *The Jews of Vienna*, p. 156; Lander, p. 218.

classes in the name of free thought and progress, in the name of justice and the equality of all citizens before the law."[288]

In 1884, Bloch began publishing the *Oesterreichische Wochenschrift*, which served as a "central organ for the general interests of Jewry."[289] This weekly periodical broadcasted his ideas until 1920, and reached Jews all over Central Europe.[290] It became the major German language Jewish newspaper in the Monarchy.[291] Bloch claimed 1500 subscriptions for its first issue and, other than an initial contribution of 500 florins from a Baron Sochor, a non-Jewish *Reichsrat* deputy from Brody, in Galicia, he never mentioned any other charitable contribution to the paper.[292] The weekly appearance of the *Oesterreichische Wochen-*

---

288 See the address by Gustav Kohn to the February 20, 1897 OIU meeting, in: *Mittheilungen der Österreichisch-Israelitische Union*, Year IX, No. 92 (March 1897), p. 3. Cited in Malachi Hacohen, "Dilemmas of Cosmopolitanism: Karl Popper, Jewish Identity and 'Central European Culture,'" *Journal of Modern History* 71, 1 (March 1999), pp. 105–49, 117; and Cahnmann, "Adolf Fischhof and his Jewish Followers," p. 130. Kohn characterized this program as based on the ideas of Fischhof.

289 These words appeared below the title on the masthead of every issue of the *Oesterreichische Wochenschrift*. Although the title changed over the years to *Dr. Bloch's Oesterreichische Wochenschrift*, and, after the Monarchy fell apart, simply *Dr. Bloch's Wochenschrift*, for simplicity's sake I will refer to the paper as the *Oesterreichische Wochenschrift* throughout this book.

290 Max Grunwald, "Josef Bloch," in *Festschrift zum 75 jährigen Bestehen des jüdischen-theologischen Seminars Fraenckelscher Stiftung*, Vol. 2 (Vienna: n.p., 1930), p. 7. This essay appeared as a supplement to the *Festschrift* due to its accidental omission when the volume originally appeared. Grunwald was Bloch's son-in-law.

291 For more on Bloch's and other Jewish newspapers in Austria, see Jacob Toury, *Die Jüdische Press im österreichische Kaiserreich: ein Beitrag zur Problematik der Akkulturation, 1802–1918* (Tübingen: J.C.B. Mohr, 1983). On the *Oesterreichische Wochenschrift* specifically, see in particular pp. 74–82. Unfortunately, Toury does not offer circulation numbers for Bloch's paper over the years.

292 Bloch, *My Reminiscences*, Vol. I, p. 181. On the subsequent pages Bloch described the financial difficulty he faced during the first year of publication, largely because his first printer tried to wrest editorial control and the copyright from him. In order to thwart this maneuver, Bloch commandeered the whole delivery of the seventh issue of December 4, 1884, as it arrived at the post office and hand copied the addresses of the subscribers (which the printer had kept from Bloch, along with the money and the financial books) before returning the papers for postal delivery. Bloch then switched printers for the next issue but had to pay a settlement of 1500 florins to the first printer to avoid a politically embarrassing criminal suit the printer had filed against him for copying the addresses from a printed edition of the paper. See Ibid., pp. 182–3.

schrift over thirty-seven years without any evidence of outside subsidies demonstrates at least its profitability, and suggests an impressive readership and thus widespread knowledge of Bloch's views.

In addition to his memoirs, speeches, private papers, and other books, the *Oesterreichische Wochenschrift* is a valuable source for Bloch's ideas. Each edition led with an editorial, most of which ran without a byline, although Bloch occasionally printed the opinions of others, including members of his editorial staff, and gave them credit. On a handful of occasions, Bloch affixed his name to a piece, but usually these were of a personal nature, such as a response to a letter to the editor that had addressed him directly. He was the source of the ideas printed in the name of the *Oesterreichische Wochenschrift*, and confirmed this fact by listing himself as the editor responsible for the newspaper's content. Furthermore, on February 22, 1895, the paper's title became *Dr. Bloch's Oesterreichische Wochenschrift*, leaving no doubt whose opinion it reflected. Thus, one can assume that unsigned editorials express Bloch's views whether he literally wrote them or not. Although during the first few years, others' names were occasionally listed as the editor, Bloch did this merely to hide his overwhelming editorial presence. In these early years, he wrote most of the news articles as well as the editorials, and edited each edition.[293]

Beginning with his campaign against August Rohling, the fight against antisemitism remained a central theme in Bloch's public ideology. He fought antisemitism throughout his career, arguing that the antisemitism of the late nineteenth century differed from earlier anti-Jewish behavior, which derived mostly from religious prejudice. Bloch identified the tripartite origins of the new antisemitism; it was at once hatred based on racial, religious, and class differences.[294] He recognized the symbiotic relationship between ethnic/racial enmity in general and the more virulent antisemitism that appeared in late nineteenth century Europe.[295] Almost weekly he railed against nationalist hatred in his newspaper and demanded that his readers fight all kinds of intolerance if they hoped to defeat antisemitism because "Jew-hatred is the

293 Lander, pp. 164–5.

294 Bloch, *Der Nationale Zwist*, p. 8.

295 Ibid., pp. 23–4.

natural child of overwrought national chauvinism."[296] The gradual transformation of earlier cultural and linguistic forms of nationalism into racism in the late nineteenth century profoundly disturbed Bloch, who lamented "race-hatred is forming a type of nationalist cramp on the head of Europe resulting from the constant growth and sharpening of nationalist thought."[297]

Nationalistic animosity had spread across Europe, and was "embedded into the flesh and blood of the current generation."[298] What Bloch called "the hallucinatory cult of nationalism" equated true patriotism with hatred of anyone perceived as a foreigner.[299] He recognized the special vulnerability of Jews in an age of general intolerance towards minorities and those seen as different or alien. "This prevailing mood among the European peoples must first and foremost take aim against the uncomfortable and indigestible Jewish minority, whose fate it is to be seen as the cause and origin of every nausea."[300]

Some Austrian Jews, in particular the Jewish establishment in Vienna, hoped that assimilation would protect them from the rising tide of nationalism.[301] In the mid-late nineteenth century, most of the acculturated Jews in the Alpine and Bohemian provinces had absorbed German culture, which offered a strong attraction to the Jews of Austria and all of Central Europe. Assimilation and emancipation were closely linked for Jews in German-speaking Europe. Since the late eighteenth century, German Enlightenment thinkers such as Christian Wilhelm von Dohm had argued that Jews should receive civil rights, but only in

296 "Gegen die 'extremen Bestrebungen,'" *Oesterreichische Wochenschrift*, Nr. 5, Year 8, January 30, 1891, p. 75. This article is but one of dozens of similar examples over the decades.

297 Bloch, *Der Nationale Zwist*, p. 20.

298 Ibid.

299 Ibid.

300 Ibid.

301 See Rozenblit, *Reconstructing a National Identity: The Jews of Habsburg Austria during World War I*, pp. 14–38, which offers a comprehensive discussion of Habsburg Jewry, region by region, in terms of cultural affiliation and ethnic identification. See also McCagg, *A History of Habsburg Jews*, and Peter Hanak, "Problems of Jewish Assimilation in Austria-Hungary," in Peter Thane, Geoffrey Crossick, Roderick Floud, eds., *The Power of the Past: Essays for Eric Hobsbawm* (Cambridge: Cambridge University Press, 1984), pp. 235–50.

return for acculturating and integrating socio-economically and politically into German society by, for example, distributing themselves across the various occupations, and fulfilling the obligations of citizenship.[302] In his 1781 tract *Über die bürgerliche Verbesserung der Juden*, Dohm called this exchange '*Verbesserung*,' a term that reflected the belief by assimilation's supporters, both Christian and Jewish, that Jews somehow needed improvement and would thus benefit from the process.

Many Central European Jews adopted the *Aufklärung* values of individual ethics and *Bildung*[303] and tried to at least absorb the culture of the society that produced it. The *Aufklärung* found its Jewish counterpart in the movement known as the *Haskalah*. The *Maskilim* believed that their Enlightenment-inspired ideas would revitalize a Jewish community that had become moribund after hundreds of years of persecution and isolation, and would earn emancipation in the manner Dohm described.[304] Many Austrian Jews willingly accepted German acculturation and identified themselves as Germans because they viewed German as the culture of Enlightenment and thus emancipation.[305] Such Jews identified themselves as Germans of Jewish faith, no less German than Catholics or Protestants because they equated being a German with participation in German culture. These German-oriented Jews simply carried forward the idea of the German *Kulturnation* that grew out of the Enlightenment.[306]

---

302 Katz, *Out of the Ghetto*, pp. 57–64.

303 George Mosse explained that "the word *Bildung* combines the meaning of the English word 'education' with notions of character formation and moral education." George L. Mosse, *German Jews beyond Judaism* (Bloomington, IN: Indiana University Press, 1985), p. 3.

304 For more on the ideology of the *Maskilim* regarding the Enlightenment and emancipation, see David Sorkin, *The Transformation of German Jewry, 1780–1840* (New York: Oxford University Press, 1987).

305 Bloch described this phenomenon in, "Deutschtum und Judenthum in Oesterreich," *Oesterreichische Wochenschrift*, Nr. 2, Year 3, January 8, 1886, pp. 13–14. See also McCagg, *A History of Habsburg Jews*, p. 177, and Beller, *Vienna and the Jews*, pp. 144–7.

306 For a discussion of this development in Germany, see Sorkin, *The Transformation of German Jewry*, and Mosse, *German Jews beyond Judaism*. There existed strong parallels in the way this phenomenon developed in Germany proper and in the Alpine and Bohemian provinces of the Monarchy.

Although he opposed the desire on the part of some Austrian Jews to identify themselves as Germans, Bloch himself was not anti-German. In his writings he demonstrated his familiarity with the German cultural pantheon.[307] In fact, he completed his university education in Munich and Zurich during the years before he came to Vienna. From the time of his youth, Bloch sought to increase his knowledge of "secular learning."[308] He quoted at length from German culture's greatest authors, such as Johann Gottfried Herder, who had described the special mission of the Jewish people.[309] Bloch cited other German writers as well, including Goethe, Hegel, Kant, and Nietzsche.[310] Although he admired and respected German culture, Bloch never viewed it as his culture.

Virtually all of Bloch's published writings, including his newspaper, appeared in German. Bloch published in German because it was the language of educated Austrian society, and, in particular, the language of the German-oriented Austrian Jews he was trying to convince to return to a Jewish *Stamm* identity. There was no need to write in Yiddish because his message was that Austrian Jews should be Jewish and Austrian but not German. Had Bloch appealed to Yiddish-speaking Jews he would have been preaching to the converted. On at least one documented occasion, however, he did make a specific point to speak to his Galician constituents in Yiddish, as a signal that their form of communication was an honorable one. As he put it, he "wanted to show that the 800,000 Jews in Galicia had a right to confer about politics with each other in their own mother-tongue."[311] The fact that most of his publications, including his newspaper, printed Biblical quotes and other assorted items with Hebrew characters demonstrated that Bloch had the

---

307 See Bloch, *My Reminiscences*, Vol. I, p. 24.

308 Ibid., p. 20.

309 Bloch, *Der Nationale Zwist*, p. 90–1. Herder was among Bloch's favorite writers, and Bloch quoted from him on a number of occasions in other writings as well. See, for example, Joseph Samuel Bloch, *Israel and the Nations* (Berlin: B. Harz, 1927), p. 52.

310 See Bloch, *Israel and the Nations*, p. 369 for Goethe, p. 416 for Hegel, p. 369 for Kant, and p. 240 for Nietzsche.

311 See Bloch, *My Reminiscences*, Vol. I, p. 216. See also Stefan Walz, *Staat, Nationalität, und Jüdische Identität in Österreich vom 18. Jahrhundert bis 1914* (Frankfurt am Main: Peter Lang, 1996), p. 123–4.

productive capacity (i.e., a press with Hebrew letters) to publish any of his works entirely in Yiddish or Hebrew, and nevertheless he chose to write in German. His mother tongue was Yiddish, and he not only learned Hebrew early in his childhood education, but also would have had to write and read it perfectly in order complete his training as a rabbi. Bloch only began to learn German at the age of seventeen.[312] Although he used German as his public language, he was not attached to it as a part of his identity because he refused to identify himself nationally as a German, unlike his German-Jewish target audience. According to Bloch, "as an *Ostjude*...I can not well consider myself a German national."[313] On another occasion, he criticized a progressive Austrian Jewish politician, Julius Ofner, for using the phrase "my German heart...."[314]

Eastern Galicia, where Bloch was born and raised, offered a very different intellectual and cultural Jewish environment than those of the more German-oriented Alpine and Bohemian provinces. The German Enlightenment did not penetrate as deeply into Galician-Jewish culture as it did into the culture of the Jews of those lands to the west.[315] This fact helps explain why Bloch did not identify himself as German. Almost all the Jews who did acculturate lived in social environments that contained a strong German bourgeoisie. Assimilation was an attempt by middle-class Jews to fit in to the bourgeois German culture of Vienna and the other cities of western Austria. By Bloch's time, Czernowitz, the provincial capital of Bukovina, was the one major location with a large population of German-acculturated Jews outside of western Austria. Despite its location on the eastern border of the monarchy, this city had a significant German minority and a largely German-oriented Jewish population dominated by an educated, secu-

---

312 See Bloch, *My Reminiscences*, Vol. I, p. 20.

313 Joseph Samuel Bloch, *Erinnerungen aus meinem Leben*, Vol. III, Morris Bloch, ed. (Vienna: Appel, 1933), p. 288. I would like to thank Dr. Michael Ley of Vienna, Austria, who made available to me a copy of this rare volume.

314 Bloch, *Erinnerungen aus meinem Leben*, Vol. III, p. 170.

315 McCagg, *A History of Habsburg Jewry*, p. 109–112.

lar-oriented middle class.[316] In the Galicia of Bloch's youth, there existed only a very small Germanophile Jewish element, along with an even smaller portion of polonized Jews concentrated in Cracow, far away from his childhood home in East Galicia.[317]

In order for Bloch to become a rabbi, he had to complete years of a rigorous traditional Jewish education. He took his rabbinical studies under Rabbi Dr. Esriel Hildesheimer, the head of the Orthodox rabbinical school in Eisenstadt.[318] Such an education was, of course, no guarantee against a desire to assimilate. Nevertheless, an adult Jew who had completed his Orthodox rabbinical training was more likely to identify himself as a member of the Jewish *Stamm* than one who had not. When Bloch encountered liberal Enlightenment ideas and found them to his liking, he was able to incorporate them into his intellectual worldview without allowing German Enlightenment culture to dominate his identity, in no small measure because he had lived in a traditional Jewish milieu for much of his early life.[319] With the exception of his rabbinical studies in Eisenstadt, during which he was also in an Orthodox environment, and his time in Munich and Zurich, he spent most of his first thirty years either in Galicia or as a rabbi in small towns in Posen, and later in Bohemia, before finally taking up residence in Vienna. In fact, although he expressed from an early age a desire to acquire both secular and Talmudic knowledge, he balanced the two in a way that did not alter his self-identification as a

---

316 See McCagg, *A History of Habsburg Jews*, p. 172–3. The province of Bukovina as a whole was one of the most diverse in the Monarchy, with roughly equal numbers of Ukrainians and Romanians (38% and 34% respectively according to the 1910 census), 20% Germans (most of whom were Jews who identified German as their language of daily use), and a smaller number of Poles (Ibid., p. 173). This unique demographic setup resulted in a political compromise among the nationalities that worked to the benefit of all, including the Jews. See Gerald Stourzh, "Der Nationale Ausgleich in der Bukowina, 1909/1910," in Ilona Slawinski, Joseph P. Strelka, eds., *Die Bukowina, Vergangenheit und Gegenwart* (Bern: Peter Lang, 1995), pp. 35–52.

317 McCagg, *A History of Habsburg Jews*, pp. 121–2. See also Israel Bartal, "'The Heavenly City of Germany' and Absolutism à la mode Autriche: The Rise of the Haskalah in Galicia," in Jacob Katz, ed., *Toward Modernity: The European Jewish Model* (New Brunswick, NJ: Transaction Books, 1986), pp. 33–43. Bartal argues that Germanization in Galicia was not at all widespread, and in fact was comparable to that in the Jewish communities across the border in Russia into the second half of the nineteenth century.

318 Bloch, *My Reminiscences*, Vol. I, pp. 19–20.

319 Ibid., pp. 11–26.

member of the Jewish people. According to Bloch, he had already largely completed his Talmudic studies in Galicia even before leaving to study with Rabbi Hildesheimer, and went there largely in search of secular knowledge.[320] Bloch's traditional Galician-Jewish upbringing thus played a large role in his strong sense of Jewish identity and his opposition to Jews' identifying themselves as members of another *Stamm.*

Bloch recognized that members of any ethnic group they tried to join would always see Jews as outsiders.

> [The Jew] will be considered a foreigner by society, never as a native. He is a step-child, Cinderella,...an adopted child whose rights are in dispute and to whom the older brothers show the door from time to time. He is never counted as a true child of the fatherland. The German, the Slav will never admit that the semitic Jew, though he has toiled in the service of a national party with selfless devotion, is of equal birth...No matter how loud we declare and proclaim our Germanness or our Polishness, we can never make them forget the Jew in us. Legal emancipation does not mean societal acceptance.[321]

In the early 1880s Bloch began a public campaign, speaking and writing in German, aimed at convincing the Jews of the Alpine and Bohemian provinces to abandon their self-identification as Germans.[322] For him, rejecting assimilation did not mean that Austrian Jews had to refrain from participating in German, Czech, or Polish culture and return to traditional Jewish culture, a demand many in his intended audience would have found intolerable, if not ludicrous.[323] He also con-

320 Ibid, p. 20.

321 Bloch, *Der Nationale Zwist*, p. 32.

322 Ibid., p. 27.

323 See also Rozenblit, *Reconstructing a National Identity: The Jews of Habsburg Austria during World War I*, p. 33. She explains how many Viennese Jews in 1914, even though they had adopted German language and middle-class culture, were ethnically Jewish in terms of "the structure of their lives" by living in Jewish neighborhoods, joining Jewish organizations, marrying Jews, and socializing among mostly other Jews. These Jews of German culture displayed an ethnic separateness, a clear boundary between themselves and Germans, despite the fact that both participated in German culture. On Viennese Jews during the war, see also David Rechter, *The Jews of Vienna and the First World War* (London: The Littman Library of Jewish Civilization, 2001).

tended that one could assimilate without converting to another religion, and that assimilation had little to do with religious observance. Bloch declared that assimilation was "a formal renunciation of religiosity as an independent national characteristic, a feeling of being integrated into the dominant nation."[324] Rather than take aim at Reform Judaism for changing traditional rituals and practices, or secular Jews who rejected their religion outright, Bloch set his sights on Jews who saw themselves as Germans, Czechs, or Poles, even if they remained practicing Jews. He wanted Jews to identify themselves as a nationality separate from any of the other Habsburg peoples. For Bloch, the implications of assimilation were above all political, not cultural or religious. In multiethnic Austria, identifying as a member of the German nationality was a political statement that he believed Jews ought not to make.

Bloch maintained that the rapidly spreading definition of nationhood based on blood ties had defined Jews out of the peoples into which they had hoped to assimilate. "As soon as the people finally decide only to offer recognition and legal consideration to their German *Stammesgenossen* (ethnic brethren), the bravest preacher of tolerance will be unable to make the people accept Jeiteles or Kohn as their kindred."[325] It was not the fault of the Jews that they remained a heterogeneous element in society, nor had they brought antisemitism onto themselves by not achieving assimilation.[326] On the contrary, Austrian Jews, especially those living in German-speaking areas, had been betrayed by a society that had demanded they adopt the cultural and intellectual values as well as the behavioral norms of the majority in order to prepare for their absorption into the mainstream, and then rejected the Jews as equal members of the community after they had done so. Bloch explained that the desire of Jews to assimilate had produced, especially among Germans, a powerful backlash that took the form of racial antisemitism.[327] "Antisemitism is a result of...our attempt to assimilate....The stronger we drive ourselves into the Christian society, the stronger the resistance."[328]

324 Bloch, *Erinnerungen aus meinem Leben*, Vol. III, p. 288.

325 Bloch, *Der Nationale Zwist*, p. 38.

326 "Assimilation und Antisemitismus," *Oesterreichische Wochenschrift*, Nr. 3, Year 2, January 16, 1885, p. 1–2.

327 Bloch, *Der Nationale Zwist*, pp 38–9.

328 Bloch, *Erinnerungen aus meinem Leben*, Vol. III, p. 158.

Assimilationist Jews had accepted the Enlightenment bargain that they abandon their sense of being a separate people as well as their cultural differences in return for civic equality and emancipation.[329] However, Bloch criticized them for having done so and regretfully noted "the Jews of Austria have formed, in a manner of speaking, an appendage of the German-Austrian people, and sometimes it appears as though Jewry and Germandom were fully identical things."[330] He lamented that many such Jews desired nothing more than to outwardly become indistinguishable from their German neighbors, and that they considered it a great compliment to hear they displayed no outstanding Jewish characteristics.[331]

These Jews of German culture worshipped literary giants such as Goethe and especially Schiller more deeply than did many non-Jewish Germans.[332] However, through their extensive acculturation and education, these Jews had made themselves different once again, in particular in Vienna, where Enlightenment rationalism had never really taken hold among the Austro-Germans.[333] As Beller put it, many Jews in Vienna "had assimilated into a great and glorious culture but the society for that culture did not exist."[334]

Although 'enlightened' German elites had promoted assimilation even into the 1880's, many people by then had begun to react against it. By this time, the majority of Austro-Germans had rejected the liberal Enlightenment ideas of individual freedom and rationalism.[335] The Enlightenment had proclaimed that anyone willing to be educated in German culture could become German. However, unlike the older, non-racial or non-biological version of antisemitism which professed its prejudice against the Jewish faith, a growing number of late nineteenth century antisemites had begun to view Jews as a genetically alien and impure element, an undesirable infiltration from the barbar-

---

329 Beller, *Vienna and the Jews*, p. 143.

330 Bloch, *Erinnerungen aus meinem Leben*, Vol. III, p. 156.

331 Ibid., p. 157.

332 Beller, *Vienna and the Jews*, pp. 150–1.

333 Ibid., pp. 134, 216–217, Jews were "at the centre of culture but the edge of society."

334 Ibid., p. 164.

335 See Andrew Whiteside, *Austrian National Socialism Before 1918* (The Hague: Martinus Nijhoff, 1962), Chapter 1.

ian East into the German *Volk*. Although he referred on occasion to the 'Jewish race,' Bloch rejected the concept of racial purity. He recognized that no pure racial types existed because people of all so-called 'races' had mixed with the others among whom they lived over the centuries. Bloch aimed this attack on racism specifically against the radical German nationalist Georg von Schönerer, whom he named as the primary progenitor of the false notion of racial purity.[336] Schönerer among others promulgated a new definition of 'German' that could not be altered by education, baptism or acculturation.[337] A German, according to these racial nationalists and antisemites, had to have German blood, a definition that consciously rejected the open, cultural definition of Germanness put forth in the German Enlightenment. By 1900, the racial definition of nationhood had become widespread among German-Austrians.[338] Although Schönerer and his political supporters constituted a fringe element in Austrian electoral politics, animosity towards Jews as perceived 'outsiders' was quite widespread. The election as mayor of Vienna of Karl Lueger, who relied heavily on antisemitic rhetoric to gain support among voters, demonstrates the strength of anti-Jewish sentiment.

Another problem faced those Austrian Jews who sought to assimilate. In late nineteenth century Austria, almost every nationality in a given region was in conflict with at least one other over such issues as language and education. Thus, in areas that had more than one other *Stamm*, Jews who had adopted another culture and hoped to assimilate completely into that other nationality faced not only the hatred of those who wanted to keep them out of their group, but also the anger of another group that came to see these Jews as part of the enemy camp.[339] Bloch predicted that, in a life and death struggle between Germans and

336 "Wo bleibt also die Race?," *Oesterreichische Wochenschrift*, Nr. 31, Year 6, August 9, 1889, pp. 573–5.

337 For more on Schönerer, see Andrew Whiteside, *The Socialism of Fools: Georg Ritter von Schoenerer and Austrian Pan-Germanism* (Berkeley: University of California Press, 1975), and Carl Schorske, *Fin-de-Siècle Vienna: Politics and Culture* (New York: Vintage Books, 1981), pp. 120–33.

338 Judson, *Exclusive Revolutionaries*, p. 226.

339 For a concise yet comprehensive region-by-region discussion of the position of Jews in the various nationalities conflicts in Austria-Hungary, see Robert Wistrich, "The Jews and Nationality Conflicts in the Habsburg Lands," *Nationalities Papers* 22 (1994), pp. 119–39.

Slavs, Jews would certainly lose.[340] In Bohemia, for example, most Germans never accepted the German-oriented Jews as fellow Germans, although Prague was an exception in that its Germans accepted Jews, if not as full-fledged members of the German *Volk*, at least as allies in the struggle between German and Czech culture.[341] Nevertheless, most Czechs did recognize those Jews as Germans and attacked them for being on the opposite side in the fight for cultural and political predominance in Bohemia. Bloch realized that Jews could never achieve security by trying to take sides in such battles, which were taking place in virtually every Habsburg province, because the peoples who were ostensibly fighting one another would always end up taking out their frustrations on the Jews.

> 'Assimilation' is understood to be above all political and national servitude, and one cannot serve two gods. If [a Jew] 'fraternizes' with the Germans or Ruthenians, the Czech mobs will smash his windows and the Pole grabs him by the throat. 'Assimilate' with the Czechs and the 'German blows' rain down. The Jewish politics of the national parties continues to remain on the level of the well-known Christian coachmen's saying— 'You ravage my Jews, I'll ravage yours.'[342]

Some Austrian Jews, however, went beyond attempting to assimilate and even joined non-Jewish nationalist parties and/or political movements in Austria. Bloch abhorred such actions, thinking it folly to believe that if Jews supported, for example, German nationalism, this support would somehow save them from antisemitism. "Certainly it was a powerful illusion...that the nationalist virus was a good vaccination to pro-

---

340 Bloch, *Der Nationale Zwist*, p. 24.

341 See Gary Cohen, *The Politics of Ethnic Survival: Germans in Prague, 1861–1914* (Princeton: Princeton University Press, 1981). For a view of Jewish identity vis-à-vis the Czech-German question that covered the whole of Bohemia, see Hillel Kieval, *The Making of Czech Jewry: National Conflict and Jewish Society in Bohemia, 1870–1918* (New York: Oxford University Press, 1988). For an examination of German, Czech, and Jewish (both Jewish-German and Jewish-Czech) ethnicity in Prague over the last two hundred plus years through the eyes of women, see Wilma A. Iggers, *Women of Prague: Ethnic Diversity and Social Change from the Eighteenth Century to the Present* (Providence: Berghahn Books, 1995).

342 Bloch, *Der Nationale Zwist*, p. 27.

tect against the antisemitic cholera; [that] through an increased dosage of the poison will the pest now completely be destroyed."[343] Jewish cooperation with Polish nationalist goals also earned a swift rebuke from Bloch. He reprinted in the *Oesterreichische Wochenschrift* a report from Lemberg describing a Galician Jew who had petitioned the local government in Lisko to remove Ruthenian language as a mandatory subject in the schools. The report criticized the action, asking "How can it benefit a Jewish population in these circumstances to work for the elimination of one of the languages of the area and to act more Polish than the Poles themselves?"[344]

Jewish German nationalists received Bloch's strongest criticism. He rebuked them for abandoning the plight of their own people, and lamented that they were "above all fanatical defenders of German predominance-regardless of the state of Judaism."[345] For example, two Jews, Heinrich Friedjung, who became a German nationalist historian, and Victor Adler, who later led the Austrian Social Democratic Party, were members of the inner circle of Georg von Schönerer's radical German nationalist party, and helped write its 1882 Linz Program. Friedjung and Adler later left when the party turned definitively towards antisemitism and racial nationalism.[346] Although Bloch denounced Jewish support for radical German nationalism throughout Austria, he held Friedjung, the editor of the *Deutsche Wochenschrift*, in particular contempt. He contrasted the national philosophy of his

---

343 Ibid., p. 38.

344 "Die Juden und der Nationalitätenhader," *Oesterreichische Wochenschrift*, Nr. 2, Year 1, October 30, 1884, p. 7. For an excellent analysis of the relations among the three major Galician ethnic groups, see John Paul-Himka, "Dimensions of a Triangle: Polish-Ukrainian-Jewish Relations in Austrian Galicia," in Israel Bartal & Antony Polonsky, eds., *Focusing on Galicia: Jews, Poles, and Ukrainians, 1772–1918* (London: Littman Library of Jewish Civilization, 1999), pp. 25–48.

345 Bloch, *My Reminiscences*, Vol. I, p. 194.

346 William J. McGrath, "Student Radicalism in Vienna," *Journal of Contemporary History* 2 (1967), pp. 183–95. This article detailed the role these and other young Jews, including Sigmund Freud, Herzl, and Gustav Mahler, played in the German nationalist movement in Austria during the 1870s and 80s. For a fuller discussion of the activities of Friedjung, Adler, Mahler and the other members of the Pernerstorfer circle during the 1870s and 80s, see McGrath, *Dionysian Art and Populist Politics in Austria* (New Haven: Yale University Press, 1974).

"Austrian Weekly" to Friedjung's "German Weekly."[347] Bloch ironically noted that despite Friedjung's fervent German nationalism, most German nationalists rejected his self-identification as a German because he, Friedjung, was a Jew.[348] Bloch condemned Friedjung's call for the Germanization of the Jewish people as "the death sentence for Jewry."[349]

When Friedjung and other German nationalist writers pointed to ancient Greece as the source of civilization, Bloch countered that the nationalistic barbarism sweeping across Central Europe in the late nineteenth century was, in fact, "purely Greek."[350] He noted that Athenians as well as Spartans had hated foreigners and did not give them equal rights in their states. This discriminatory policy contrasted with that of ancient Israel, which, according to Bloch, treated foreigners and natives equally. "The opposition between Greeks and Israelites is reflected in the opposition between the devout nationalist and the cosmopolitan-humanist world-view."[351] The Greeks were the "forefathers of chauvinism," while the Israelite world-view followed from the belief that all peoples and nations are descended from Adam and Eve, and thus equal.[352] On this basis Bloch denounced Friedjung and other Jewish proponents of national chauvinism as "severed from the Jewish spirit."[353] Bloch relied often on Biblical sources to justify his support for equal rights and the rule of law, Enlightenment views that for him derived from Jewish traditions.

When Jewish-German nationalists such as Friedjung supported the German cause in Bohemia, Bloch condemned them as practitioners of the worst kind of political short-sightedness, and referred to them on one occasion as "semitic Teutons."[354] As a vulnerable and visible minority, Jews should have been the strongest proponents of compromise between Czechs and Germans, so as to reduce nationalist tension

---

347 "'*Deutsche Wochenschrift*' contra '*Oesterreichische Wochenschrift*,'" *Oesterreichische Wochenschrift*, Nr. 5, Year 1, November 21, 1884, p. 1.

348 Ibid.

349 Bloch, *Der Nationale Zwist*, pp. 51–2.

350 Ibid., p. 83.

351 Ibid., p. 85.

352 Ibid.

353 Ibid., p. 51.

354 "Die Juden im nordwestlichen Böhmen," *OW*, Nr. 9, Year 2, February 27, 1885, p. 3.

in Bohemia and Austria as a whole.[355] Bloch decried the illusion that Jews could remain safe in Bohemia by taking sides in the language issue. "We cannot present ourselves as either 'German-national' or 'Czech-national' without becoming a ridiculous caricature, and for our co-nationals in Bohemia it is only logical...to take up a position outside all national parties."[356]

In a speech to the *Reichsrat* given February 11, 1890, Bloch bemoaned the centuries-old role Jews had played as representatives of the German language and culture in the East. He directly attacked German racial nationalism and antisemitism as contradicting the essence of the national idea, which was first and foremost to promote the growth and expansion of the nation and its culture. Bloch contrasted the French idea of an inclusive civic nationalism with the small-mindedness of the Bohemian Germans, many of who rejected Jewish attempts to identify as fellow Germans despite centuries of Jewish loyalty to the German language.[357] Bloch explained that through their use of Yiddish, with its predominantly German vocabulary and grammar, Jews had earned the mistrust of the largely Slavic peoples among whom they lived after their medieval expulsions from much of German-speaking Central Europe.[358] As the speech reached its climax, Bloch illustrated the uncivilized character of exclusionary German nationalism.

> We have fought for Germanism in all the countries of Europe (Herr Hevera: 'Unfortunately!'—Great mirth.) Herr Hevera is right: yes, unfortunately...We Jews were martyrs for Germandom. German became our mother tongue. How was our loyal national devotion finally repaid? We awoke one day and a

---

[355] Bloch, *Der Nationale Zwist*, pp. 36–37.

[356] Ibid., p. 40.

[357] Joseph Samuel Bloch, *Documente zur Aufklärung, Nr. 3, Talmud und Judenthum in der Oesterreichische Volksvertretung, Dr. Bloch's Parlamentsreden* (Vienna: Oesterreichische Wochenschrift, 1900), pp. 27–28.

[358] The fact that Ashkenazi Jews had adopted German (which came to be known as Yiddish) in the medieval period suggests that they had already adopted German culture, and in that sense made an attempt at assimilation approximately one thousand years ago. That first attempt ended with their expulsion from Western and Central Europe, the second had even more dire results.

> new party had arisen with a new doctrine of salvation. How did this doctrine go? Like all great ideas, it too had the foresight to be short, clear and understandable to all;...Hepp! Hepp! That is the highest achievement of the nineteenth century. (Resounding mirth.) Hepp! Hepp! It is the purest outpouring of nationalist thought. (Laughter.) Hepp! Hepp! It is the greatest triumph and renown of Germanism. Hepp! Hepp! It is a sound out of the depths of the German national soul. (General mirth.) Hepp! Hepp! is inherently German, neither can it be translated into Czech nor Polish. (A great period of extended mirth.)[359]

Bloch then pointed out the absurdity of German intolerance of foreigners in light of the fact that millions of Germans lived as minorities scattered throughout Russia and Eastern Europe. He attacked the antisemitic Deputy Türk, who, earlier in the day, had praised the Czar for oppressing Jews, by reminding him that hatred of foreigners had also created hardships for Germans in Russia. Finally, Bloch compared German intolerance with the laws of ancient Israel. "The Jewish state had another program. One set of rights and laws for natives and foreigners."[360]

This speech garnered Bloch much publicity and bolstered Jewish self-esteem in Austria. Both Jews and non-Jews acknowledged the power of his arguments.[361] Never before had the *Reichsrat* witnessed a Jew respond so forcefully and directly to the remarks of an antisemite and rhetorically trounce his opponent in a public debate over antisemitism.[362] The *Reichsrat* stenographic record parenthetically noted the following comment at the end of the text of the speech:

---

359 Ibid. "Hepp Hepp" was shouted over and over during the 1819 antisemitic riots in Germany, and served during the nineteenth century as a catch phrase for German antisemitism. The phrase originated in the medieval period as an anagram of 'Hierosolyma est perdita.' Thanks to Aviel Roshwald for the information on the term's medieval origins. Although 'Hepp' is often spelled with one 'p,' I have preserved Bloch's original spelling.

360 Ibid., p. 29.

361 Wistrich, *The Jews of Vienna in the Age of Franz Joseph*, p. 292.

362 Ibid., 293. See also Bloch, *My Reminiscences*, Vol. I, p. 248–257.

"Lively applause on the right. Speaker is congratulated from all sides."[363] This notation makes clear that the "mirth" and "laughter" of the deputies reflected their approval of Bloch's statements; they agreed with his biting and sarcastic assessment of German nationalism. Bloch also received personal congratulations from Ritter von Jaworski, Chairman of the *Reichsrat* Polish Club (of which Bloch was a member), who thanked him, and told him "you have been a credit to us today."[364] The Jewish response was overwhelming. Bloch received over one thousand telegrams from Jews across Austria and Hungary who were grateful and proud that someone had so powerfully exposed "the meanness of antisemitism."[365] Bloch was particularly proud to receive a congratulatory message from Fischhof.

In addition to criticizing Jewish support for German culture, Bloch also spoke out against the seemingly blind loyalty of some of his co-religionists to the *Verfassungspartei*, the party of German liberals.[366] German liberals had strongly supported legal equality for all citizens, including Jews, and applauded that principle's enshrinement in the 1867 Constitution. In the late nineteenth century, Jewish-German liberals viewed the spread of Enlightenment liberalism and German culture as one and the same. As late as 1899, the *Neue Freie Presse*, edited by two Jews, was still able to declare that "despite the difficulty of fight-

---

363 Bloch reprinted the text of the speech in the *Oesterreichische Wochenschrift* on February 14, 1890 (Nr. 7, Year 7), pp. 134–46, and the above comment appeared at the end of the text on p. 146. Bloch published the speech again as a supplemental addition to the paper the following week entitled "Reden gegen den Antisemitismus," and later included it in the *Documente zur Aufklärung* collection.

364 Bloch, *My Reminiscences*, Vol. I, p. 252. As a deputy from Galicia in the 1880s and 90s, Bloch had no choice but to join the Polish Club. In his 1907 bid to win election to the *Reichsrat*, this time from Vienna, Bloch defended his membership in the Polish Club saying that he had been forced to join, and, in any case, had done so with the approval of Adolf Fischhof (demonstrating at least Bloch's belief that Fischhof's name carried sway). See *Oesterreichische Wochenschrift*, "Zur Reichsratswahl im fünften Wahlkreis. Ein Wort der Abwehr, von Dr. Josef S. Bloch," Nr. 13, Year 24, March 29, 1907, pp. 213–17.

365 Letter to Bloch from Adolf Fischhof, February 14, 1890. Bloch, *My Reminiscences*, Vol. I, p. 254. See also *Dr. Josef S. Bloch, Auswahl aus seiner Briefsammlung*, Max Grunwald, ed. (Vienna: Ludwig Hirschfeld, 1930), a collection of dozens of letters Bloch received over the years. Many of them congratulated him for his public opposition to antisemitism and discrimination.

366 Bloch, *Erinnerungen aus meinem Leben*, Vol. III, p. 156.

ing simultaneously for Germandom and liberty, being liberal and thinking liberal is not a fashion, but rather the realization of the human ideal, and truly German."[367] In western Austria the Jews remained loyal to the Verfassungspartei because they saw it as the party of both liberalism and Germandom. They did so even after many non-Jewish Germans among them had abandoned the party for antisemitic parties such as the Christian Socials. Most of those Germans who remained in the *Verfassungspartei* did not actively oppose antisemitism, an ideology that contradicted the principles of civic equality enshrined in the Constitution for which the Liberals had fought. Bloch argued that Jews ought not reflexively support such a party.

Bloch condemned the Liberals for embracing nationalist and antisemitic elements during and after the 1880s.[368] German liberalism in Austria had always had a strong connection to German nationalism.[369] After 1867 German Liberals were forced to decide whether they could function as the leadership for a multiethnic state in which, according to the law, each nation was to have equal rights. They ultimately proved unable to put aside their sense of German cultural superiority when, in 1867, the new Cisleithanian constitution gave significant power to the *Reichsrat* in which they had a majority.

Bloch feared that the increasing strength of nationalist prejudice would undermine the idea of an Austrian state that enforced the equal rights of all its citizens and placed all its cultures on equal legal grounds. However, the German Liberals had never really accepted that idea in the first place. They instead envisioned an Austrian state that, while offering all its citizens civic equality as individuals, would nonetheless promote the spread of German culture, the culture of Enlightenment progress, to the 'backward' Eastern parts of the Monarchy. The German Liberals, and their Jewish liberal counterparts, were never able to separate their liberal polit-

---

367 *Neue Freie Presse*, August 7, 1899 (morning edition), p. 1. The quotation was a part of an editorial celebrating the 150th anniversary of Goethe's birth; cited in Steven Beller, "Germans and Jews as 'Mitteleuropäisch' Elites," in Peter Stirk, ed., *Mitteleuropa* (Edinburgh: Edinburgh University Press, 1994), pp. 61–85, quotation on p. 70.

368 For a more wide-ranging discussion of the Liberals' politics regarding Austrian Jews, see Peter Pulzer, "The Austrian Liberals and the Jewish Question, 1867–1914," *Journal of Central European Affairs*, 23 (1963), pp. 131–42.

369 See Judson, *Exclusive Revolutionaries.*

ical principles from their belief in the superiority of German culture.[370] Even Fischhof proved unable to do so. As they began to lose seats in the *Reichsrat*, many German Liberals increasingly used nationalist rhetoric to hold on to as many German votes as possible. They were not concerned that such rhetoric would turn away non-Germans, because the Liberals had already alienated them with their pro-German policies.[371] Bloch lamented, "The parties did not hesitate one moment to substitute liberal terminology with nationalist nomenclature."[372]

Despite the Liberal party's infidelities with nationalism and antisemitism, the liberal 'German' Jews of Austria could not easily abandon it in the voting booth.[373] For example, in 1896 Moravian Jews voted for the German Liberals in the local *Landtag* elections, even though that party had made an electoral alliance with the antisemitic *Deutschvolkischen* party. Out of loyalty to the German Liberals, Jews actually cast votes that helped put antisemites in power.[374] Bloch described the emotional, almost romantic feelings that bound Jews to liberalism, and the sense of loss experienced by those who acknowledged that it had abandoned them.

> For the Jew, liberalism was more than a political doctrine, a comfortable principle and a popular opinion of the day--it was his spiritual asylum, his protective port after thousands of years of homelessness, the final fulfillment of the futile yearning of his forefathers, his patent of freedom after a servitude of indescribable severity and shame, his Goddess-Protector... One morning he awoke to a shrill, hateful tone bombarding his ear, like the cries of a wild beast. He glanced up and saw his

370 See Beller, "Patriotism and the National Identity of Habsburg Jewry." Beller argues that the acculturated liberal Jews of western Austria predominantly identified themselves as German-Austrians, and took the German side in political conflicts between the nationalities.

371 Judson, pp. 269–70.

372 Bloch, *Der Nationale Zwist*, p. 25.

373 For more on Jewish voting patterns over these decades, see Walter B. Simon, "The Jewish Vote in Austria," *Leo Baeck Institute Year Book*, 16 (1971), pp. 97–122.

374 "Jüdischer Idealismus: Zu den mährischen Landtagswahlen," *Oesterreichische Wochenschrift*, Nr. 45, Year 13, November 6, 1896, p. 887–8; This event is also cited in Beller, "Germans and Jews as 'Mitteleuropäisch' Elites," p. 80.

> beloved Goddess-protector lying dead on the floor...all her former supporters and friends had taken flight and gone over to the nationalist camp.[375]

Bloch had an antagonistic relationship with the German Liberal party throughout his career. Although he fought for such liberal principles as constitutional government, the rule of law and civil equality, he stood against the Liberal party as an institution because he believed that it placed the narrow interests of the German people above the neutral application of those principles. Bloch believed that the Liberals' stance conflicted with a true commitment to liberalism, and stood in the way of the development of a culturally neutral Austrian consciousness based on common citizenship and equal rights. He argued that during the 1870s and 80s the Liberals "saw their sole task as defending 'the German position' without examining whether this 'position' bequeathed by absolutism was still tenable and whether the Slav nations, which had now come of age, were not entitled to claim equal treatment from the state."[376] Furthermore, Bloch decried the passivity of the Liberal party as an institution in the fight against antisemitism, rebuking it for standing aside "without any powerful retort, without a word of defense."[377] He allied only with individual German Liberals whom he felt fully supported equal rights and fought discrimination. One such person was Josef Kopp, a well-respected Liberal politician and veteran of the 1848 revolution who served as Bloch's attorney during the Rohling affair.[378]

---

375 Bloch, *Der Nationale Zwist*, pp. 25–6.

376 Bloch, *My Reminiscences*, Vol. I, p. 27.

377 Bloch, *Documente zur Aufklärung*, Nr. 3. p. 82. Speech of October 20, 1891.

378 Bloch offered effusive praise of Kopp after Rohling dropped his libel suit. See "Deutschtum und Judenthum in Oesterreich," *Oesterreichische Wochenschrift*, Nr. 2, Year 3, p. 14. For a longer tribute to Kopp, see Bloch, *My Reminiscences*, Vol. I, pp. 90–101. Kopp also wrote a detailed account of the Rohling affair, see Josef Kopp, *Zur Judenfrage nach den Aktenprozesses Rohling-Bloch* (Leipzig: J Klinkhardt, 1886). Kopp, then leader of the Liberal coalition in the *Reichsrat*, stood up to oppose antisemitism in the person of Schönerer, and in 1883 challenged the antisemite's reelection to the central committee of the *Deutscher Schulverein*. Many German politicians at the time saw Schönerer's reelection as a referendum on whether Jews could be considered Germans. Schönerer won reelection, despite Kopp's best efforts. See Judson, *Exclusive Revolutionaries*, pp. 229–30.

Any politician that Bloch believed would sincerely fight antisemitism and nationalist hatred could earn his support. For example, the candidates Bloch endorsed in Vienna in the 1891 municipal elections included nominees of both the Liberal party and the Democratic party. He argued simply that Jews should not blindly vote for the Liberals because, as a group, they had betrayed them. Rather they should choose individual candidates, whatever their party affiliation, if they supported equal rights and stood up to antisemitism.[379]

The German Liberals fell from power in 1879, and a new government, headed by Count Eduard Taaffe, took the reins.[380] The government coalition consisted mostly of Czechs, Poles, aristocratic conservatives, and clericals, in other words, exactly the groups who opposed the German Liberals. Taaffe, a descendant of an Irish noble family that had emigrated to Bohemia, proclaimed as his goal the reconciliation of the nationalities and supported some measures to decentralize the Austrian state in order to satisfy the Slavs, in particular the Czechs who were demanding parity for their language in Bohemia. He succeeded to a degree. First and foremost he convinced the Czechs to end their boycott and return to the *Reichsrat*, and he created a Czech half of Prague's Charles University among other concrete, if not spectacular measures.[381]

Bloch defended Taaffe's nationalities policy, a stand that placed him in direct opposition to the dominant German liberal orientation of the Viennese Jewish establishment.[382] He claimed that the Jewish establishment viewed opposition to the German Liberals "not only as heresy but as treason against the Jews."[383] Bloch related that his political position had inspired such scorn among the Viennese Jewish establishment that they vehemently protested when, in 1884, Taaffe planned to appoint him Professor of Hebrew Antiquities at the Philosophical Faculty of the

379 See "Die Wahlbewegung-In letzter Stunde," *Oesterreichische Wochenschrift*, Nr. 9, Year 8, February 27, 1891, pp. 157–9.

380 For more on the Taaffe era, see Okey, pp. 268–76.

381 William Jenks, *Austria under the Iron Ring, 1879–1893* (Charlottesville: University Press of Virginia, 1965), p. 308.

382 Beller, "Patriotism and the National Identity of Habsburg Jewry," pp. 229–32.

383 Bloch, *My Reminiscences*, Vol. I, p. 27. He cites as his source for this remark: Comp. Dr. Ad. Brill, *Populär-wissenschaftliche Monatshefte*. Organ des Mendelssohn-Vereines in Frankfurt a. M. 1884, Nr. 8, p. 188.

University of Vienna. According to Bloch, Adolf Jellinek, Chief Rabbi of Vienna from 1856 until 1893, informed the Ministry of Ecclesiastical Matters that such an appointment "would be no less than a provocation of the Viennese Jews."[384] In the end, the appointment went to a Dr. D.H. Muller, Docent of Arabic. Dr. Georg Jellinek, the Chief Rabbi's son, was appointed Assistant Professor. Bloch also remarked that the senior Jellinek expressed regret for his actions in this affair and often praised Bloch's political activities subsequently.[385]

When the German liberals went into opposition in 1879, liberal Jews went with them. Even Fischhof stood against Taaffe, whose rule hurt Fischhof's "German interests and brothers."[386] Bloch, on the other hand, hoped to bring Jewish support away from the German liberals and towards the Minster President as part of his plan to wean west Austrian Jews, presumably including Fischhof, from their German identities. With the 1867 Constitution, the German liberals had achieved most of their 'liberal' goals, civic equality, constitutional government and a broader, but not universal, suffrage. Their only remaining task became making sure the government supported their 'German' goals, i.e. the strengthening of German culture in Austria. The German-oriented Jews of Austria could not abandon liberalism so they continued to back the German cause as inseparable from liberalism itself.

Bloch claimed that Taaffe had offered on two occasions to cooperate with the *Verfassungspartei* on a policy to stamp out antisemitism, but they rejected these overtures. Following this rejection and the continued opposition of Jewish (as well as German) Liberals to his government, Taaffe took a passive approach toward the growing antisemitic movement in Austria.[387] Bloch argued that the Jewish establishment should have abandoned the German Liberals, who, after all, had not stood up to the growing antisemitic movement, and instead supported Taaffe, who had offered to do so in exchange for the political support of the Viennese Jewish leadership.[388] Bloch believed that

384 Ibid., p. 156.

385 For the details of this affair, see Ibid., pp. 155–7. See also Grunwald, "Josef Bloch," p. 6, which corroborated Bloch's version of the affair.

386 Charmatz, pp. 344–6.

387 Bloch, *My Reminiscences*, Vol. I, p. 152.

388 Ibid., p. 159.

Taaffe was the best hope for compromise and reconciliation among the nationalities.

The *Oesterreichische Wochenschrift* called on Jews to rally behind Taaffe.[389] In addition, Bloch's newspaper reprinted statements the Minister President made that reaffirmed the support of his government for equal rights for all citizens.[390] Furthermore, Bloch maintained that Taaffe wanted Jewish support. He claimed that Taaffe had said confidentially that he was willing "to take strict measures against antisemitism for that purpose."[391] There is no independent confirmation of this confidential statement. However, the Viennese Jewish establishment, because of what Bloch described as their "position as 'Germans,'" refused to have anything to do with Taaffe's government.[392] Bloch regretted that, in the 1880's, "Viennese Jewry, reared and educated in the traditions of German liberalism, felt itself in the innermost part of its soul to be a part of the German *Volk*."[393] He summarized their position as follows: Anyone who supported Taaffe and promoted compromise between the Slavs and Germans in Austria "injured German hegemony and was therefore a bad Jew."[394]

Although he likely exaggerated the extremeness of his opponents' position, the split on this issue nevertheless illustrates an important distinction within Habsburg Jewry. Most Jews expressed a deep loyalty to the Habsburg Monarchy until its fall in 1918. However, an important difference remained between the majority of acculturated Jews of Vienna

389 See, for example, "Die Antwort des Grafen Taaffe," *Oesterreichische Wochenschrift*, Nr. 20, Year 6, May 24, 1889, pp. 369–71.

390 See, for example, *Oesterreichische Wochenschrift*, Nr. 22, Year 6, June 6, 1889, pp. 423. Bloch maintained his public support for the Taaffe regime until almost the very end. He lost patience with Taaffe a few months before the fall of the Minister President, and greeted the change in government with relief at the time (see "Rücktritt des Ministeriums Taaffe," *Oesterreichische Wochenschrift*, Nr. 44, Year 10, November 3, 1893, p. 855). However, Bloch was quickly disappointed by the Windischgrätz coalition government that followed (see "Das Ende der Coalition," Nr. 25, Year 12, June 21, 1895, p. 457–8). The overwhelmingly positive assessment in the memoirs he wrote after the fall of the Monarchy reflected Bloch's feelings about Taaffe in comparison to those politicians who came both before and after him during the last decades of Austria-Hungary.

391 Bloch, *My Reminiscences*, Vol. I, p. 159.

392 Ibid., p. 160.

393 Bloch, *Erinnerungen aus meinem Leben*, Vol. III, p. 74.

394 Bloch, *My Reminiscences*, Vol. I, p. 79.

and the Alpine and Bohemian provinces, who promoted the German character of the Austrian state and those, like Bloch, who opposed assimilation and politically identified themselves purely as Austrians. The distinction becomes clearer when one compares Bloch's rejection of a German identity to those Jews who began a Purim service in Brünn in 1898 with the words "Join hands, Germans, in free Austria..."[395]

The Jews who endorsed a pro-German orientation for the state thought themselves to be true Austrians as well. For example, Adolf Jellinek wrote an article called "Jewish-Austrian" in which he explained how Jews should express their Austrian consciousness. He contended that Jews represented a "political (Austrian) nationality." They would therefore always support a strong centralized government, which, after all, "voted for the Bill of Rights. The provincial diets didn't do it!"[396] Jellinek criticized those who supported a decentralized system of government in the name of reaching a compromise that would satisfy the non-German nationalities, characterizing them as people "to whom the pre-eminence of the German element is a thorn in the flesh."[397] Jellinek expressed strong support for a centralized Austria dominated by its Germans, an idea at odds with Bloch's call for an Austrian state and society in which all of its nationalities would receive equal treatment and participate fully in the government and administration.[398]

---

[395] Report of Berthold Feiwel, *Die Welt*, June 17, 1898, pp. 7–8, cited in Beller, "Patriotism and the National Identity of Habsburg Jewry," p. 234. Feiwel was a Zionist eager to denounce liberal Jews, but the words he claimed to have heard do not appear out of line with the sentiments of German-oriented Jews that Bloch described in his own writings.

[396] Adolf Jellinek: "Jüdisch-Österreichisch," *Die Neuzeit*, No. 24, June 15, 1883; cited in Cahnmann, "Adolf Fischhof and his Jewish Followers," p. 116. Jellinek wrote a number of books and countless articles in addition to this one. See for example Adolf Jellinek, *Der jüdische Stamm. Ethnographische Studien* (Vienna: Herzfeld & Bauer, 1869).

[397] Adolf Jellinek: "Zur Wahlkampagne," *Die Neuzeit*, No. 23, June 6, 1879; cited in Cahnmann, "Adolf Fischhof and his Jewish Followers," p. 116.

[398] For more on Jellinek, see Marsha L. Rozenblit, "Jewish Identity and the Modern Rabbi: The Cases of Isak Noa Mannheimer, Adolf Jellinek and Moritz Güdemann in Nineteenth-Century Vienna," *Leo Baeck Institute Yearbook* 35 (1990), pp. 103–31. Rozenblit argued that, unlike Bloch, Jellinek denied that Jews were an ethnic group, and viewed them only in terms of their common religion. Ibid., p. 115. Jellinek and Bloch were political allies on many issues, despite their different approaches to German and Jewish identity. See, for example, Jellinek's article in *Die Neuzeit*, February 13, 1891, pp. 62–3, cited in Ibid., p. 111. In that sense, their relationship parallels that of Fischhof and Bloch.

Historians have failed to emphasize the difference between a supraethnic Austrian (Bloch) and an Austro-German (Jellinek) political identity for Habsburg Jews. For example, Schorske generalized Habsburg Jews as "the supra-national people of the multinational state" without any reference to disagreements over the meaning of that 'supra-national' consciousness.[399] Werner Cahnmann referred to the above comments by Jellinek and then noted, "the Jews of Austria were soon to be the only 'Austrians' left."[400] He seems to have conflated Jellinek, despite his German sympathies, with an Austrian identity. However, Jellinek's support for the German national cause contradicted Bloch's conception of a supraethnic Austrian consciousness, one that was more consistent with the *Staatsidee* of Austria. Although they both proclaimed an Austrian identity, Jellinek identified with German centralism in Austria, while Bloch did not.

In the last decades of the nineteenth century, the position of Jellinek reflected the dominant position of the German-acculturated bourgeois Jews of Vienna, Bohemia, and Moravia, the group that served as the political, social, and economic leaders of Austrian Jewry. These people considered themselves Jewish by religion, to be sure, but not as members of a separate Jewish *Stamm*. They identified as Austro-Germans of the Jewish faith.[401] Thus, Bloch's call for Jews to adopt a supraethnic Austrian identity stood in direct opposition to the German-Austrian consciousness espoused by most of the Jewish political establishment in Vienna and most of the German-oriented segment of Habsburg Jewry in general. His ideas only began to gain ground among them when the German liberals' antisemitic sympathies became too obvious to ignore.[402] Although both types of Jews were, of course, loyal Austrians who favored the continuation of the multiethnic state, the difference between the two identities demonstrated that the Jews themselves disagreed on what it meant to be an Austrian, and revealed how complex the issue of identity was for Habsburg Jews.

399 Schorske, *Fin-de-Siècle Vienna*, p. 129.

400 Cahnmann, "Adolf Fischhof and his Jewish Followers," p. 116.

401 Beller, "Patriotism and the National Identity of Habsburg Jewry," pp. 227. In this article, Beller explored the differences between the 'German' and 'Austrian' approaches to Jewish national identity in Austria. This article is seminal to understanding the issues for Jews relating to identity in multiethnic Austria. For a prototypical example of a Jew who rejected the idea that Jews formed a separate ethnic group, see Heinrich Jaques, *Denkschrift über die Stellung der Juden in Oesterreich* (Vienna: C. Gerold, 1859).

402 Ibid., pp. 229–230.

Chapter 4

JOSEPH SAMUEL BLOCH: THE SOLUTION TO THE PROBLEM OF RACIAL NATIONALISM AND ANTI-SEMITISM IN AUSTRIA

Bloch laid out his conception of identity for the Jews of Austria and a new mission for the Austrian state in *Der Nationale Zwist und die Juden in Österreich* (1886), a collection of articles that had appeared during the first two years of the *Oesterreichische Wochenschrift.* He issued this book as an attack "against Austrian antisemitism and against every kind of racial hatred and national narrow-mindedness."[403] The Taaffe government appreciated Bloch's political support and reciprocated by paying for the printing of this publication and calling attention to it in the government newspapers.[404] In fact, Taaffe was a powerful supporter of Bloch throughout his years as Minister-President.[405]

Der Nationale Zwist und die Juden in Österreich reflected the influence of Fischhof on Bloch. Bloch endorsed Fischhof's plan to federalize Austria, and criticized the liberal Jews of western Austria who rejected it in favor of a centralized, German-language government system.[406]

---

403 Bloch, *My Reminiscences*, Vol. I, p. 158.

404 Ibid., p. 159, and Isidor Schalit, "Erinnerungen von Ehrenburschen Medizinalrat Isidor Schalit," in Ludwig Rosenhek, ed., *Festschrift zur Feier des 100 Semesters der akademischen Verbindung Kadimah* (Mödling: n.p., 1933), p. 53. Because Bloch was a member of the *Reichsrat* Polish Club, he was officially part of the government coalition during the Taaffe era.

405 Grunwald, "Josef Bloch," p. 4, and Cahnmann, "Adolf Fischhof and his Jewish Followers," p. 127, corroborated Bloch's claim that Taaffe supported his activities.

406 Ibid., p. 60. On liberal Jewish support for German centralism, see Beller, "Germans and Jews as 'Mitteleuropäisch' Elites," pp. 79–80.

Bloch particularly lamented the failure of Fischhof to win followers for his ideas among German liberals. After attending the July 16, 1882, meeting at the *Musikvereinsaal* during which Fischhof had announced his new pro-federalization movement, Bloch regretfully noted that it had met with "the greatest animosity" from both the German Liberals and the liberal Jewish establishment.[407]

The achievement of reconciliation among the nationalities, which had been Fischhof's cause, became one of Bloch's highest priorities as well. As early as 1881–2, Bloch had begun to see Fischhof's plans to reorganize Austria along federal lines as the only comprehensive political solution to the nationality issue.[408] In a similar vein, Bloch recognized "the right of self-determination for peoples."[409] To balance autonomy for the nationalities on matters of language, culture and education, he also emphasized the importance of having a functioning central legislature whose members looked to the common interests of all Austrians. He urged political leaders of all backgrounds to "serve the general public and not the particularistic interests of one class of the population, one individual nation or confession."[410] Bloch expressed a strong commitment to democracy, and believed that only a party organized solely around a belief in democratic principles, such as the one envisioned by Fischhof in 1882, could cut across ethnic lines and engineer such a reconciliation.

> Democracy is not the party of a particular nationality, rather in it lay the rights of every nationality; it is thus a truly Austrian party. It sees in the national agitations the greatest danger to the future of our fatherland. It fights against every national chauvinism...It advocates for a fair national compromise, for the creation of a nationalities' law that would satis-

---

[407] Bloch, *My Reminscences*, Vol. I, p. 58.

[408] Toury, "Josef Samuel Bloch und die Jüdische Identität im österreichischen Kaiserreich," p. 43.

[409] "Zur Nachmahnung," *Oesterreichische Wochenschrift*, Nr. 29, Year 8, July 24, 1891, p. 519.

[410] Ibid.

> fy all sections...It stands as an Austrian party according to the concept of a political life that encompasses the greater, the entire state.[411]

Fischhof and Bloch differed in one profound respect. Bloch sought to convince Austrian Jews to embrace their Jewish ethnic identity rather than seeing themselves as Germans, Czechs or Poles of Jewish confession. He found absurd the position of assimilationism, which, as he described it, claimed that "Jews should be allowed to be good, true Germans, good true Magyars, as well as nationally-Polish and nationally-Czech, but not nationally-Jewish."[412] Bloch considered Jews to be a separate *Stamm* linked by a shared historical tradition and descent from the ancient Hebrew tribes.[413] He expressed a Jewish ethnic consciousness, and he sought to inspire "a feeling of kinship among all those who belonged to the Jewish race."[414] However, he rejected Jewish nationalism, i.e. a political movement focused on specifically Jewish goals such as a Jewish state, as well as assimilation as potential options. Only one choice remained. "The nationalist parties, which with the sensation of race-hatred stand opposite one another...allow us no other choice than—to become Jews once again, Austrian Jews."[415]

Bloch condemned the passivity of leading Jewish public figures in the face of increasing antisemitism in Austria in the 1870s and early 1880s.[416] He called on Jews to respond to antisemitic statements and actions, rather than remain quiet in the hope that ignoring it could defeat prejudice. In December 1882, Bloch criticized Jewish members of Parliament for not speaking out against attacks on their Jewish brethren. Arguing that, "the unfortunate nationalities disputes have blinded their eyes," he declared them incapable of properly assessing

---

411 "Der Demokratische Centralverein," *Oesterreichische Wochenschrift*, Nr. 47, Year 6, December 6, 1889, p. 856.

412 Bloch, *Erinnerungen*, Vol. III, p. 74.

413 Ibid., p. 158.

414 Bloch, *My Reminiscences*, Vol. I, p. 182.

415 Bloch, *Der Nationale Zwist*, pp. 27–8.

416 McCagg, p. 184. See also Toury, "Troubled Beginnings: The Emergence of the Österreichisch-Israelitische Union," p. 467. Toury described a policy among many Viennese Jews that preferred silence to public confrontation.

the situation. "They have not defended the cause of Jewry, perhaps they have even damaged it. They have forgotten their Jewishness and dreamt that the enemy does not notice it either."[417]

His aggressive attacks in 1883 against the antisemitic lies of Rohling made Bloch a public figure. It brought him so much publicity simply because no other Jews in Austria had spoken out forcefully against antisemitism. In the first issue of the *Oesterreichische Wochenschrift*, on October 15, 1884, Bloch issued "A Warning and a Call of Alarm."[418] He declared that Jews faced a direct attack by antisemites and would have to take positive steps to fight them. It was no longer enough to rely on the government alone to protect the rights of Jews. "We will build a Jewish civic union (*Bürgerverein*) to defend our political and social rights, which are under such strong attacks!"[419] Discussions among like-minded Jewish leaders swiftly followed Bloch's proclamation and led directly to the foundation of the *Österreichisch-Israelitische Union* in 1886.[420]

According to Bloch, "to become Jews once again," meant more than just being politically active. He demanded that Jews not only act, but also think differently, that they change the conception of their own identity. Jews needed to reclaim (or maintain) their Jewish *Stamm* identity and demand equal rights for all citizens by organizing as a group to fight antisemitism and ethnic prejudice in general. As evidence that his was the correct approach, Bloch claimed that Galicia then exhibited both the strongest Jewish ethnic consciousness and the weakest antisemitism.[421]

---

417 Joseph Samuel Bloch, *Gegen die Anti-Semiten: Eine Streitschrift* (Vienna: D. Löwy, 1882), p. 4. This publication was collection of articles that had earlier appeared in the *Wiener Allgemeine Zeitung*. The above quotation appeared in the introductory essay, dated December 20, 1882.

418 "Unsere Situation- Ein Mahn-und Weckruf," *Oesterreichische Wochenschrift*, Nr. 1, Year 1, October 15, 1884, p. 1–3.

419 Ibid., p. 3.

420 See Lander, pp. 186–93 for a further discussion of the founding of the organization and Bloch's role. Lander focused on Bloch's activities relating to specifically Jewish issues, and argued that he, rather than Herzl, had provided the impetus for a new kind of consciously Jewish politics in Vienna ten years before the publication of *Der Judenstaat*. She also contended that Bloch provided a bridge between the assimilationist liberals who preceded him and the Zionists who followed.

421 Bloch, *Der Nationale Zwist*, p. 31.

He later realized the inaccuracy of the latter claim, made in 1886, and railed against Galician antisemitism throughout the 1890s and beyond. Nevertheless, Galicia and Bukovina provided Bloch with his most receptive audience, largely because of the strength of Jewish identity that already existed there.[422] He aimed his message particularly at pro-German Jews in Bohemia, where, as he described it, neither of the two major nationalities were "our kindred, and we ought not covet such an honor. We are neither Germans nor Slavs but—Austrian Jews or Jewish Austrians!"[423]

In characterizing his people as 'Austrian Jews or Jewish Austrians,' Bloch underscored the equal importance of the Jewish and Austrian aspects of his conception of identity, as well as its flexibility. In a non-political setting, the ethnic, cultural and/or religious elements of identity were primary, whereas in a political or civic context, being an Austrian and thus identifying with the needs of the whole society was to predominate. Jews were to be members of the Austrian civic nation yet preserve their awareness as members of the Jewish *Stamm*. The ethnic element was divorced from politics, in that, although Bloch wanted Jews to feel what today might be called ethnic pride and solidarity, they were not to pursue particularistic Jewish interests in the political arena. For example, he did not endorse Jewish political autonomy or call for measures that would specifically benefit Jews. Rather he operated according to universal principles such as equality before the law that, while certainly improving the lot of Jews, would benefit all of the peoples equally as well as strengthen the foundation of the state. He remained consistent in his support for equal rights in all instances, including those where Jews might have benefited from a little inequality.

For example, Bloch supported universal male suffrage despite his fear that such a reform might, in the short term at least, worsen the plight of Austrian Jews. As early as 1899, he argued that Austria should move toward "universal, equal and direct suffrage."[424] In late 1905, he

422 Beller, "Germans and Jews as 'Mitteleuropäisch' Elites," p. 79.

423 Bloch, *Der Nationale Zwist*, p. 40.

424 "Die Verfassungskrisis," *Oesterreichische Wochenschrift*, Nr. 34, Year 16, August 25, 1899, pp. 618. Although he did not address the issue of women's suffrage directly, one can assume that by universal Bloch likely meant universal male suffrage.

again called for full and equal suffrage in Austria. Bloch supported universal male suffrage even as he predicted that a *Reichsrat* elected on that basis would be less supportive of legal equality and more likely to support discrimination against Jews than one based on the then-limited franchise.[425] He believed that the unrepresented poor were even more susceptible to antisemitic demagoguery than the general population. When universal male suffrage became a reality in Cisleithania on January 20, 1907, Bloch praised it as the beginning of a new era in Austrian politics, literally a "new-Austria."[426]

As this issue makes clear, Bloch held to the principle of civic equality even when he thought its application conflicted with the direct interests of Jews because he believed that principle to be central to his vision of the Austrian state. If the interests of the civic and ethnic elements of Bloch's identity conflicted in a political setting, the needs of the common polity had to stand above the needs of one group as long as the policy in question did not violate constitutional principles of equality for individuals and nationalities.

The call for the Jews of Austria to embrace a Jewish ethnic consciousness was, for Bloch, intimately linked to his call for the embrace of an Austrian civic consciousness. He argued that anti-Jewish prejudice combined with political rivalries among the peoples would lead Jews not only to identify ethnically as Jews but also to turn politically "to the standpoint of the Austrian."[427] He emphasized that a heightened Jewish self-awareness in no way conflicted with a sense of being Austrian, or with loyalty to the Austrian state. In fact, because of the Jewish ideas of tolerance and universal brotherhood, "the proud words I am a Jew do not undermine...the bonds of love for our beautiful Austria..., on the contrary, it can only strengthen these bonds."[428]

---

[425] "Der Kampf des Proletariates für seine Rechtsgleichheit," *Oesterreichische Wochenschrift*, Nr. 48, Year 22, December 1, 1905, p. 757. For more on the enactment of universal male suffrage in Austria, see Beller, *Francis Joseph*, pp. 169–71.

[426] Bloch, *Erinnerungen aus meinem Leben*, Vol. III, p. 155. For more on the introduction of universal male suffrage in Austria in 1907, see Okey, pp. 348–9.

[427] Bloch, *Der Nationale Zwist*, p. 40.

[428] *Oesterreichische Wochenschrift*, Nr. 10, Year 1, December 26, 1884, p. 7. Excerpt from a speech Bloch delivered to the Jewish student organization *Kadimah*, at the Weißes Roß Hotel, December 17, 1884.

Furthermore, Bloch declared "'to be a Jew' also means that in the realm of politics one stands firmly for peace and brotherhood among all the Austrian peoples."[429]

Through his writings, political speeches and other public commentaries, Bloch carried out a steadfast campaign to wean the Jews of the Alpine and Bohemian provinces from their self-identification as Germans.[430] Of course, not all of the Jews in these areas identified as Germans, nevertheless the resistance he faced in the early years of his campaign demonstrates the strength of the opposing position. Bloch demanded that these so-called Germans of the Jewish faith instead identify themselves as members of the Jewish *Stamm*, and, equally importantly, become the core of a new civic Austrian nation. "The Jews alone are Austrians *sans phrase*, without a second national adjective that conflicts with the first. If one could construct a specifically Austrian nationality, the Jews would constitute its foundation."[431]

The Jewish 'national adjective' did not conflict with the Austrian because, according to Bloch, no specifically Jewish interests existed, territorial or otherwise, separate from those of Austria. One could be both a Jew and an Austrian without any hesitation. This concept bears a striking similarity to the idea of hyphenated identities (Italian-American, African-American, Mexican-American, Korean-American, etc.) so common in the United States and elsewhere today. Bloch recognized that his notion of a hyphenated identity for Austrians had strong parallels to circumstances in the United States in his own time. He cited the example of Irish Americans, whose American patriotism made them no less Irish, just as their support for Irish independence from Britain made them no less American.[432] This was no different for Bloch than the contemporaneous situation of the so-called subject peoples of Austria-Hungary (i.e. those other than the Germans and Magyars), who sought cultural autonomy while remaining loyal and patriotic to the state as a whole.

In fact, Bloch looked to the United States as a model for the society he wanted Austria to become. Bloch reprinted a speech by Theodore

---

429 Bloch, *Erinnerungen aus meinem Leben*, Vol. III, p. 159.

430 Beller, "Patriotism and the National Identity of Habsburg Jewry," p. 229.

431 Bloch, *Der Nationale Zwist*, p. 41.

432 Bloch, *Erinnerungen aus meinem Leben*, Vol. III, p. 288–9.

Roosevelt that expressed the American ideals of a community of citizens making one nation, as well as equal treatment of all citizens, presumably with the hope that Austria might follow the American example.[433] What Bloch saw as America's pure state patriotism and a national identity shared by all citizens regardless of their ancestral background offered a parallel to the civic Austrian nationalism he sought to create. Although the concept of American national identity at that time did contain a strong push for cultural conformity, Bloch saw that even if immigrant Jews became culturally more Americanized in terms of language, dress, and public behavior, nothing stopped them from continuing to practice their religion as they saw fit and preserving their sense of peoplehood. He thus praised America for having made good citizens out of Jewish immigrants while allowing them to retain the fundamental aspects of their Jewishness.[434]

Bloch cited the American patriotism of Irish-Americans specifically to demonstrate the parallel with the patriotism of Austrian Jews, and to refute the claims by antisemites that European Jews in general were somehow less than fully loyal to the various countries in which they were citizens. Bloch explained that the desire of some Jews to recreate their ancient homeland did not reflect a lack of commitment and patriotism to the countries of their birth in the diaspora. He argued that, at least in Austria, a love of Zion in no way impinged on a Jew's loyalty to the country that granted and protected his or her rights as a citizen.[435] "Bloch described how the diaspora had become the homeland (*Heimat*) for most Jews, and the rights they had won there at great cost were achievements worth preserving.[436] He declared "For millennia here we have fertilized our homeland with the martyr blood of our forefathers."[437] Bloch emphasized the deep love Austrian Jews had for their

433 "Präsident Roosevelt über die Nationalitätenfrage," *Oesterreichische Wochenschrift*, Nr. 10, Year 22, March 10, 1905, pp. 146–7.

434 Joseph Samuel Bloch, *Ein Besuch beim Judenthum in New-York und Umgebung* (Vienna: Verlag der 'Oesterreichischen Wochenschrift,' 1912) pp. 23–4, 73.

435 "Das letzte Streitobjekt," *Oesterreichische Wochenschrift*, Nr. 15, Year 4, April 22, 1887, p. 234.

436 Bloch, *Erinnerungen aus meinem Leben*, Vol. III, pp. 97–8.

437 Ibid., p. 100.

Heimat, and emphasized that Jews had lived in Austria for 2000 years, as long as either Germans or Slavs.[438]

Bloch countered claims of Jewish particularism by declaring that "the so-called exclusive Jewish interests are in every way congruent with the vital interests of the Fatherland. We Jews have no greater interest and no concerns other than that all the peoples, different races, and confessions within the boundaries of our fatherland live peacefully alongside one another."[439] According to Bloch, the protection of equal rights for all Austrians was the only Jewish interest. "As Jews we can stand up for nothing other than the rights of all the races in the state."[440] He explained that Jewish interests were consistent with those of all other Austrian citizens and the Austrian state, and noted that Jews possessed a deep "consciousness of community with the other residents of the state."[441]

Bloch espoused the creation of a single Austro-Jewish identity with two components that coalesced into one. Many Habsburg Jews, mostly the Orthodox and Hasidim, retained their traditional Jewish *Stamm* identity. A small percentage of Habsburg Jews became Zionists or Jewish nationalists, and many acculturated Jews came to see themselves as simply Germans or Czechs of the Jewish faith. Although an overwhelming majority of Jews in each of these categories expressed a deep loyalty to the Habsburg Monarchy, Bloch demanded a more comprehensive Austrian consciousness. He espoused a vision of Austrian identity that supported the interests of the multinational state above those of any individual nationality. He recognized a real commonality of interest between Jews and all other Austrian citizens, as well as the state they shared. Bloch wanted to "invigorate patriotic feelings, to strengthen the unbreakable bond that ties [Jews] to the destiny of this great Empire and its numerous peoples."[442] He sought to enhance and

---

438 "Arier- und Juden-Heimat," *Oesterreichische Wochenschrift*, Nr. 42, Year 13, October 16, 1896, pp. 825–6.

439 "Der Antisemitismus in Nöthen," *Oesterreichische Wochenschrift*, Nr. 3, Year 1, November 7, 1884, p. 2.

440 Bloch, *Der Nationale Zwist*, p. 42.

441 "Das Regierungsprogramm und der Antisemitismus," *Oesterreichische Wochenschrift*, Nr. 6, Year 10, February 10, 1893, p. 95.

442 "Nur nicht Oesterreichisch," *Oesterreichische Wochenschrift*, Nr. 2, Year 5, January 13, 1888, p. 18.

spread the feeling of a common political identity that would link Austrian citizens across all ethnic and religious boundaries. Thus, Bloch's formulation of identity represented the strongest expression of a supraethnic Austrian consciousness.[443]

According to Bloch, Habsburg Jews had consciously chosen their Austrian identity, and thus held it more strongly. "We are not Austrians through the mere accident of birth, through the application of external pressure. We are Austrians through the deepest heart-felt desire, with the clearest recognition that each decline, each paralysis of this Empire means a deep injury to our own vital interests."[444] He expressed pride that his identification as an Austrian followed from a conscious choice rather than a less 'rational' feeling such as ethnic solidarity or dynastic loyalty.

Bloch urged his fellow Austrian Jews to abandon the siren call of nationalism on the grounds that it conflicted with both parts of their identity. After all, "Jewry does not bow before the idols of a nationalist idea; on the contrary, it places itself and its rich arsenal in the service of Austrian state patriotism."[445] Furthermore, Bloch contended that supporting this idea would demonstrate that the Jews were "truly Austrian, the most loyal of Habsburg patriots."[446] Indeed it was "the mission of Israel" to fight ethnic prejudice and hatred among the peoples and instead to promote "the consanguinity of one single family of peoples to which we all belong-the Slav, the Teuton, the Roman, the man of brown, or red, or yellow complexion...."[447] Austrian Jews, according to Bloch, were to fight for Jewish interests, which did not mean increased political power for Jews, but rather equal rights for all the peoples and citizens of Austria.

> Fate would have it that, as we fight for Jewry, we are fighting not only for religious and human rights, for the freedom of the spirit, but also for the fundamental ideas without which the

[443] McCagg called him "the ultimate 'Habsburg Jew!'" McCagg, *A History of Habsburg Jewry*, p. 184. The ultimate 'Austrian Jew' would have been more accurate.

[444] Bloch, *Der Nationale Zwist*, p. 41.

[445] Ibid., p. 49.

[446] Ibid., p. 43.

[447] Bloch, *Israel and the Nations*, p. 402–3.

> continued existence of the Austrian state is unthinkable...We [Jews]...are fighting for something that is more than just for us, that stands higher than one individual nationality, a fight for us, but at the same time for the ideas of reciprocal tolerance between confessions, the peaceful coexistence of races and peoples in one large Imperial state, ideas that we, as true Austrians, as Habsburg patriots, would rank above all others. [448]

Success in this fight would serve the Jewish interest, as well as that of the Austrian state, both of which required the strengthening of the idea of equality for all citizens and compromise among the nationalities. Bloch maintained, "The final victory of these ideas will secure the future of Jewry as well as the continuation of the Austrian Imperial state."[449] In fact, he argued that the victory of the idea of civic equality, of a true *Rechtsstaat*, would be "the highest and most shining triumph of the idea of Judaism."[450]

Without doubt, Bloch's ideas demonstrate strong support for the Habsburg state. However, he was not simply a dynastic patriot. Although he expressed a deep fidelity to Franz Joseph, Bloch did not espouse a blind love of *Kaiser und Reich*. The Emperor had earned Bloch's devotion through his support for equality, especially after antisemitism grew more powerful during the 1870s and 80s. Bloch noted every instance when Franz Joseph rebuked antisemitic prejudice or publicly reaffirmed that he would protect the rights of Jews and/or the equal rights of all citizens.[451]

Bloch did occasionally overstate Franz Joseph's championing of equal rights. For example, he praised the Emperor for having begun the process of Jewish emancipation in 1848.[452] The then-young ruler, how-

---

448 Bloch, *Der Nationale Zwist*, p. 42.

449 Ibid.

450 Ibid., p. 49.

451 See the following editions (among others) of the *Oesterreichische Wochenschrift*: Nr. 36, Year 2, September 17, 1885, p. 6-7; Nr. 25, Year 8, June 26, 1891, p. 463; Nr. 38, Year 11, September 21, 1894, p. 727, Nr. 48, Year 15, December 2, 1898, p. 869. See also, among many other examples from his memoirs, *Erinnerungen aus meinem Leben*, Vol. III, p. 140.

452 *Oesterreichische Wochenschrift*, Nr. 44, Year 5, November 9, 1888, p. 695–6.

ever, had not only prorogued the Kremsier Constitution in 1849, nullifying its emancipation of Jews, but, in 1851, rejected a document drawn up by an advisor, Karl von Kübeck, that would have emancipated the Jews without broader reforms or diminutions of his monarchic powers.[453] Nevertheless, Bloch's misreading of those events, even if willful, underscored his belief that Franz Joseph deserved loyalty because he championed equal rights, not for his piety, his divine right to rule, or any of the other traditional motivations for dynastic fealty. Bloch could have revoked his loyalty had the Emperor's policies and statements changed. He did not love Franz Joseph as a child-like subject bowing before a divinely sanctioned father and ruler, but rather as a politically aware citizen pledging to serve a constitutional monarch who, during the time of Bloch's public life, stood as a countervailing force against antisemitism and ethnic hatred.

Rather than old-fashioned allegiance to a monarch, Bloch expressed a state patriotism based on his belief that Austria offered Jews choices that the nation-states of Europe could not. "Austria, as it is now constituted, a state in the most modern sense of the idea, a state with different ethnic groups and nationalities, confessions, languages and races on one territory...a state that has the mission to unite the heterogeneous elements; [it] is for Jews the happiest Fatherland."[454] Bloch urged his fellow Jews to identify with Austria because it recognized them as full and equal citizens and because its multiethnic composition allowed them to preserve their Jewish *Stamm* consciousness without branding them as separatists. In fact, he turned the meaning of *Habsburgtreu* on its head by measuring true Habsburg loyalty not by devotion to the monarch, who, in theory, was not necessary in order to have a *Rechtsstaat*, but by a commitment to the principles that were essential to the preservation of Austria, namely equal rights and brotherhood among the peoples.

Bloch expressed a civic Austrian nationalism. This differed from Habsburg patriotism, according to which one always followed the wishes of the ruling dynast. An Austrian nationalist, like any nationalist, is loyal to a collective group of people and ideas that exists separate

453 Beller, *Francis Joseph*, p. 56.

454 "Zu den deutsch-czechischen Ausgleichsverhandlungen," *Oesterreichische Wochenschrift*, Nr. 1 Year 7, January 3, 1890, p. 2.

from any particular government. Whereas a dynastic patriot is merely a servant of the ruler, a passive subject waiting for instructions, a nationalist actively participates in shaping the destiny of the nation, and has just as much of a stake in its future as does any other member of the nation. Bloch tried to cultivate a sense of *Verfassungspatriotismus*, or constitutional patriotism, rather than traditional *Habsburgtreue*.

Although his writings, in particular his newspaper, focused primarily on Jews and the problems they faced, namely antisemitism, Bloch aimed his message of tolerance and civic unity not just at Jews, but all the Habsburg nationalities. In some of his editorials he targeted non-Jews specifically and sought to convince all Austrians of the wisdom of his ideas. For example, in a piece on an upcoming election, Bloch called not only on his fellow Jews, but also "all liberal voters," to follow his recommendations.[455]

In the early part of his career, Bloch made a number of presentations to non-Jewish and/or religiously mixed audiences in order to spread his ideas throughout all segments of Austrian society.[456] On March 10, 1885, he spoke at a meeting of the *Deutscher Schulverein*, an organization that sought to promote German language and cultural education in the schools.[457] Bloch condemned the nationalist parties and organizations for turning the schools into another political battleground in the nationalities struggle. He argued that individual schools should not be 'German' or 'Czech' and teach only that language, but rather should teach all the languages in a given region to their students.[458] Such a policy, he believed, would in the long-term aid communication and the cultivation of civic ties across *Stamm* and religious lines.[459]

---

455 "Die n.ö. Landtagswahlen," *Oesterreichische Wochenschrift*, Nr. 43 Year 29, October 24, 1902, p. 691.

456 Bloch's appearances before non-Jewish groups (excluding the *Reichsrat*) became less frequent after the mid-1880s, perhaps because he became focused on representing his largely Jewish constituency in the *Reichsrat* while also becoming involved with the OIU and running his newspaper.

457 Joseph Samuel Bloch, "Elementar-Schule bei den alten Völkern," in *Aus der Vergangenheit für die Gegenwart: Social und literarhistorische Vorträge und Essays* (Vienna: Verlag von Hugo Engel, 1886), p. 93–120. In addition to their invitation to lecture, the *Deutscher Schulverein* invited Bloch to join their association, but he declined.

458 Ibid., p. 93.

459 Ibid., p. 117–20.

Throughout his career Bloch expressed a belief that knowledge and understanding of other peoples' cultures, religions, and histories would create a more cooperative political environment and a more unified society built on basic human fellowship.[460]

Bloch also reached out to a non-Jewish audience on issues of social justice and workers' rights. He hoped both to broaden his base of support for the fight against antisemitism and facilitate the creation of strong citizenship bonds across lines of class in addition to those of nationality. He criticized the Liberal party, and Jewish liberals in particular, for ignoring the needs of labor and the working class.[461] In the early part of his career, Bloch also gave lectures to workers about how Jewish tradition emphasized fair treatment for laborers and legal equality for all citizens. On August 12, 1882, he delivered a lecture entitled "Der Arbeiter bei den alten Völkern," to a gathering of workers that had packed the largest hall in Floridsdorf.[462] He repeated it for an assembly of Viennese and Lower Austrian iron and metal workers held in the hall "zum Grünen Lager" on August 20, 1882.[463] In these presentations Bloch argued that the workers' fight for social justice and the battle against antisemitism were part of the same battle for equality, so workers should join with Jews, not give in to hatred against them.[464] He declared, "No, not the fight against Semitism but for it would bring the most beneficial results to the working population and to the welfare of the state."[465]

Bloch's interactions with Viennese workers provide further evidence that he reached a wide audience. He later received invitations to speak to other workers' organizations, but remarked that "the Police Head Quarters gave me a hint not to lecture any more to workmen."[466] Bloch's lectures also appeared in the socialist papers, of which thousands of copies appeared, shortly after he delivered them, and they

---

460 See also Lander, p. 110.

461 Bloch, *My Reminiscences*, Vol. I, p. 27.

462 Ibid., p. 32.

463 Ibid., p. 51.

464 He later published this lecture in a collection of essays. See "Der Arbeiter bei den alten Völkern," pp. 7–46, in Bloch, *Aus der Vergangenheit für die Gegenwart.*

465 Bloch, "Der Arbeiter bei den alten Völkern," in *Aus der Vergangenheit für die Gegenwart*, p. 46.

466 Bloch, *My Reminiscences*, Vol. I, p. 51.

were read on numerous occasions at workers' gatherings.[467] Bloch claimed that antisemites gave him credit for convincing Viennese workers to remain outside the antisemitic ranks.[468]

In other writings Bloch again reached out to the working class. He published an extensive essay in 1884 entitled "Das Recht auf Arbeit,"[469] in which he expressed his support for workers' rights, and even argued that the state was obligated to find work for those who had tried and could not find it themselves.[470] He later offered effusive praise for Theodor Hertzka's utopian tract *Freiland* because it sought to create a society based on "the fullest possible economic and social justice."[471]

In addition, Bloch sought to include the poor in his Austrian civic nation, criticizing what he called "the war against the poorest" as a violation of the shared religious tenets that commanded Jews and Christians to help the disadvantaged.[472] He fought poverty throughout his career. In his aborted 1907 bid to return to the *Reichsrat*, Bloch described his economic program in general terms as based on the Jewish obligation to care for the needy and oppressed people in society, to fight for their legal rights and economic well-being.[473]

---

[467] Ibid., p. 51–3. Bloch cited an article published in the *Oesterreichische Volksfreund* (No. 47, 1883) by Pater Eichhorn, an "antisemitic agitator," who complained of the widespread publicity Bloch's lectures had received in the socialist papers.

[468] Ibid., p. 52. Bloch referred the above Eichhorn article as well as a pamphlet published in Vienna in 1886 by a German nationalist, Kornelius Vetter. See also, Wistrich, *The Jews of Vienna in the Age of Franz Joseph*, p. 280.

[469] This essay appeared in four parts, one in each of the first four issues of the *Oesterreichische Wochenschrift* (Nos. 1–4, Year 1: October 15, October 30, November 7 and November 14, 1884). This essay also later appeared in the collection *Aus der Vergangenheit für die Gegenwart.*

[470] "Das Recht auf Arbeit, Part I," *Oesterreichische Wochenschrift*, Nr. 1, Year 1, October 15, 1884, p. 15.

[471] "Freiland und die Freilandbewegung," *Oesterreichische Wochenschrift*, Nr. 25, Year 8, June 26, 1891, p. 451.

[472] "Der Kampf gegen die Aermsten" *Oesterreichische Wochenschrift*, Nr. 46, Year 11, November 16, 1894, p. 883.

[473] Bloch, *Erinnerungen aus meinem Leben*, Vol. III, p. 161. This speech originally appeared in the February 18, 1907 edition of the *Oesterreichische Wochenschrift*, pp. 122ff. Bloch stood for election in the Leopoldstadt district in Vienna along with three other Jewish candidates, but dropped out for fear that the Jewish vote would be split and the Christian Social candidate would win. He recounted the campaign in *Erinnerungen aus meinem Leben*, Vol. III, pp. 153–196.

In an early essay, he focused on the plight of the Viennese poor, many of whom had left their villages to look for urban jobs only to find themselves destitute and homeless without *Heimatrecht* in the city in which they resided.[474] *Heimatrecht* is not easily translated, but it referred to the right to receive poor relief from the community of one's birth. Bloch cited a figure of between eleven and thirteen thousand poor people expelled from Vienna each year because they lacked *Heimatrecht*, and claimed that two-thirds of the Viennese poor fell into that category. Austrians received *Heimatrecht* in their place of birth, and could only transfer it when moving to another municipality by paying a fee the poor could not afford. Although citizens had the right to live anywhere in the Monarchy as long as they could support themselves, cities such as Vienna could send the destitute back to the place where they possessed *Heimatrecht*, and were not legally obligated to support people they considered another town's responsibility. Bloch condemned this practice and called for full freedom of movement and residence for all citizens without regard to income.[475] He contrasted the Austrian policy with that of ancient Israel, which offered the right of residence in any locality for all citizens. Bloch preferred the Hebrew law because it "tied the relationship of persons to the whole not indirectly through the connection with one municipality, one location, but rather directly to the state itself through the idea of a political community (*Staatsgemeinschaft*), which all members embrace spiritually."[476]

Other politicians besides Bloch criticized the *Heimatrecht* law and/or the plight of the poor in general. However, he condemned the law in part because of its deficiency in developing the overall Austrian *Staatsgemeinschaft*. It would have certainly been possible to criticize the *Heimatrecht* law without bringing up this point, but Bloch's statement reflected his commitment to creating a common civic consciousness. Whether speaking against antisemitism, reaching out to workers

---

474 Bloch, "Über Heimats- und Armenrecht," in *Aus der Vergangenheit für die Gegenwart*, pp. 90–91. For more on the poor in turn of the century Vienna see Michael John, "Obdachlösigkeit-Massenerscheinung und Unruheherd in Wien des Spätjahrhundertzeit," in Hubert Ehalt, Gernot Heiss, Hannes Stekl, eds., *Glücklich ist, Wer vergiss-?: das andere Wien um 1900* (Vienna: Böhlau, 1986), pp. 173–94.

475 Bloch, "Über Heimats- und Armenrecht," p. 60.

476 Ibid.

or decrying the plight of the poor, Bloch sought to strengthen the bonds of the Austrian *Staatsgemeinschaft*.

Bloch spoke out to both Jews and non-Jews alike trying to convince them that Austria had to combat antisemitism. Hatred of Jews was only one aspect of the nationalist prejudice that threatened the multiethnic state and the Austrian community Bloch wanted to create. His ideology did not force one to choose between his or her ethnic and civic consciousness because the two elements complemented one another, nor did it require or even encourage the adoption of a particular *Stamm* identity. Thus, Bloch believed that anyone could identify both as a member, for example, of the Czech *Stamm* and the Austrian civic nation, and he hoped that all Austrians, Jewish and non-Jewish, would do so.[477] Bloch's own Jewish *Stamm* consciousness made clear to him that most people wanted an ethnic identity that offered them a sense of community with the members of that group. He did not seek to create a society of de-ethnicized, cosmopolitan Austrians. Bloch's concept of Austrianness was to be another layer on top, but not in lieu, of ethnic consciousness. Furthermore, it neither privileged nor targeted any particular nationality. Bloch proclaimed, "our battle cry thus should not be taken as 'against the Germans,' or 'against the Slavs,' but rather **for Austria**, [emphasis his] the whole common Fatherland. He who does not want to be an Austrian is the enemy!"[478]

Onl y a sense of unity among all Austrians, Bloch contended, could defeat the ethnic rivalries that set the peoples against one another. The nationalities strife endangered the Jews of Austria, as an exposed and dispersed minority group. He maintained, however, that these prejudices also threatened the survival of the Austrian state itself, which "can exist and flourish only if the various ethnic groups and nationalities, confessions, languages, and races who live amongst each other on her territories take one another by the hand towards an easing of the oppositional nature of their political, national, and religious interests."[479]

477 See also Lander, p. 13, 119.

478 "Deutschtum und Judenthum in Oesterreich," *Oesterreichische Wochenschrift*, Nr. 2, Year 3, January 8, 1886, p. 14.

479 Bloch, *Der Nationale Zwist*, p. 41.

This axiom applied to Bloch's political ideology as well. He proclaimed that, since ethnic prejudice was inimical to the interests of the Austrian state, those who expounded it were anti-Austrian. He often returned in his editorials to the innovative and strategically attractive theme that racial hatred of any kind, including antisemitism, was not only morally wrong but unpatriotic, even treasonous against Austria. Bloch explicitly tied Austria's survivability to its rejection of antisemitism and the protection of the rights of all its citizens, including its Jews. He proclaimed "race-hatred is a disintegrative and destructive element which, at its innermost core, is an anti-Austrian idea, against which the Austrian state must take a hostile stand."[480] He admitted that perhaps antisemitism could serve as an integrating factor in a state such as Germany, built around one ethnic nation, but in Austria it would "act as a more centrifugal force weakening the idea of the state as a whole."[481]

Bloch thus sought to isolate antisemites and convince non-Jews that antisemitic violence and discrimination threatened them and their Fatherland, as well as the Jews it directly targeted. He demanded that non-Jews do more than refrain from supporting antisemitism, they had to work actively against it. In fact, there existed a number of non-Jewish Austrians who opposed antisemitism, some of whom created an organization, the *Verein zur Abwehr des Antisemitismus*, specifically to demonstrate that point.[482] The *Verein* strongly encouraged Jews to take a passive role in the fight against antisemitism, arguing that Gentile opposition would make a more powerful statement. While such a stance contradicted Bloch's own belief that Jews should play an active role in the struggle against prejudice, he nevertheless praised the members of the *Verein* for joining the fight in the first place.[483]

---

480 "Der Antisemitismus in Nöthen," *Oesterreichische Wochenschrift*, Nr. 3, Year 1, November 7, 1884, p. 1. On other occasions Bloch labeled antisemitism an "anti-Christian" idea. See, for example, "Antisemitismus und Christenthum," *Oesterreichische Wochenschrift*, Nr. 4, Year 1, November 14, 1884, p. 2. He also linked antisemitism to anarchy, see "Anarchismus und Antisemitismus," *Oesterreichische Wochenschrift*, Nr. 35, Year 12, August 30, 1895, pp. 629–30.

481 "Ein Warnungsruf," *Oesterreichische Wochenschrift*, Nr. 51, Year 9, December 16, 1892, p. 914.

482 Jacques Kornberg, "Vienna, the 1890s: Jews in the Eyes of Their Defenders. (The Verein zur Abwehr des Antisemitismus)," *Central European History* 28 (2), pp: 153–73.

483 Ibid, p. 156.

The racialist German nationalists, whose "Jew-hatred and hatred of Austria share the same origin," earned Bloch's particular contempt. In addition, he took aim at the Christian Socials and the so-called 'black-yellow' (the Habsburg colors) antisemites, who "embrace the enemies of Jews and the enemies of Austria in a more quiet attachment and faith."[484] Bloch ridiculed the attempt by the conservative clerical newspaper, *Das Vaterland*, to argue that it propagated a "patriotic, loyal antisemitism" as opposed to the pan-German, blatantly pro-Hohenzollern and anti-Habsburg antisemitic program of Schönerer.[485]

> An 'Austrian' antisemitism is the same sort of nonsense as a 'Christian' antisemitism, a contradiction in and of itself. The Austrian state is a state of nationalities. Here, the peaceful relationship among the races is the highest postulate of the state's existence, mutual concern and esteem among the nationalities is the first condition of domestic peace...Race hatred...is destructive to the Austrian state.[486]

According to Bloch, Austria's ethnic diversity served as its defining characteristic, one that clearly separated it from the national states that surrounded it and also bestowed upon it a clear purpose, namely to serve as "a refuge of free and brotherly united peoples."[487] He juxtaposed the Austrian idea of equality for all its peoples with the *Staatsidee* of a national state, which promoted the interests of the dominant nationality over those of minorities. Bloch condemned the very idea of the nation-state, proclaiming,

> the nationality principle has, so far as it has been carried out to this point in Europe, brought nothing other than severe calamity. It has led to bloody wars, poisoned the lives of indi-

---

484 "Antisemitischer Patriotismus," *Oesterreichische Wochenschrift*, Nr. 46, Year 8, November 20, 1891, p. 846.

485 "Das 'Vaterland' in Nöthen," *Oesterreichische Wochenschrift*, Nr. 21, Year 5, May 25, 1888, p. 234.

486 Ibid.

487 Bloch, *Der Nationale Zwist*, pp. 45–6.

> vidual peoples during times of peace and has everywhere obstructed the quiet development of culture.[488]

He contended that national states "whether they want to or not," must seek to suppress the heterogeneous elements that inevitably exist in every country.[489] For this reason, "the national state knows...only one law- the law of the stronger. [It] is therefore unsuited to become a *Rechtsstaat*."[490] Bloch compared such a state to a state of nationalities, "the state pure and simple, the state without trimmings," which he likened to a mother who equally loved all her children despite their differences.[491] Bloch believed that Austria, because of its diversity, had a special mission to carry out.

> The Austrian Mission is this, for the first time in history to carry out the idea of the *Rechtsstaat* to the fullest, [to be] a state that protects the rights of its citizens without regard to their language, race, confession, and ethnic origin. Such an ideal mission awaits our Fatherland, ideal like no other. It is called upon to passionately foster and cultivate the idea of rights...to offer a worry-free asylum. And if it is true, as it is written on the *Burgtor* of the shining Imperial city on the Danube: '*Justitia regnorum fundamentum*,' (Justice is the foundation of kingdoms) so it applies first and foremost to our state, which...presents itself to us as the predestined *Rechtsstaat*.[492]

The Austrian mission, Bloch believed, was to save mankind from nationalist hatred. In his eyes, the Austrian state's primary purpose for existing was to convince its many peoples to view themselves as a sin-

---

488 "Rumänen, Magyaren und Juden," *Oesterreichische Wochenschrift*, Nr. 32, Year 10, August 11, 1893, p. 595.

489 Bloch, *Der Nationale Zwist*, p. 47.

490 Ibid., pp. 47–8. Six decades later Hannah Arendt echoed Bloch's view on the inability of such states to respect the rights of its minority peoples. See Arendt, *On the Origins of Totalitarianism* (New York: Harcourt, Brace, 1951), pp. 230–1.

491 Bloch, *Der Nationale Zwist*, p. 48.

492 Ibid.

gle civic nation. In order to carry out this mission, to present to the world an alternative to racial hatred and ethnically-defined nation-states, Bloch called for the cultivation in all its citizens of a new kind of supraethnic, civic Austrian identity.

> Elsewhere the state is completely submerged in one nationality and thus disappears behind it. Here...the idea of the state remains in unadulterated form in full view. Elsewhere the tie that binds the parts to the whole, that makes one unified whole, is the ethnic, racial and blood community....Here, where such a thing does not prevail, it is simply the love and devotion to the soil that produced us and to which our reminiscences hasten—it is the pure, integral, unsullied, absolute idea of the state that unites the parts into a whole. Here is the much sought after "Austrian state patriotism:" the "state" patriotism completely without regard to nationality or confession,...which has not yet been brought into existence.[493]

Bloch hoped to build a new Austrian nation around this sense of state patriotism and civic consciousness. He did not claim that this nation already existed, or that Austria was already the ideal state he described above. Furthermore, Bloch was not naive enough to believe it would be easy to instill a supraethnic Austrian identity in the minds of people who identified with an ethnic group, a province or kingdom, a town, a religion, or any number of other points of identification for citizens of Austria at that time. Nevertheless, he believed Austria could do it. He described his concept of the Austrian idea as "incompatible with national intolerance," and argued that

> only the state which is not national, but rather sees its salvation in the civil equality of all its citizens, which is not German and not Slavic, not Catholic and not Protestant...must encourage the positive cultural and spiritual development of each nationality;

493 Ibid., p. 46–7.

> it has likewise cosmopolitanism as its foundation and builds a higher synthesis between nationality and world citizenship.[494]

In laying out this new mission for Austria, Bloch was offering an indirect, yet powerful critique of current and previous policy on the part of the Monarchy's leaders, including the man wearing the crown. A government that 'sees its salvation' in equality would have to behave very differently from one that sought simply to play the peoples off one another in order to achieve short-term political gains. Such a government would have to seek a solution to the nationalities strife as its highest priority, as the precondition to the fulfillment of its mission.

According to Bloch, the *Reichsrat* and other common democratic institutions could serve as focal points around which citizens could develop these civic bonds. However, not only the government, but also the citizenry would have to play an active role if Austria was to fulfill the mission to which Bloch had assigned it. He referred to voting as a citizen's "holiest and most and important duty."[495] Bloch urged his fellow Austrians to vote for candidates who championed his Austrian mission by supporting equal rights for all citizens regardless of nationality and confession, as well as the equal opportunity for the development and advancement of each *Stamm*.[496] Only an active civil society could support the kind of changes that Bloch believed Austria needed to make in order to survive.

---

494 Ibid., p. 46. The section of *Der Nationale Zwist*, pages 46-48, from which the last few quotations were taken, bears an almost verbatim resemblance to an editorial, "Die ideale Mission des österreichischen Kaiserstaates," by Bernhard Munz (listed as a University administrator in Graz) that ran in the *Oesterreichische Wochenschrift* on February 20, 1885 (Nr. 8, Year 2), pp. 1–2. However, when Bloch reprinted these words in *Der Nationale Zwist*, he did not credit Munz. Although this action called into question Bloch's publishing ethics, it made clear that, whoever wrote these words originally, Bloch publicly proclaimed them as his own. Thus, for the purposes of this book, the fact that Bloch recopied someone else's words as opposed to forming the sentences himself is of little importance. Nevertheless, Dr. Bernhard Munz deserves credit for his contribution to *Der Nationale Zwist*, even if over one hundred years late. See also Lander, p. 119, and Toury, "Josef Samuel Bloch und die Jüdische Identität im Österreichischen Kaiserreich," p. 53, n. 38, and p. 59, for similar discussions of this issue.

495 "Zu den *Reichsrat*hwahlen," *Oesterreichische Wochenschrift*, Nr. 21, Year 2, May 29, 1885, p. 1–2.

496 Ibid., p. 1.

Bloch tried to nurture and cultivate horizontal bonds based on citizenship that would unite all Austrians. Believing that this common consciousness would come into being only if Austria fully enforced the Constitution that guaranteed civil rights and equality before the law for all citizens, he would not tolerate any violation by the state of the principle of equality, and condemned any breach of the constitutional rights upon which an Austrian civic consciousness would have to rest. He maintained that the ideas of laws, rights and justice had become deeply imbedded in the consciousness of Austrian citizens, but asserted that this consciousness could only be continue to be viable if these laws and rights were applied equally without regard to nationality, class and confession.[497]

Bloch initially laid out his ideas on Jewish and Austrian identity in the early 1880s, and remained steadfastly committed to them throughout his career. He continued his crusade over the next decade with a sense of optimism that Austrians would overcome their ethnic and religious prejudices and form an inclusive civic nation. However, in the mid- to late 1890s, he increasingly came to doubt that Austria would win the fight against the ethnic hatreds that threatened its existence, as well as the safety of its Jews, although he never altered his view of the importance of that struggle. He saw with increasing frequency that Jews faced not only prejudice, but also legal discrimination in violation of the equal rights mandated by the 1867 Constitution.

The unofficial exclusion of Jews from public office, as well as other violations of their civil rights during the 1890s, brought swift polemical responses from Bloch. In 1893, he criticized the absence of Jews in the administration of the *Südbahn*, a government-run railroad, as an example of hiring discrimination by the state.[498] He exposed a case of blatant discrimination only two years later. A government advertisement for a physician in a salt mine in Hallstatt stated that a baptismal certificate was required for the job. Bloch decried this violation of Article III of the 1867 Constitution, which stated that all public

497 "Justitia regnorum fundamentum!," *Oesterreichische Wochenschrift*, Nr. 41, Year 12, October 9, 1895, pp. 741.

498 "Arische Privatbeamte," *Oesterreichische Wochenschrift*, Nr. 11, Year 10, March 17, 1893, pp. 191–2.

positions must be equally accessible to all citizens. He discussed the issue with his fellow members of the *Reichsrat* Polish Club, in order to decide how best to bring it to the public consciousness. Eventually, they decided to have Deputies Kronawetter and Pernerstorfer protest directly to Ernst von Plener, the Finance Minister, whose department had announced the position. As a result of the protests, Plener removed the baptismal requirement for the position. Bloch offered the following commentary on the affair, "For us Jews this incident is a new and serious warning that we may not relax in the defense of our civil rights."[499] He expressed frustration that, although the affair was eventually settled successfully, the Polish Club had told him that it was not a Galician affair, and should not concern him. Bloch considered this event not merely an affront to Jews, but an attack on the principle of legal equality, an issue that should have concerned patriotic Austrian citizens of every nationality and religion because he believed that equality was the foundation upon which the legitimacy of the Austrian state rested.[500]

By the early 1890s Bloch had lost faith in the Taaffe administration. He would have most preferred the emergence of a truly multiethnic democratic party such as the one Fischhof had advocated in 1882. In 1889, Bloch had praised the *Demokratische Centralverein*, hoping it would be able to do what the German Liberal party could not, attract members of all the nationalities into a single democratic party.[501] However, no such party or coalition ever emerged.

His disillusionment with Taaffe combined with the ultimate weakness of the *Demokratische Centralverein* led Bloch to offer support on more than one occasion for the Social Democrats, a new development in his political strategy. As discussed earlier, he had publicly reached out to the workers and supported their rights from early on in his career. In the early 1890s, Bloch began to look more favorably on the SDP as a political party. In 1893 he explained that Jews were being "forced into

---

499 "Ein Erfolg im Kampfe für die Staatsgrundgesetze," *Oesterreichische Wochenschrift*, Nr. 12, Year 12, March 22, 1895, p. 209. Bloch also described this event in *My Reminiscences*, Vol. I, pp. 337–9. (See pp. 337–9).

500 "Ein Erfolg im Kampfe für die Staatsgrundgesetze," *Oesterreichische Wochenschrift*, Nr. 12, Year 12, March 22, 1895, p. 209.

501 "Der Demokratische Centralverein," *Oesterreichische Wochenschrift*, Nr. 47, Yr. 6, December 6, 1889, p. 855.

the ranks of Social Democracy" because neither the liberals nor the government, then still led by Taaffe, would not protect their rights.[502] Bloch took great pains to note the basic conservatism of Jews and their widespread aversion to revolution, arguing that Jewish support for the SDP resulted from what they saw as a lack of all other options.[503] In 1895 he went further and endorsed the Social Democrats in an election for the Vienna City Council as the only force capable of and willing to stand up to Lueger's Christian Socials and fight for equal rights.[504] He praised the Social Democrats, in particular when compared to the antisemites, a number of times during the 1890s and in the years leading up to 1914.[505] In fact, his ideas on Austrian identity were quite compatible with those expressed by Karl Renner.[506]

Although his optimism about the future of the Austrian political system had begun to ebb with the fall of Taaffe, two other events led Bloch to harbor stronger doubts about the future of civil rights and equality in Austria. First, in June 1895 the Chairman of the Polish Club, Zaleski, finally bowed to the pressure of Prince Liechtenstein and other powerful antisemites in the *Reichsrat* and forced Bloch to resign his seat based on what the latter described as the manufactured pretext of questions about the most recent election.[507] Bloch had to stand in a special election in his district. During the election campaign his opponents

---

502 "Man drängt uns in die Reihen der Socialdemokratie, I," *Oesterreichische Wochenschrift*, Nr. 41, Yr. 10, October 13, 1893, pp. 800–01; "Man drängt uns in die Reihen der Socialdemokratie, II," *Oesterreichische Wochenschrift*, Nr. 43, Yr. 10, October 27, 1893, pp. 839–41.

503 "Man drängt uns in die Reihen der Socialdemokratie, I," *Oesterreichische Wochenschrift*, p. 800.

504 "Was ist zu thun?," *Oesterreichische Wochenschrift*, Nr. 14, Year 12, April 5, 1895, pp. 249–50.

505 See, for example "Eine Pflicht der Wiener Juden," *Oesterreichische Wochenschrift*, Nr. 39, Year 29, September 27, 1912, pp. 653–4. For more on ideological parallels between Bloch and the Social Democrats, see Lander, pp. 131–2.

506 See Chapter 5.

507 Bloch, *My Reminiscences*, Vol. I , pp. 340. No comprehensive academic study of the Polish Club and its dealings with Galician Jewish *Reichsrat* members exists. For a less than objective picture, see Saul R. Landau, *Der Polenklub und seine Hausjuden* (Vienna: n.p., 1907), and Max Rosenfeld, *Die Polnische Judenfrage* (Vienna: R. Löwit, 1919). Both of these are highly polemical works that are extremely critical of the Polish Club, and especially its Jewish members, as well as the Club's attitudes towards Jews.

practiced voter intimidation of the most brutal kind. Bloch lost his seat and Austrian Jews lost their most powerful voice in the *Reichsrat*. He believed that his enemies had sought to remove him from office because he "had the gall to declare himself a Jew."[508] This affair certainly helped convince Bloch of the weakness of the democratic process in Austria by the 1890s.

The crisis that followed the Badeni language ordinances further increased Bloch's pessimism. The crisis began on April 5, 1897, when the Minister President, Casimir Badeni, ordered that all administrative communications within the Bohemian provinces be conducted in both Czech and German. In order to make this possible, the government required all civil servants in Bohemia to become bilingual by 1901. As most educated Czechs had already learned German, the burden would be on the Germans to learn what most of them considered a culturally inferior Slavic language or else lose their jobs.

Shortly after the issuance of the ordinances, Germans rioted all over western Austria. German deputies ground parliamentary business to a halt by obstructing all discussions, debates and procedures. By the fall of 1897 they had turned the *Reichsrat* into a circus.[509] On November 29, 1897, Badeni resigned and the government withdrew the ordinances. Subsequently, Czechs began to riot throughout Bohemia and inflicted violence in particular against Jews, whom they viewed as having supported the German cause.[510] In the end, German remained the sole language of internal administration in Bohemia and the riots stopped, but the crisis in many ways signaled the end of a functioning parliamentary life in Austria. As concerned the Jews, events followed exactly the pattern Bloch had predicted in *Der Nationale Zwist und die*

---

508 "Prinz Liechtenstein und die Reichsrathswahl in Kolomea," *Oesterreichische Wochenschrift*, Nr. 44, Year 12, November 1, 1895, p. 806. The *Oesterreichische Wochenschrift* discussed the affair, and Bloch described it in detail in *My Reminiscences*, Vol. I, pp. 335–50. Although his depiction may be somewhat one-sided, I am more concerned with how these events, which he saw as clearly unconstitutional and discriminatory, affected his outlook on civic life and equality in Austria.

509 For a more detailed discussion of this crucial affair, see Okey, pp. 305–09.

510 "Die Judenhetze in Böhmen," *Oesterreichische Wochenschrift*, Nr. 50, Year 14, December 10, 1897, pp. 1001–2. On the riots in Prague, see also Cohen, *The Politics of Ethnic Survival*.

Juden in Österreich more than ten years earlier, namely that when the peoples fight each other, the Jews suffer.

Bloch had little sympathy for Badeni as a politician and noted that, as Governor of Galicia, Badeni had utilized violence and extraconstitutional means against him during the special election only two years earlier.[511] Bloch did argue, however, that the Badeni ordinances made sense in light of the two languages spoken by the population of Bohemia. He believed that the civil servants of the province should become bilingual, a stand consistent with statements throughout his career on the need for Austrians to learn their neighbors' languages.[512] However, the Germans of Austria, still the most powerful and numerous of the Cisleithanian nationalities, had made clear by their opposition to the Badeni ordinances that they disagreed.

The obstructionist tactics employed by the German deputies during the Badeni Crisis had literally crippled the *Reichsrat*. Other factions quickly realized they could do the same to block legislation they opposed, and parliamentary activity at the central level ground to a halt.[513] Bloch denounced obstructionists of every party for threatening to destroy the *Reichsrat*. He thundered, "each Austrian...who maintains a sense of the honor and the reputation of his Fatherland...must turn red from shame as a result of the parliamentary excesses, the likes of which would not be possible in the civilized world."[514]

Bloch believed Austria, if it was to be a *Rechtsstaat*, must have a constitutional government. He condemned the creeping replacement of the parliamentary system by absolutist rule through the use of Paragraph 14 of the Constitution.[515] This clause allowed the Emperor to rule by decree when the *Reichsrat* was not in session. After 1897 Franz Joseph prorogued the *Reichsrat* whenever obstruction brought activity

---

511 "Die Nemesis," *Oesterreichische Wochenschrift*, Nr. 49, Year 14, December 3, 1897, pp. 981–3, and Bloch, *My Reminiscences*, Vol. I, pp. 346.

512 "Die Juden und der österreichische Sprachenstreit," *Oesterreichische Wochenschrift*, Nr. 20, Year 14, May 14, 1897, pp. 405–6.

513 "Der Verfall Oesterreichs durch die antisemitische Verhetzung," *Oesterreichische Wochenschrift*, Nr. 9, Year 17, March 2, 1900, pp. 157–8.

514 Ibid., p. 158.

515 "Die Verfassungskrisis," *Oesterreichische Wochenschrift*, Nr. 34, Year 16, August 25, 1899, pp. 617–8.

to a standstill. Before the *Reichsrat* reassembled, the Minister President negotiated agreements so that the decrees could be approved *ex post facto* when the deputies gathered once again.[516] Although he did not criticize the Emperor by name, Bloch's unstinting criticism of Franz Joseph's moves toward absolutism and the use of Paragraph 14 to rule by decree demonstrated his commitment to constitutional rule and his refusal to blindly support the Emperor under any circumstances.

As part of his support for constitutional and parliamentary government, Bloch emphasized the particular importance of the *Reichsrat,* which he referred to as "the common Austrian state institution."[517] Bloch had hoped to build a common civic Austrian identity around the two pillars of the *Reichsrat* and the Constitution. At the turn of the twentieth century, both appeared impotent in the face of nationalistic and antisemitic hatreds. The war between the nationalities had weakened these two institutions, and thus weakened the very *Staatsidee* that buttressed Bloch's Austrian *Rechtsstaat.*[518]

As Bloch saw it, the mission of the *Reichsrat* was to enforce the equal rights guaranteed in the Constitution.[519] However, he commented as early as 1895, that "Austria is called a state of laws and a constitutional state, but many points of the Constitution continue to exist only on paper and the rights described within them often reflect the opposite of the situation in reality."[520] By 1904, the situation had worsened. Bloch declared that for years the *Reichsrat* had not carried out its mission of protecting civil rights and that Austria no longer possessed a working parliament.[521] The decline of the *Reichsrat* and the lack of enforcement of the Constitution, perhaps as much as anything else, ren-

---

516 Beller, *Francis Joseph*, pp. 160–1.

517 "Der Verfall Oesterreichs durch die antisemitische Verhetzung," *Oesterreichische Wochenschrift*, Nr. 9, Year 17, March 2, 1900, p. 158.

518 "Zur Auflösung des österreichischen Parlamentes," *Oesterreichische Wochenschrift*, Nr. 37, Year 17, September 14, 1900, pp. 651–2.

519 "Ein Rückblick," *Oesterreichische Wochenschrift*, Nr. 52, Year 20, December 25, 1903, pp. 827–8.

520 "Cilli und Saybusch," *Oesterreichische Wochenschrift*, Nr. 28, Year 12, July 12, 1895, p. 513.

521 "Meister Stampiglius in der österreichischen Delegation," *Oesterreichische Wochenschrift*, Nr. 5, Year 21, January 29, 1904, p. 65.

dered impossible the creation of Bloch's civic Austrian nation. By the turn of the century, he was no longer calling for the creation of a new identity to fight ethnic and racial hatred on a philosophical level. Instead Bloch turned to a defensive and reactive strategy of fighting antisemitism one incident at a time.

By the beginning of the twentieth century, Bloch's pessimism about the future of the *Rechtsstaat* in Austria had grown stronger. He called for greater education of the citizenry on the importance of the rule of law, but at the same time admitted the difficulty of doing so "in a country in which the corruption of the public spirit is built directly into the political system."[522] As early as the end of 1903, he sounded doubts about the long-term viability of the Austrian state in the face of nationalism.

> Centrifugal forces have awakened...in this multilingual *Reich.* There are moments in which it appears almost impossible to hold this complicated organism together, moments in which the complete dissolution, the war of all against all, looms. The national principle, which works in such effective ways against the strengthening of the state, has achieved incalculable devastation here.[523]

Twelve months later saw the end of Minister President Koerber's years in office, at which time Bloch offered a grim picture of developments in Austrian politics between 1900 and 1904: "The nationality feuds grew immeasurably, the Parliament remained a hotbed of the most wasteful obstruction, governmental authority was severely weakened and economic need has reached a level that is barely still tolerable."[524] Although he recognized that constitutional government and the parliamentary system in Austria were in a sorry state, Bloch remained a steadfast supporter of those institutions as the best means of enforcing equal rights.

522 "Die Ursachen des Verfalles," *Oesterreichische Wochenschrift*, Nr. 6, Year 21, February 5, 1904, pp. 81–2.

523 "Ein Rückblick," *Oesterreichische Wochenschrift*, Nr. 52, Year 20, December 25, 1903, p. 827.

524 "Das neue Ministerium," *Oesterreichische Wochenschrift*, Nr. 1, Year 22, January 6, 1905, p. 1.

> It is a shortsighted wisdom that says that enlightened absolutism is better than the unbridled parliamentarism we have had for five years. If we were to grant that a working Parliament, as it is currently composed, poses a serious threat to Jews..., the civil rights of our fellow believers nevertheless remain tenable only on a constitutional basis, and the future fate of the Jews is inseparably linked to the survival and growth of constitutional organizations.[525]

Furthermore, despite what he described as the antisemitic mood of the recent Parliament, Bloch declared "we are not able or even permitted to wish for the unparliamentary condition of unbounded rule through Paragraph 14 or a totally naked absolutism because we do not want to be downgraded once again from free and equal citizens to *Schutzjuden*."[526] Bloch remained absolutely committed to constitutional government in Austria.

By 1905 Bloch had become much more pessimistic about the future of constitutional government in Austria than he had been twenty or even ten years earlier. Nevertheless, for him the solution remained the same, perhaps because he could imagine no other alternative. In Bloch's mind multiethnic Austria offered the only hope for Central European Jews in their quest to be treated as equal citizens and be safe from discrimination and prejudice. As he had for two decades, he continued to maintain

> the fate of the Jews will be also the fate of this state, because no element of the population is as selflessly patriotic, as unquestionably Austrian as the Jews. We desire no special legal rights, we have no borders across which we stare yearningly, we are no national autonomists, we are Austrians all the same!—and thus we are reviled and oppressed![527]

---

[525] Ibid.

[526] Ibid. The term referred to the status of Jews before emancipation, in which they lived under the monarch's special protection, and possessed no rights as citizens *per se*.

[527] Ibid., p. 2.

In the last decade leading up the outbreak of the First World War, Bloch's assessment of Austria's future remained bleak.[528] He railed against the election-related violence, corruption, and intimidation of voters in Galicia in 1907, an egregious example of which was the election of a radical Polish nationalist and antisemite from an East Galician district that was 18% Ukrainian and 65% Jewish.[529] In 1911, Bloch condemned a police inspector who disparaged Jews as a people in an official report.[530] Bloch was particularly distressed by the existence of "official k.k. antisemites," because he relied on the state as the last bastion of support for the principle of equal rights against an increasingly hostile populace.[531]

In editorial after editorial, Bloch lamented the corruption and the ethnic and racial hatred that he saw strangling Austrian society. In particular, he blamed the Christian Social party for having destroyed public life.[532] Bloch declared "all the problems in public life today can be

---

528 Many in the Austrian ruling establishment, defined by Solomon Wank as the traditional elites plus the German-Austrian bourgeoisie, shared Bloch's doubts about the future of Austria and the negative impact of the lack of a common identity. See Solomon Wank, "Pessimism in the Austrian Establishment at the Turn of the Century," in Solomon Wank, Heidrun Maschl, Brigitte Mazohl-Wallnig, Reinhold Wagleitner, eds. *The Mirror of History: Essays in Honor of Fritz Fellner* (Santa Barbara: ABC-Clio, 1988), pp. 295–314. Wank cited a letter from Ulrich Klepsch, Habsburg military attaché at St. Petersburg to his friend, Baron Alois Lexa von Aehrenthal, later Foreign Minister, in which the former lamented, "It seems as if only the love of the peoples for the person of the Emperor was the bond, the only one, which held Austria together," and added, "that is not *good*." (Haus-, Hof- und Staatsarchiv, Nachlass Aehrenthal, Carton 2, Klepsch to Aehrenthal, 28 December 1887, emphasis in original, cited in Wank, p. 297).

529 "Misbrauch der Amtsgewalt. Der Wahlrechtsraub im 30. Reichsratswahlbezirk des Königreiches Galizien. Eine öffentliche Anklage," *Oesterreichische Wochenschrift*, Nr. 22, Year 24, May 31, 1907, pp. 357–60; "K.K. Anarchisten," *Oesterreichische Wochenschrift*, Nr. 23, Year 24, June 7, 1907, pp. 373–5.

530 "Der Polizist als Antisemit," *Oesterreichische Wochenschrift*, Nr. 46, Year 28, November 17, 1911, pp. 757–8.

531 Ibid., p. 758. The term "k.k.," or "*kaiserlich und königlich*" translates as "imperial and royal." It referred to the status of Franz Joseph's civil officials as servants of an institution that represented the Emperor of Austria and the King of Hungary and served as shorthand for any institution of the Monarchy.

532 See, among many others, "Christlichsoziales Panama in der Bukowina," *Oesterreichische Wochenschrift*, Nr. 43, Year 27, October 28, 1910, p. 707.

traced with certainty to Christian Social origins."[533] He also warned that the influence of Christian Socialism over the government was leading Austria towards "a frightful form of racial strife and a war of life and death."[534] Bloch came to see the Emperor himself as the only public institution not corrupted by antisemitism and nationalist hatreds.[535] By the summer of 1914, he no longer spoke of creating a civic Austrian nation because civic life as he understood it had ceased to exist in Austria.

The outbreak of war in August 1914 gave him new energy, and breathed life into his hope for the creation of a united Austrian community. Although they had not previously united around democratic principles and constitutional institutions, perhaps the Habsburg nationalities would do so in a great conflict against a terrible enemy, namely Russian czarism.[536] Bloch wanted brotherhood and peace among the Austrian peoples however it was achieved. With the outbreak of war he triumphantly declared that the peoples of the entire Monarchy, both the Austrian and Hungarian halves, had unified themselves into a single nation.[537] Many Austrians made triumphant and patriotic statements when war broke out in August 1914. Bloch could simply have gloried in future military triumph or the virtue of the Monarchy and its allies. However, he also celebrated what he believed was the creation of a new supraethnic nation that bound the peoples to one another and their com-

---

533 "Von Pfister bis Sviha," *Oesterreichische Wochenschrift*, Nr. 21, Year 31, May 22, 1914, p. 358.

534 "Du sollst nicht jubeln, wenn dein Feind gefallen ist!" *Oesterreichische Wochenschrift*, Nr. 10, Year 27, March 11, 1910, p. 170.

535 "Der achtzigste Geburtstag des Monarchen," *Oesterreichische Wochenschrift*, Nr. 33, Year 27, August 19, 1910, pp. 545–6.

536 Bloch hated Russia above and beyond all other countries because of its terrible mistreatment of its Jews. He berated the treatment of Russian Jews at least once a month in his newspaper, and often more frequently than that. Even a partial listing of such editorials would be too numerous to offer here. After July 1914 Bloch became silent about Romania, the state against which he had railed over the years almost as often as he had Russia, until Romania entered the war against the Central Powers in the middle of 1916. Bloch then launched a series of editorial attacks over the following months reminding his readers that, after Russia, Romania was the second great enemy of Jews and was now an enemy of the Austrian war effort as well. For a summary of Bloch's invective against the treatment of Jews in Romania, see *Erinnerungen aus meinem Leben*, Vol. III, pp. 120–52.

537 "Der Kaiser Franz Josef I," *Oesterreichische Wochenschrift*, Nr. 33, Year 31, August 14, 1914, p. 561. See the first page of the introduction for the actual quotation.

mon state, which to him would have been the greatest victory Austria could achieve.

Bloch hoped that the wartime unity he saw among the peoples would lead to a greater acceptance of Jews as part of this new Austro-Hungarian nation. Throughout the war he decried the plight of *Habsburgtreu* Galician Jewish refugees forced to flee from the Russian occupation forces.[538] These Jews faced terrible treatment at the hands of the Czarist armies, and Bloch called on the Austrian government to take care of its citizens. He declared that they were "loyal Austrians and bitter enemies of sinister Russia," and thus deserved "the eager assistance of the Fatherland."[539] Bloch appealed for aid for these fellow members of the Austrian community, once again by attempting to create a conception of community that included Jews. As he called on Austria to help its Jewish citizens, he also exhorted Austrian Jews to help their country. Bloch regularly implored his readers to support the Austrian war effort and printed ads encouraging them to buy war bonds as a way of showing their loyalty. In one particularly blunt example, he ran an advertisement that read, "every loyal Jew will subscribe to the 4th Austrian War Bond."[540]

During the war Bloch returned to the tactic of branding antisemites as disloyal and unpatriotic. He accused Viennese antisemites of placing prejudice and hatred above the needs of the country, and once again linked antisemitism to the larger nationalities strife that threatened the Austrian state.[541] According to Bloch, internal peace and the future of Austria would only be secure "when all will have learned that they are not permitted to hate or stir up any group or class, absolutely not, that the law must be followed fully and unconditionally, even as regards the Jews."[542]

---

538 See also Marsha L. Rozenblit, "The Dilemma of Identity: The Impact of the First World War on Habsburg Jewry," in Ritchie Robertson & Edward Timms, eds., *The Habsburg Legacy: National Identity in Historical Perspective* (Edinburgh: Edinburgh University Press, 1994), pp. 144–57, see pp. 147–48.

539 "Das jüdische Opfer des Krieges," *Oesterreichische Wochenschrift*, Nr. 36, Year 31, September 4, 1914, pp. 609–10.

540 *Oesterreichische Wochenschrift*, Nr. 20, Year 33, May 19, 1916, p. 334.

541 "Biehloweks Hetze gegen Juden und Sozialdemokraten," *Oesterreichische Wochenschrift*, Nr. 9, Year 32, February 26, 1915, p. 154.

542 "Der Gerichtsaal und die Burgfrieden," *Oesterreichische Wochenschrift*, Nr. 44, Year 33, November 10, 1916, p. 732.

He had not labeled antisemitism an anti-Austrian idea during his period of pessimism, perhaps because he thought such a charge held little weight in light of the particularism of most of the nationalist leaders in the post-Badeni era. His return to this strategy signified his belief, or at least his hope, that a viable sense of an Austrian community existed, and that he might be able to isolate antisemites by placing them outside that community.

At least in his newspaper, Bloch maintained a positive attitude towards Austria's future until the very end of the war. The desire to appear loyal during the war certainly affected what one would or would not say in public, as did the press censorship that tightened in wartime. However, when the *Reichsrat* reopened in 1917, some members openly called for independence for their various peoples. Bloch, had he felt that way, at least had the option to be more negative and critical of Austria without fear of repercussions from the government. His optimism appears sincere, if increasingly unrealistic.[543] He printed a glowing obituary of Franz Joseph following his death, in which he praised the Emperor for protecting the Jews as equal citizens and for upholding the principle of equality to the fullest.[544] Bloch also expressed his hope that, under the new leadership of Emperor Karl, Austria would finally enact the political reorganization it required in order to deal with the nationalities question, although he did not offer any specific plans in this regard.[545]

Bloch believed that constitutional and parliamentary government remained necessary in order for Austria to solve its internal conflicts and guarantee its survival as a state. He hoped that the reopening of the *Reichsrat* in May 1917 would quickly lead to a reform of the Austrian state structure that would satisfy the various nationalities.[546] By the summer of 1917, he thought he saw "the outline of a new Austria tak-

---

543 Other Jewish writers also maintained their public support for a reformed and continued Austria down to the end. See Rozenblit, "The Dilemma of Identity: the Impact of the First World War on Habsburg Jewry," pp. 145–50.

544 "Kaiser Franz Joseph I," *Oesterreichische Wochenschrift*, Nr. 46, Year 33, November 24, 1916, pp. 761–2.

545 Ibid.

546 "Eine neue Gruppe im Herrenhaus?" *Oesterreichische Wochenschrift*, Nr. 22, Year 34, June 8, 1917, pp. 357–8.

ing shape, in which the peoples will be able to live with one another in joyful community in a polity built on solid foundations," although he did not provide evidence to support this observation.[547] On May 3, 1918, Bloch ran an optimistic editorial encouraging compromise and reform in Austria, and declared that hope still remained for the future of a multiethnic Austrian state.[548] Even as late as October 4, 1918, Bloch clung to the fantasy that "on the political horizon of our Monarchy the contours of a new organization are becoming ever more distinct and comprehensible."[549] Based on his predictions over the years, he must have feared that the breakup of Austria-Hungary and the impending creation of national states in Central Europe would bring disaster to the region, particularly to its Jews. Bloch simply held on to his hope for the survival of multiethnic Austria until the bitter end.

On October 18, 1918, the last issue of *Dr. Bloch's Oesterreichische Wochenschrift* appeared, and on October 25, 1918, four days after the Austro-Germans established a national assembly to organize what would become their new German-Austrian state, the first issue of *Dr. Bloch's Wochenschrift* replaced it. Another article in that edition, written by Dr. Heinrich Schreiber, openly mourned this development.[550] Bloch had not commented in print on Emperor Karl's manifesto of October 16, 1918, which announced the federalization of the Monarchy's Austrian half. He did not write the editorial that appeared in the October 18 issue, and by the following week the various nationalities had clearly rejected the manifesto and made it a dead letter.

Bloch had originally chosen the title "Austrian Weekly" specifically to emphasize the Austrianness of his political philosophy. His removal of 'Austrian' from the title of his newspaper symbolized that Bloch had finally acknowledged the death of his Austria. On November

547 "Zur Verfassungsänderung," *Oesterreichische Wochenschrift*, Nr. 29, Year 34, July 27, 1917, pp. 470–1.

548 "Es wird weitergehetzt," *Oesterreichische Wochenschrift*, Nr. 17, Year 35, May 3, 1918, pp. 261–2.

549 "An die Arbeit!" *Oesterreichische Wochenschrift*, Nr. 39, Year 35, October 4, 1918, pp. 625–6.

550 *Oesterreichische Wochenschrift*, Nr. 42, Year 35, October 25, 1918, pp. 673–5, cited also in Rozenblit, "The Dilemma of Identity: the Impact of the First World War on Habsburg Jewry," p. 150.

8, 1918, three days before Emperor Karl I officially renounced his authority to govern in Austria, Bloch declared, "the past is over."[551] He did not publicly mourn the old Monarchy, because doing so would only have placed his loyalty to the new Austrian state, in which he chose to reside, into doubt. Bloch had no choice but to hope that the new Austria would allow him and his fellow Jews to live peacefully.

In many ways, the end of Austria-Hungary signaled the end of Bloch's career.[552] The Republic of Austria in which he resided after November 1918 was not a multiethnic state, and its relative homogeneity rendered Bloch's supraethnic vision no longer relevant. The Austrian Republic contained a population dominated by ethnic Germans. These Germans wanted nothing more than to join their rump Austrian state to the German *Reich*, but the Treaty of Versailles proscribed such an *Anschluss*. Bloch found himself cut off from his Galician Jewish supporters, who were now citizens of a reconstituted Poland. He continued to publish his newspaper until February 20, 1920. On that date the editorial board announced that the paper would go on a "long hiatus" while its editor traveled abroad in support of Jewish causes.[553] With the exception of a special edition on November 7, 1920, celebrating Bloch's 70th birthday, the newspaper, and Bloch's active public career in Austria, came to an end.[554]

Looking back at his legacy, Bloch's vision for a new civic Austrian nation did not become reality. Although he did offer some specifics,

---

551 "Am Schweideweg: Ein jüdisches Parlament," *Oesterreichische Wochenschrift*, Nr. 44, Year 35, November 8, 1918, p. 706.

552 For more on the ideas of Bloch and/or other Austrian Jews after the Monarchy's dissolution, see Rozenblit, "The Dilemma of Identity: the Impact of the First World War on Habsburg Jewry," pp. 150–4, and David Rechter, "Kaisertreu: The Dynastic Loyalty of Austrian Jewry," in Klaus Hödl, ed., *Jüdische Identitäten: Einblicke in die Bewusstseinslandschaft des österreichischen Judentums* (Innsbruck: Studien-Verlag, 2000), pp. 189–208. To summarize, Bloch did not alter his views on Jewish identity, and continued to see Jews as an ethnic community (*Stammesgemeinschaft*). See *Oesterreichische Wochenschrift*, Nr. 51, Year 35, December 27, 1918, p. 824, cited also in Rozenblit, "The Dilemma of Identity," p. 152.

553 *Oesterreichische Wochenschrift*, Nr. 7, Year 37, February 20, 1920, p. 89.

554 According to Bloch, the end of the Monarchy allowed the new successor states to take measures to block out Viennese newspapers, which naturally hurt his paper's profitability. See Bloch, *Erinnerungen aus meinem Leben*, Vol. III, p. 268.

such as the need for bilingual education, he neither fully answered the admittedly difficult question of how to depoliticize ethnic identity while preserving its cultural and communal integrity, nor described exactly what concrete steps, beyond political reforms, Austrian society would have to take in order to inculcate the sense of a common consciousness that was central to his fight against racial nationalism and ethnic prejudice.

Bloch's most fertile intellectual period occurred during the Taaffe era, in particular during the early to mid-1880s when he felt most optimistic about the possibility of solving the nationalities question through some form of political compromise. Perhaps because he emphasized rhetoric rather than putting forth specific legal and/or institutional solutions, his ideas on the nationalities question and in particular his vision of a civic Austrian identity did not fundamentally change even when political and social circumstances did. In terms of politics, he did grow more willing to embrace and support Social Democratic candidates after the mid-1890s, although even his early speeches to the workers of Vienna and Lower Austria demonstrated some compatibility with aspects of Social Democratic ideology. While his faith in Austria's ability to solve its problems weakened, he continued to prescribe mostly the same solutions during the First World War as he did during the 1880s, namely support for constitutional and parliamentary government, the legal equality of all citizens, and some form of compromise that would allow all the nationalities to feel that the state treated them equally as ethno-cultural entities.

During the last decades of the Monarchy Bloch's ideas resonated among the audience upon which he focused most of his attention, his fellow Habsburg Jews. Bloch drew support from nationalist Jewish students, including the Jewish nationalist student union, *Kadimah*, which had expressed their admiration for him before either his election to the *Reichsrat* or the founding of his newspaper.[555] Orthodox Rabbis and their congregants, as well as nationalistically-oriented Jewish politicians in the western and eastern parts of Austria also supported him.[556]

555 Toury, "Troubled Beginnings: The Emergence of the Österreichisch-Israelitische Union," p. 461, n. 16.

556 Wistrich, *The Jews of Vienna in the Age of Franz Joseph*, p. 288.

Furthermore, Bloch won adherents among Viennese workers and democratic politicians of different faiths, most notably Josef Kopp. In addition, his newspaper, which Rozenblit called "the most important Jewish weekly newspaper in Vienna,"[557]

The civic organization Bloch helped found, the *Österreichisch-Israelitische Union*, played a significant social and political role in Vienna and throughout Austria.[558] In 1910 the OIU claimed to have interceded in 5,000 cases of discrimination against Jews during the first twenty-five years of its existence, and to possess a membership of 7,000.[559] It thus had an impressive 4% of the entire Viennese Jewish community, which numbered 175,318 in 1910, on its membership rolls.[560] Less than four years after its founding, it came to dominate the leadership positions in the Viennese Israelitische Kultusgemeinde, demonstrating the influence of Bloch's vision among Viennese and Austrian Jewry. With the IKG elections of November 1889, the OIU-nominated candidates won all seven contested races and saw the election of its candidate, Alfred Stern, as president. This feat gave the OIU a solid majority on the IKG board, and led to peaceful relations between the two organizations.[561] The OIU became the largest and by far most important Jewish organization in all of Austria in the early 1890s. It remained such for at least the next fifteen years, when more nationalistically oriented groups began to come to the fore and claim a position alongside the OIU, which nevertheless remained prominent until the end of the Monarchy.[562]

Furthermore, Bloch received multiple mandates from Galician Jews to represent them in the *Reichsrat*, and leading antisemites in that body considered him important enough to target for removal from

---

557 Marsha L. Rozenblit, "Review Article: The Jews of the Dual Monarchy," *Austrian History Yearbook* 23 (1992), pp. 160–180, quotation on p. 162. See also Toury, *Die Jüdische Press im österreichische Kaiserreich: ein Beitrag zur Problematik der Akkulturation, 1802–1918*, p. 82; and McCagg, p. 184.

558 Rozenblit, *Vienna and the Jews*, p. 159.

559 Ibid., p. 158.

560 Ibid., p. 17.

561 See Toury, "Years of Strife: The Contest of the Österreichisch-Israelitische Union for the Leadership of Austrian Jewry," p. 183. See also Bloch, *My Reminiscenses*, Vol. I, p. 168, and Wistrich, *The Jews of Vienna in the Age of Franz Joseph*, p. 291.

562 Toury, "Years of Strife: The Contest of the Österreichisch-Israelitische Union for the Leadership of Austrian Jewry," p. 196.

office. Evidence also exists of his influence, presumably concentrated in the Jewish community, in the English-speaking world, in particular the United States, which he visited on more than one occasion and wrote about in *Ein Besuch beim Judenthum in New-York und Umgebung*. During his 1912 visit to New York, he received certificates honoring his work on behalf of the Jewish people from the First Hungarian Congregation Ohab Zedek (February 17, 1912), as well as from the Federation of Galician and Bucovinaen (sic!) Jews in America (February 20, 1912).[563] In addition, an English version of his two-volume memoirs appeared in 1923, the year of his death, and his book *Israel and the Nations* was translated only four years later. These books, which had been published in German only in 1922, were thus translated not as historical documents, but as ideas that resonated at that time.

Bloch used the public platform his political career and his newspaper gave him to alter the way Habsburg Jews perceived their own identity. By the late nineteenth century, the Jewish attempt to assimilate into Austro-German society had been rejected by the Austro-Germans themselves. These Jews had not and could not become Germans. Another alternative, Zionism, offered them a strong Jewish identity, but seemed to reject, at least at some point in the future, the homeland and Austrian state towards which many of them felt great loyalty. Bloch's conception of identity contained an ethnic Jewish and a civic Austrian element that complemented rather than contradicted one another. Being a member of the Jewish *Stamm* did not make Austrian Jews any less Austrian, because all Habsburg citizens were members of one *Stamm* or another. Furthermore, to him being Austrian meant embracing membership in a civic community that valued all the people of the Monarchy equally, and thus did not require the renunciation of one's Jewishness. After successfully challenging the position of the assimilationist establishment in the 1880s, Bloch watched his understanding of identity become predominant among Austrian Jews during the last twenty-five years of the Monarchy's existence.

Two distinct sources served as the roots of Bloch's ideas: the Enlightenment-derived political ideals of democrats such as Adolf

563 See Central Archives for the History of the Jewish People, Jerusalem, File no. P/150/3, Papers of Joseph Samuel Bloch.

Fischhof, and the moral and religious teachings of traditional Judaism. Bloch balanced the universalistic principles he took from the Enlightenment with a desire to preserve his Jewish identity and heritage. In fact, he characterized his ideas on nationalism and identity as not only based on Enlightenment-derived principles but also on what he learned from Talmudic law and Jewish thought. Bloch was able to do so because he, like the liberal Jews who sought to assimilate, saw in Enlightenment philosophy the fulfillment of Jewish tradition. However, he developed an alternative interpretation of Enlightenment liberalism that rejected its assimilationist thrust, the idea that Jews had to shed their Jewishness to become full members of human society.

In terms of the broader Austrian political spectrum, Bloch shared a belief with German liberals in certain political ideals, such as constitutional government, the rule of law, and civic equality, all of which are elements of the *Rechtsstaat*. Furthermore, he saw Fischhof's plan for the decentralization of Austria as the most appropriate compromise solution to the nationalities question. However, unlike Fischhof and German liberals in general, Bloch separated these ideals from a belief in the superiority of German or any other culture. He sought to create a culturally neutral sense of Austrian nationhood based on constitutional patriotism. Bloch laid out the ideological framework for a unifying Austrian identity based on constitutionally guaranteed civil rights and equality before the law, democratic and parliamentary government, and equal treatment of all cultures, languages, and religions as collective entities. He envisioned a mission for this multiethnic Austrian state that, instead of playing down or ignoring ethnic prejudice and racially-based nationalism, confronted them by offering as an antidote a civic, supraethnic definition of nationhood that he considered morally superior to the idea of homogeneous societies posited as the ideal by the nation-state principle. This vision offered the Austrian state a powerful and attractive *raison d'être*, one that could have combined with constitutional and democratic reforms to create a real sense of unity among the diverse Habsburg peoples.

Even though they drew at least in part on Jewish theology, and reflected most urgently the alienation Jews felt in an era of increasing ethnic prejudice and hatred, Bloch's ideas on Austrian identity must not be 'ghettoized' as purely Jewish history. The views of any of the

Monarchy's citizens on the nationalities question developed to some degree out of the specific circumstances faced by his or her ethnic group, as well as from that group's cultural and intellectual heritage. Bloch made a serious contribution to the overall discourse on Austrian identity by calling for full equality among the peoples, democratic and civil rights for all citizens, a full commitment on the part of all citizens to the state they shared, and the development of a civic Austrian consciousness that would unify members of more than a dozen nationalities into a single political nation. Furthermore, Bloch rejected the national state as the ideal form of government and argued that the main purpose of Austria's existence was to demonstrate the moral superiority of the multiethnic state to the nation-state idea.

Bloch was a true believer in Austria. He rejected the attempt at assimilation in favor of the embrace of Jewish ethnicity; thus he could not fall back on the hope of assimilating into the surrounding peoples if Austria fell apart. He rejected Zionism; thus he could not fall back on a Jewish nation-state if Austria fell apart. As a result, in terms of his understanding of Jewish identity, multiethnic Austria was his only option. Furthermore, Bloch needed Austria in a way that reformers of other nationalities, who at least in theory had a territorial base on which to build a new polity should the Monarchy disappear, did not. He did not put forth a particular reform plan other than endorsing Fischhof's because he wanted whatever kind of reform the peoples could agree to as long as it included his bedrock principles of civil equality for individuals and collective equality for cultures. He wanted constitutional reforms so that all the Habsburg nationalities would be satisfied living in multiethnic Austria and accept it as the proper home for their peoples. Only at that point could the truly important work begin, namely the development of constitutional patriotism among the citizenry and the transformation of the diverse population of Austria into a cohesive civic nation, of which the members of all its ethnic, cultural, and religious groups would be equal and full members.

Chapter 5

'OTHER VOICES': THE IDEAS OF OTHER POLITICAL THINKERS ON AUSTRIAN REFORM

The following discussion builds on Robert Kann's well-known analysis of various Austrian reform proposals.[564] It goes beyond Kann's work, however, by examining what each reformer to be discussed here had to say about a number topics in addition to his specific reform plan, including nationalism and national identity as abstract concepts, what sort of *Staatsidee* a reformed Austria would rely upon as its ideological foundation, and, finally, what form a common Austrian consciousness, if such a thing were to develop, might take.

The 'nationalist' figures in this chapter: Iakiv Holovatskyj, Frantisek Palacký, Joseph Eötvös, and Aurel Popovici presented and in some cases formulated positions that, for the most part, the political leadership of their nationalities adopted, although certainly there existed a range of opinion among leaders of each ethnic group, and those opinions also changed over time as a result of alterations to the political and cultural landscape. An examination of their ideas, in addition to those of Fischhof and Bloch, covers either directly or indirectly virtually all of the numerically significant Habsburg peoples. Bloch represented the ethnically conscious Jewish position, while Fischhof expressed that of the German liberals, both Jewish and non-Jewish, in terms of the German cultural identity he envisioned for the Austrian state. Most other German liberals shared this vision of Austria as a bastion of German culture, but simply sought to achieve it through the maintenance of a centralized administration rather than the decentral-

564 See Kann, *The Multinational Empire*, Vol. II.

ization Fischhof advocated. The needs of Holovatskyj's Ukrainians largely paralleled that of the other numerically small and mostly peasant Slavic nationalities of the Austrian half of the Monarchy, such as the Slovenes, Dalmatian Croats, and the Romanians of Bukovina, while the Hungarian Romanians, represented here by Popovici, shared the same fate as the other non-Magyar peoples of post-1867 Hungary: the Slovaks, Croats, Serbs, and sub-Carpathian Ukrainians, all of whom faced a policy of intense Magyarization. Palacký was Czech and Eötvös Magyar. The Poles, or at least the nobles who ran the province, were largely satisfied with their unofficial self-rule after 1867, but never really gave up their dream of a reunited Poland (before 1867 their interests roughly paralleled those of the Magyars, in that they dominated their own province for which they sought as much autonomy as possible). The Italians in the Habsburg lands that remained after the unification of Italy during the 1860s did not express a comprehensive vision of an Austria that could satisfy their people's desires perhaps because, like the Poles of Galicia, many of them hoped to join their territory to their national homeland at some future date, and so they simply concentrated on improving their position in the Habsburg territories they populated without regard to larger Empire-wide reforms. The ideas of Karl Renner and Otto Bauer represent, in general, the position of the Social Democratic Party, the largest supraethnic political organization in the Monarchy. Furthermore, with the exception of Holovatskyj, who nevertheless largely formulated the pro-Austrian position among Ukrainians, these figures were well-known and influential both inside and outside the circles of their own nationality and/or political party.

The proposals put forth by each reformer reflect in large measure the interests of the ethnic group with which he identified, as well as the circumstances of the era in which he wrote. Even more importantly, despite the differences in the specifics of the reform plans, there existed a significant consensus across political and ethnic lines on the need to preserve a multiethnic Austrian state and create some form of common supraethnic identity. This consensus suggests that the peoples of the Monarchy may have been able to resolve their differences and reform the Austrian state, if their ruler had given them the opportunity and the authority to do so.

Iakiv Holovatskyj (aka Havrylo Rusyn)

Iakiv Holovatskyj (1814–1888) was one of three poets collectively known as the Ruthenian Romantic Triad. In 1837 this trio produced *The Dniester Nymph (Rusalka Dnistrovaia)*, a collection of folk literature credited with sparking the revival of Ukrainian national culture.[565]

Unlike the other figures to be discussed in this chapter, he did not propose a comprehensive reform plan for the Habsburg state. However, Holovatskyj's early writings laid out the basic ideology of Austro-Slavism, the position that developed among pro-Austrian Ukrainians and other Slav nationalists in the Monarchy, including Czech leaders such as Palacký and Karel Havlicek.[566] In fact, Holovatskyj had been in contact with Havlicek, and his ideas echoed those that the Czech leader had expressed in the immediately preceding months and years.[567] Austro-Slavism called upon the Monarchy to provide for the equal cultural and material development of all its peoples and offered the loyalty of its Slavs in return. Such an arrangement would increase domestic stability, thus improving Austria's international standing and ensuring its survival. This basic formula, which received one of its first public airings by Holovatskyj, stood at the heart of virtually every reform plan that endorsed some form of federalism and/or autonomy for the various peoples of the Monarchy. Although later in his career Holovatskyj transferred his allegiance from Austria to Russia,[568] pro-Austrian Ukrainians, including for example the late nineteenth century Ukrainian nationalist Ivan Franko, relied on the

565 Piotr S. Wandycz, *The Lands of Partititoned Poland, 1795–1918* (Seattle: University of Washington Press, 1974), pp. 254–55.

566 Ivan Rudnytsky, "The Ukrainians in Galicia under Austrian Rule," in Andrei Markovits, Frank Sysyn, eds., *Nationbuilding and the Politics of Nationalism, Essays on Austrian Galicia* (Cambridge: Harvard University Press, 1982), 23–67.

567 Ibid., pp. 28–29.

568 Wandycz, p. 255.

basic ideology he had developed earlier in justifying their loyalty to Vienna.[569]

In 1846 Holovatskyj, under the alias Havrylo Rusyn, published an article on the condition of Ukrainians in Galicia in which he laid out the reasons why his people were loyal to the Austrian state, and proposed steps that Vienna should take to strengthen those feelings.[570] He had a clear sense of Ukrainian peoplehood, and proclaimed that Ukrainians on both sides of the Austro-Russian border formed a single nationality.[571] Holovatskyj began by detailing the wretched level of cultural and educational development among his people. However, he exonerated Vienna of responsibility for this situation and praised "Austria's mild rule."[572] Holovatskyj called on Ukrainians to throw off their apathy, but bemoaned the lack of leadership and a central organization around which to build a national and social movement.

Holovatskyj explained that the polonization of the Greek Catholic (also known as Uniate) high clergy in Galicia during the previous centuries had deprived Ukrainians of what should have been their most obvious national leadership.[573] Most Ukrainians in Galicia were mem-

---

[569] Leonid Rudnytsky, "The Image of Austria in the Works of Ivan Franko," in Markovits and Sysyn, pp. 239–254. Franko presented a mixed image of Austria over his career, more critical during the 1880s and early 1890s, then growing more positive after the middle of that decade when Franko began to collaborate with Austrian newspapers and came into contact with other Austrian intellectuals such as Hermann Bahr, Viktor Adler, and Martin Buber. He even referred to "we Austrians" on a number of occasions (See ibid., p. 253). Franko's support for Austria reflected the same concept of Austro-Slavism put forth by Holovatskyj two generations earlier.

[570] Havrylo Rusyn (Iakiv Holovatskyj), "Zustände der Russinen in Galizien," *Jahrbücher für Slavische Literatur, Kunst und Wissenschaft* (Leipzig, 1846), pp. 361–389.

[571] For a recent analysis of the development of Ukrainian ethnic consciousness in Galicia, see John-Paul Himka, *Religion and Nationality in Western Ukraine. The Greek Catholic Church and the Ruthenian National Movement in Galicia, 1867–1900* (Montreal: McGill-Queen's University Press, 1999). For a recent analysis of the development of Polish ethnic consciousness among Galician peasants, see Keely Stauter-Halstead, *The Nation in the Village: The Genesis of Peasant National Identity in Austrian Poland, 1848–1914* (Ithaca: Cornell University Press, 2001).

[572] Rusyn, p. 362.

[573] For a more detailed analysis, see Himka, *Religion and Nationality in Western Ukraine. The Greek Catholic Church and the Ruthenian National Movement in Galicia, 1867–1900.*

bers of the Greek Catholic Church, organized during the late sixteenth century when Polish Catholics sought to bring the Orthodox Ruthenians of the Polish-Lithuanian Commonwealth into the Roman Catholic Church. Greek Catholics followed Orthodox rites but recognized the spiritual supremacy of Rome, and were, in a sense, a way-station between Orthodoxy and Catholicism. The Greek Catholic Church provided the Ukrainians of Galicia with a basis for their distinctiveness from both Poles and Russians. Despite their lack of either a native nobility (all the nobles in the area had long since come to consider themselves Poles by the nineteenth century, even if in some cases their ancestors had once spoken Ukrainian or Lithuanian as their native tongue) or an ethnically consciousness clerical class to lead their national movement, Holovatskyj proudly noted that Galician Ukrainians had nevertheless made progress in developing their national consciousness during the years since 1772 when the province passed to Austria in the first partition of Poland.[574] He thanked in particular Joseph II, "the great Kaiser who never forgot that Galicia was not a Polish province, but rather the former Rus' kingdom of Halych and Wladymir."[575]

Ukrainians, Holovatskyj emphasized, had demonstrated their steadfast loyalty to Austria during the 75 years of Habsburg sovereignty over Galicia.

> The Ruthenians willingly bore all sacrifices for the whole [*gesammten*] Fatherland, without a word of protest. One remembers the fateful year 1809 [during which Austria led an ill-fated campaign to liberate Central Europe from Napoleonic France], in which the Ruthenians demonstrated their loyalty and devotion.[576]

He contrasted Ukrainian support for the Habsburg cause with the behavior of the Galician Poles who had abandoned Austria to follow

---

574 Rusyn, p. 365.

575 Ibid. These sentiments were echoed by Franko, who stated "Our people have not forgotten [Joseph II], and they still speak of his wise and humane treatment of his subjects." As quoted in Rudnytsky, p. 25.

576 Rusyn, p. 368.

Napoleon. Holovatskyj noted that Ukrainians, "when treated well are loyal and thankful."[577]

Holovatskyj suggested that the Monarchy support the intellectual, literary, and cultural development of Galician Ukrainians and all the Austrian Slavs by allowing them to be educated in their own language.[578] He pointed to the bleak outlook for his people in the Russian Empire, where they "have no hope for their literature and nationality. Muscovitism tramples over everything, and Ruthenians' complaints of the violation of their rights are numerous."[579] Holovatskyj railed against the complete subjugation of the Ukrainian Orthodox clergy to Moscow as well as the brutal serfdom of the peasantry, and noted that Ukrainians in Galicia were well aware of this oppression and the relatively better conditions they enjoyed in Austria.[580]

This situation presented Vienna with a clear opportunity, and Holovatskyj encouraged the Monarchy to take advantage. "Thus the entire hope for the Ukrainian nation and literature is Austria, which protects and shelters each nation. Insightful Ukrainians feel this very strongly. Austria can, through promoting Ukrainian literature, also gain influence in Russian Ukraine, and find sympathy there."[581] Holovatskyj urged Austria to support the "emancipation and uplifting of the Ruthenian peasants....The Ruthenians in Galicia have not lost hope in Austria."[582] He argued that Austria could strengthen its position and ensure its long-term stability by resolving the nationalities question rather than playing one group against another, and declared "it is in the political interest of the Empire to hold the various peoples in relatively equal standing."[583] Holovatskyj closed with the patriotic epigram "Austria above all others, if it only desires [to be]."[584]

This document cannot be taken as a purely objective report of Ukrainian conditions in Galicia. By writing in German rather than

577 Ibid.

578 Ibid., p. 376.

579 Ibid., p. 378.

580 Ibid., p. 379.

581 Ibid.

582 Ibid.

583 Ibid., p. 376.

584 Ibid., p. 379. "Österreich über alles, wann es nur will!"

Ukrainian, Holovatskyj targeted the government in Vienna rather than the reading public among his own people, and thus he exaggerated the positive aspects of Austrian rule for political reasons. Austria, too, had censorship, and neither did it 'protect and shelter' its Slavs during the 1840s, nor in any way nurture the Slavic peoples' national movements. Nonetheless, Holovatskyj, who was keenly aware of the cultural and economic oppression Ukrainians suffered at the hands the Polish nobility (*szlachta*) in Galicia and as well as the dreadful conditions they faced under the Russian autocracy across the border, recognized that the Austrian government could be a valuable potential ally of his people. This strategic calculation helped shape the ideas he put forth in the 1846 article.

The article focused more on the cultural/linguistic rather than economic grievances of Galician Ukrainians, although it did ask for the emancipation of the peasants from their feudal obligations. It is questionable whether issues of culture and language mattered more than their material needs to a majority of Holovatskyj's people, or rather reflected his recognition that, in 1846, requesting support for Ukrainian literature seemed a less threatening request than demanding land redistribution for the peasants.[585] Holovatskyj did not mention the *jacquerie* of February 1846, which occurred during the year his article was published. It is unclear whether he wrote the article before this peasant (mostly Ukrainian) uprising that stopped an incipient revolt led by the Polish nobility against Austria. He wanted the article to emphasize the loyal rather than the revolutionary qualities of his people.[586]

---

585 John-Paul Himka asserted that the major issues for Ukrainians in Galicia were overwhelmingly economic, and that the Ukrainian national movement itself was a social movement in which the peasantry came to play a leading role in the late nineteenth century. See Himka, *Galician Villagers and the Ukrainian National Movement in the Nineteenth Century* (Edmonton: Macmillan Press, 1988). Jan Kozik, on the other hand, argued for the importance of both economics and culture, and in the end considered the cultural issues more important during the pre-1848 period. Jan Kozik, *Ukrainian National Movement in Galicia, 1815–1849* (Edmonton: Macmillan Press, 1986). For an earlier analysis focused more specifically on the revolutions of 1848–9, see Martha Bohachevsky-Chomiak, *The Spring of a Nation: The Ukrainians in Eastern Galicia in 1848* (Philadelphia: Shevchenko Scientific Society, 1967).

586 The peasants received some support from Vienna, although the government suppressed the violence before it turned into a full-scale social revolution. See Wandycz, pp. 133–6.

Holovatskyj called on the Austrian government to recognize that a policy of cultural equality could engender greater loyalty among its subject peoples, in this case, Ukrainians. He focused on ethno-cultural rights rather than the rights of historic provinces because increased autonomy for Galicia would, if anything, have worsened the plight of Ukrainians. Galician autonomy would have placed the Ukrainians even more at the mercy of the Polish nobility who, thanks to their legal and political privileges as nobles, dominated political life in the province. The call for cultural equality and autonomy made the most sense for nationalities that saw themselves threatened more by a neighboring people amongst whom they lived in a given province than by the central government. Holovatskyj's ideological position on the nationalities question and the reform of Austria thus derived from the political circumstances faced by the members of his ethnic group.

To a good degree, the position of Ukrainians in Galicia paralleled that of the Romanians in Hungary, as well the other peoples of the Monarchy who possessed a certain amount of territory in which they were numerically dominant, yet found themselves oppressed by a more powerful nationality within a historic province-kingdom. Their position explains why Holovatskyj, like Popovici a half-century later, preferred a system of ethnic-territorial federalism that divided the Monarchy into ethnically defined territories irrespective of the borders of the historic provinces. In such a system, each ethnic group would have an area of their own in which they exercised autonomy over local affairs, in particular over cultural, educational, and linguistic matters. Ethnic-territorial federalism differed both from a federalism based on the historic provinces and from Karl Renner's idea of 'personal autonomy,' according to which each individual received linguistic and cultural rights irrespective of where in the Monarchy he or she lived.

Holovatskyj's analysis of the needs of his people had a decisive influence on the Austro-Slavist position that became dominant among Ukrainians until the end of the Monarchy. Although he did not focus on the need to create a common identity or deal with questions of democracy and participatory government, his ideas on autonomy and equality are compatible with those of Bloch. Holovatskyj's offer of increased loyalty in return for equal treatment and cultural freedom meshed well with the Austrian idea put forth by Fischhof in the late

1860s and refined by Bloch in the 1880s and 90s, namely that Austria make equality among the nationalities the foundation of its *Staatsidee*.

Frantisek Palacký

Frantisek Palacký (1798–1876) was the dominant founding figure in the Czech national movement, a man Thomas Masaryk, the founder and first President of Czechoslovakia, proclaimed "the father of the nation."[587] Palacký served as one of the Czech leaders during the 1848–9 revolution and contributed greatly to the drafting of the Kremsier Constitution in 1849. At the outset of the revolution he made clear his loyalty to Austria and his belief that only a multiethnic state could solve the problems faced by the Central European peoples. On April 11, 1848, Palacký offered his famous dictum, "Truly, had the Austrian state not already existed for so long, we would have had to hasten to create it in the interest of Europe and of humanity!"[588]

During the 1848–9 period Palacký produced a number of draft proposals for the reform of the Habsburg state and the solution of its nationalities question. Although before the revolution and through the spring of 1848 he had preferred a solution based on autonomy for the historic provinces, at that point he altered his thinking and at Kremsier made his groundbreaking proposal based on ethnic federalism.[589] In the

[587] Thomas G. Masaryk, *Palacký's Idee des böhmischen Volkes* (Prag: Verlag von IUC Aug. Zalud, 1899), p. 73. See also Hugh L. Agnew, *Origins of the Czech National Renaissance* (Pittsburgh: University of Pittsburgh Press, 1993), p. 4. For a more detailed, if somewhat dated discussion of Palacký as nationalist historian, see Joseph F. Zacek, *Palacký: The Historian as Scholar and Nationalist* (The Hague: Mouton, 1970). For a recent study, see Georg J. Morava, *Franz Palacký: eine Frühe Vision von Mitteleuropa* (Vienna: Österreichische Bundesverlag, 1990). Morava also has written a biography, *Palacký: Cech, Rakusan, Evropan* (Prague: Vysehrad, 1998). The title neatly encapsulated Palacký's multilayered identity: Czech, Austrian, European.

[588] Frantisek Palacký, *Oesterreichs Staatsidee* (Prag: n.p., 1866), p. 83, Appendix A. This appendix reprinted a letter Palacký wrote in which he rejected an invitation to join the Frankfurt Parliament as a delegate from Bohemia, which was then a part of the German Confederation.

[589] Kann, *The Multinational Empire*, Vol. II, p. 28–9. His earlier draft of September, 1848, reflected a move in this direction. It placed equal weight on the rights of historic provinces and nationalities, and also factored geographic concerns into the equation.

Kremsier constitutional committee Palacký declared his belief in "the equal right of the nationalities," and further argued "we have to construct Austria in such a way that the peoples like to live there, this must be our leading idea."[590]

With this idea as his guiding principle, Palacký's final Kremsier draft proposed a federal scheme that divided power between a central government and eight state units to be drawn based on ethnicity without regard to the borders of the historic province-kingdoms. The state diets, whose members were to be directly elected, would send delegates to serve as the deputies in the central parliament. The central government would deal only with Empire-wide issues such as foreign affairs, military issues, trade, and finance. All else, including the administration of the justice system and education, would devolve to the states. The would states include: 1) German Austria: the Alpine provinces and the German-inhabited parts of Styria, Carinthia, Tyrol and the Bohemian lands; 2) Czech Austria: the Czech parts of the Bohemian provinces as well as Slovak Hungary (Palacký considered Czechs and Slovaks to be one people); 3) Polish Austria: all of Galicia and Bukovina (he failed to recognize Ukrainians as a separate people or that Bukovina had only a small Polish minority); 4) Illyrian Austria: areas within Carniola inhabited by Slovenes; 5) Italian Austria: South Tyrol and Lombardy-Venetia; 6) Southern Slav Austria: Croatia, Dalmatia, Voivodina; 7) Magyar Austria: the Magyar inhabited parts of the Hungarian kingdom, including parts of Transylvania; 8) Romanian Austria, including both territories in Hungary and other Habsburg lands.[591]

Despite its inconsistencies, most notably the omission of Ukrainians as a people separate from the Poles, as well as the omission of the issue of minorities mixed into a particular territories (such as the Germans of Transylvania among numerous other examples), the plan stands out for two reasons above all. First of all, it encompassed the entire Habsburg patrimony, including Hungary and Lombardy-Venetia, and thus endorsed the idea of a unified Austrian state. Second, Palacký

---

590 Cited in ibid., p. 325, n. 63.

591 Palacký reproduced his final Kremsier proposal as Appendix B in *Oesterreichs Staatsidee*, pp. 87–98. See also Kann, *The Multinational Empire*, Vol. II, pp. 28–30, and 324, n. 61.

held to the ethnic principle and divided German-Bohemia from the rest of the Bohemian kingdom, an offer Czech leaders would not make again.

Although Czechs were an oppressed nationality to whom the ethnic solution offered the chance to develop freely, many Czechs, including Palacký, who wrote the first comprehensive modern history of Bohemia, also felt drawn to the provincial solution because the Bohemian province was, like Hungary to the Magyars, a national and historic kingdom which they hesitated to divide. The concept of the historic state rights of Bohemia, which the Habsburgs had abolished in the years after their crushing defeat of the indigenous Bohemian nobility at the Battle of White Mountain in 1620, offered a powerful reason for Czechs to support provincial federalism. In fact Palacký changed his mind and endorsed this system in 1865, although he claimed his reversal reflected the political reality that ethnic federalism could not be achieved.[592] He argued that the idea of autonomy for the historic provinces, which he credited to Eötvös, had won such widespread support by 1865 that the ethnic solution had become impossible to implement. Certainly, the Magyar leaders would never have consented to the division of Hungary. Perhaps Palacký hoped that autonomy for Hungary would come within an overall plan for equal autonomy for each province, thus preserving a unified system for the whole Monarchy. He denied being an inflexible ideologue, and stated his willingness to compromise in order to achieve his goals of equality and reform. Palacký characterized the move as a tactical maneuver rather than an ideological shift.

During Palacký's career the Czechs occupied a position that was politically weaker than that of the Magyars, who could dominate their province-kingdom, yet stronger than that of groups such as Holovatskyj's Galician Ukrainians and Popovici's Hungarian Romanians, whose only hope was equality and/or autonomy for each *Stamm*, to be achieved by dividing the Monarchy as much as possible into ethnically defined territories. Palacký's support at different times for ethnic and provincial federalism thus reflected the somewhat middling political position of the Czechs vis-à-vis the other peoples. It is to Palacký's great credit that during the crucial revolutionary period he was willing to compromise

[592] Palacký, *Oesterreichs Staatsidee*, p. 37.

the historic rights of his province, once a powerful and independent kingdom of which he was a nobleman, for a far-sighted solution that could have perhaps satisfied both Czechs and Germans by providing autonomy for each.

The Kremsier constitution differed from Palacký's plan in terms of some specifics and in the former's omission of Hungary and Lombardy-Venetia from its scope, but the two derived from the same basic principles, and the Constitution's final draft included the division of Bohemia into German and Czech districts. Franz Joseph, however, tore up the constitution and Austria entered into the decade known as neo-absolutism, which ended in 1859 with Austria's defeat by Piedmont and France. The subsequent seven years witnessed some experimentation with various constitutional reform schemes, and came to an end with the introduction of dualism as prescribed by the 1867 *Ausgleich.*

During the period of constitutional experimentation in the early and mid-1860s, politicians felt that they had an opportunity to help shape the reform process for the first time since the end of the 1848–49 revolutions. Palacký had spent much of the neo-absolutist period working on his history of Bohemia. In April and May of 1865 he wrote a series of essays that he published the following year as a collection called *Oesterreichs Staatsidee*. In these essays he put forth his vision for a reformed Austrian state. In these essays Palacký denounced dualism, which was then under discussion, as an alternative to the centralized system then in place because both contradicted the principle of equality. He recognized that dualism would simply replace German dominance with a shared dominance of the Germans and Magyars.[593] Contending that such a system would be "ruinous for the whole Empire,"[594] Palacký condemned anyone who supported it as a traitor for whom "national sympathies or antipathies are more powerful than the concern he pretends to have for the preservation of the unity and power position of the whole of Austria," and accused them of being "secret or open enem[ies] of Austria and the ruling dynasty."[595]

---

593 Ibid., p. 37.

594 Ibid., p. 50.

595 Ibid., p. 52.

Palacký contended that federalism alone could achieve equality for all the nationalities.[596] Arguing that Austria had to adhere to the principle of equality if it wanted to survive, he asserted, "only justice can be a lasting foundation for the Empire."[597] Palacký declared that Austria must "consider itself a mother equally to all, and as stepmother to none...the government in Austria can be neither German nor Magyar, not Slavic or Romanian, rather in the highest and most general sense Austrian, i.e. it should be equally just towards all of its members."[598] This statement defined "Austrian" as an ethnically and culturally neutral concept that stood above the nationalities in exactly the same sense that Bloch used the term. Such a concept seemed to leave room in Palacký's worldview for a supraethnic Austrian identification alongside individual *Stamm* identities.

According to Palacký, Austria needed as its new *Staatsidee* "the principle of equality of all the peoples."[599] He pledged the loyalty of the Czech people to an Austria based on that *Staatsidee*:

> We Bohemians [Böhmen] sincerely wish for the preservation and unity of Austria, because we believe that with our own power we would hardly be able to achieve a separate, sovereign state. We could never and in no way better preserve our particular nationality and our own culture, or even our autonomous way of life than in Austria—mind you in a free Austria organized according to principles of autonomy and equal justice. We have no hope and political perspective outside of Austria... However, if someone says to us that we are only friends of

---

[596] Ibid., p. 69. On this occasion he offered his support for autonomy for the historic provinces based on the October Diploma of 1860. See ibid., pp. 57–9. Palacký called for a system of provincial self-government that placed power largely in the hands of aristocratically-dominated *Landtage*, with central power limited to common affairs such as war, trade, finance, and foreign affairs. The central government's power would reside with Franz Joseph and a weak but all-Austrian *Reichstag*. Palacký's support for this undemocratic plan reflected the increased political conservatism of his later years, during which he drew closer to the Czech nobility. For more on the October Diploma, see Beller, *Francis Joseph*, pp. 80–83.

[597] Palacký, *Oesterreichs Staatsidee*, p. 52.

[598] Ibid., p. 27.

[599] Ibid., p. 17. See also Masaryk, pp. 44–5.

> Austria out of selfishness, we would heartily assent; but politicians who are not naive will grant to us that exactly such friends tend to be the most loyal and reliable...Our interests lead us, exactly as in 1848, to decide for a single and undivided Austria, for an empire of equal nations and countries.[600]

In this statement Palacký laid out the both the depth and the limitations of his identification with Austria. That loyalty was conditioned on Austria providing equality for his people, but also on the geo-political conditions of Central Europe. The Czechs needed Austria because Germany and Russia surrounded them. Palacký in fact saw Austria primarily as a bulwark against so-called Eastern and Asiatic elements, presumably including Russia.[601] Unlike Bloch, he expressed neither a deeply held attachment to Austria because it was a multiethnic state, nor the strong desire to create an integrated community of all the Habsburg peoples. To Palacký, Austria was simply the best option that existed at that time for the Czechs. However, as he noted, rational, interest-based loyalty is often the most reliable.

Palacký identified the Austrian state as congruent with his interests as a Czech. He also recognized the need for an Austrian *Staatsidee* more meaningful than the dynasty alone could provide. Palacký stated neither a desire to create a common Austrian consciousness nor any opposition to such an idea. He confined himself to the question of what constitutional structure could give the Czechs self-rule within an Austria still strong and unified enough to protect it from its neighbors. He left the question of an Austrian identity to others. However, in his famous April 11, 1848 letter he had identified himself as "a Bohemian of Slavic stock [*Stamm*]."[602] Such a formula derived from his conception of 'Bohemian' as an identity that could unify all citizens of the Bohemian provinces because it included both a political and ethnic element. According to Masaryk, Palacký hoped to apply this formula, whose hyphenated identity resembled that of Bloch, to the whole of Austria.[603] According to this concept, a Habsburg

600 Palacký, *Oesterreichs Staatsidee*, p. 55.

601 Ibid., Appendix A, pp. 83, 86.

602 Ibid., Appendix A, p. 80.

603 See Masaryk, pp. 45–6.

citizen would identify him or herself as an Austrian, as a resident of a given province, and a member of an ethnic group.

Palacký himself took great pride in his eloquent statement of Austria's necessity, claiming it as his contribution to the preservation of the state.[604] He best summed up the reasons why the Habsburg state stayed together as long as it did, and helped provide Czechs and other Slavs with a justification for supporting the continued existence of the Monarchy as long as hope for future reform existed. However, Palacký's ideas differed from the ideas of Bloch because they still assumed that national states were the ideal, and only the relative weakness of the Czechs and the other small nationalities of the Habsburg lands justified the existence of a multiethnic Austrian state. Such a position neither precluded the construction of a deeper common Austrian consciousness, nor provided for it a strong foundation.

Joseph Eötvös

Joseph Eötvös (1813–1871) was one of the most important Hungarian liberal politicians and thinkers of the nineteenth century. In fact, one historian referred to him as "perhaps the noblest of all in Hungary's great generation of reform."[605] His liberalism showed through right from the outset of his career, as he called for the reform of the penal code in his 1838 essay, *Prison Reform*, and his 1845 novel, *Village Notary*[606] He served as Minister for Public Instruction (education) and Religious Affairs in Hungary from April to September of 1848. In late 1848 Eötvös withdrew from the revolutionary movement led by Louis Kossuth because he opposed Hungary breaking from the Habsburg Monarchy, the integrity of which he saw as crucial for the peaceful development of his kingdom.[607] He also opposed Kossuth's attempt to pre-

---

[604] Palacký, *Oesterreichs Staatsidee*, p. 24.

[605] Peter F. Sugar, ed., *A History of Hungary* (Bloomington: Indiana University Press, 1990), p. 195. This book offers a highly readable broad survey of the history of the Hungarian state over the last thousand years. See pp. 209–94 for the history of Hungary from 1848 to 1918.

[606] Ibid., p. 200.

[607] Paul Bödy, *Joseph Eötvös and the Modernization of Hungary, 1840–1870*, 2nd ed. (New York: Columbia University Press, 1985; orig., 1972), p. 48.

serve noble domination of Hungary through the preservation of their privileges as a class.[608] Eötvös published a series of intellectual and political treatises in the 1850s and early 60s that scientifically analyzed the relationship among nationalism, liberalism, and states.

After the *Ausgleich* he served again as Hungarian Minister for Public Instruction and Religious Affairs from 1867 to 1871 and in that capacity wrote the initial drafts of the 1868 Nationalities Law and the 1868 Public Education Act that proclaimed linguistic and cultural equality for all the peoples of Hungary.[609] Although the final version of these laws offered somewhat less in the way of guarantees for equality than had Eötvös' original draft (Deák had had to moderate them somewhat to mollify Magyar nationalist tendencies among members of the Diet), these laws were nevertheless incredibly tolerant towards the non-Magyar languages and cultures of Hungary.[610] In its final version, the Public Education Act prescribed compulsory education for children between the ages of six and fifteen, and guaranteed students the right to an education in their native tongue as long as that language was "prevalent" in a given area, as well as money for schooling and textbooks for those who could not afford it.[611] The final version of the Nationalities Law provided that, although Hungarian was the state language and the language of parliamentary debate and legislation, laws

---

608 Ibid., pp. 51–53. Bödy blamed Kossuth, in particular his unreasonable demands in negotiations with the central government, for the failure to peacefully modify and codify a new relationship between the Monarchy and Hungary. Bödy argued that Kossuth undermined the moderate Batthyány ministry, supported by Eötvös, Deák, and Széchenyi, which sought a compromise with Vienna. Bödy praised the views of Eötvös and his moderate colleagues on domestic issues as superior to the ethno-culturally intolerant and undemocratic policies of Kossuth, and lamented their inability to mobilize support for their views as opposed to those of Kossuth (pp. 54–7). See also Bela K. Király, *Ferenc Deák* (Boston: Twayne Publishers, 1975), for an analysis of these various figures, albeit one with Deák, the eventual leader of the Hungarian political elite by the mid-1860s, as the central focus.

609 Bödy, pp. 5–7. On Eötvös see also Steven B. Vardy, *Baron Joseph Eötvös, A Literary Biography* (Boulder, Co: Social Sciences Monographs; distributed by Columbia University Press, 1987); Johann Weber, *Eötvös und die ungarische Nationalitätenfrage* (Munich: Oldenbourg, 1966).

610 For an overview of Eötvös' and Deák's role, as well as of the laws themselves, see Király, pp. 186–88.

611 Ibid., p. 187.

would be issued in all the languages of the kingdom, and the vote of 20% of the legislators in a county assembly could designate a second official language for debate in that body. Furthermore, any county legislator could be heard (although perhaps not understood) in his native tongue. The law also declared that anyone could petition any level of the government in his or her native language. Unfortunately for the non-Magyars of the kingdom, those who governed Hungary after 1868 ignored most of the provisions of these laws, and they remained largely unenforced after their promulgation.[612]

Politically, Eötvös represented the moderate position within the Magyar nationalist leadership. He viewed Hungary as a state of nationalities rather than a Magyar national state, and actively tried to win the loyalty of the non-Magyars for the Hungarian state.[613] Eötvös also accepted Austria as a political entity above Hungary rather than considering it simply as a separate state or agglomeration of states that happened to share the same monarch. He believed that Hungary's demands for self-rule could be balanced within a unified Austrian state system.[614] Greatly influenced after 1848 by Palacký's ideas on how the Monarchy should be organized (and vice versa), Eötvös sought to preserve a single constitutional structure for Austria.[615]

This book concerns itself with Eötvös' vision of the Austrian state as a whole, what role Hungary should play within it, and his theoretical ideas on issues relating to nationalism and identity. It will thus focus on the Austrian-wide proposals he made before the *Ausgleich*. Afterwards, as a Hungarian government minister for the remaining four years of his life, Eötvös could not realistically call for any fundamental changes to the dualist structure for which his fellow Magyars had fought so hard. He produced his major treatises on the reform of Austria and the solution of its nationalities question during the neo-absolutist period, a time when Franz Joseph ruled Austria as a centralized state and administered it through a unified, German-speaking bureaucracy. Eötvös rejected both the centralized and German aspects

---

612 Ibid., p. 188.

613 Sugar, p. 270.

614 Bödy, pp. 48, 54–57.

615 Ibid., p. 59.

of this system. The non-German peoples, he contended, felt as though they lived under a foreign government because it spoke a language different from their own.[616] By decentralizing its government, Austria could lessen and perhaps avoid this kind of alienation. He accepted that the more advanced economic development and more widespread education and literacy among the Austro-Germans would necessarily lead to a disproportionate political role for them within Austria. Echoing Fischhof, however, Eötvös cautioned that the best way for the Germans to maintain this position was for the government to stop imposing the German language and culture on the other peoples.[617]

Eötvös believed that a centralized, Germanized system engendered so much resentment that it threatened the unity of the Austrian state.[618] He also rejected a territorial division of the Monarchy based on ethnic lines for two reasons. First, constant migration over the centuries had led, in particular in Hungary, to a complex ethnic patchwork that could not be divided into clearly defined territories. Second and more importantly for him, such a solution would require the destruction of the legal rights and boundaries of the historic province-kingdoms. Furthermore, he claimed that these political units, because of their centuries of existence as independent or at least autonomous entities, had generated a powerful sense of solidarity that bound the peoples of each historic kingdom into a nationality.[619] This conception of the so-called 'historic nations,' peoples such as the Magyars who had created kingdoms in the medieval period and thus claimed to possess legal rights that derived from that era, was of course most powerful among those individuals who actually enjoyed the right to participate in the political process, namely the nobles of the various provinces. Hungary among all the Habsburg kingdoms had most successfully retained its traditional rights and Eötvös' support for provincial rather than ethnic-territorial autonomy reflected his status as a Magyar noble. Among that nobility, however, he was one of the most democratic and progressive politicians on virtually every issue.

---

616 József Eötvös, *Die Garantien der Macht und Einheit Oesterreichs* (Leipzig: F.A. Brockhaus, 1859), pp. 69–71.

617 Ibid., p. 72.

618 Ibid., p. 107.

619 Ibid., pp. 82–3.

In order to preserve the historic rights of the province-kingdoms, Eötvös proposed a federal system based on provincial autonomy. He maintained that the dynastic Habsburg state rested on the principle of historic rights and legitimacy for its very existence, and could not survive if it violated that principle.[620] This argument reflected Eötvös' conservatism in the non-political sense of the word, namely the idea that what did not already exist could not be created out of thin air. Such a principle worked in favor of preserving the Habsburg state, itself a creation of history that counted legitimacy as well as inertia as two of the strongest forces holding it together.

In an early work published in 1851, Eötvös called for a unitary state structure that balanced the need for enough power at the center to defend the borders with the historic rights of the province-kingdoms to govern themselves on internal matters. Such a system required a single constitution for the whole of the Monarchy, a common parliament, and a central administration to deal with issues of common concern.[621] In an 1859 publication that appeared before the Austrian military defeats by the Franco-Piedmontese alliance at Solferino and Magenta, Eötvös detailed his constitutional reform plan. He reiterated the need for balance between the interests of the whole Monarchy and those of the historic states, and even placed the former ahead of the latter, as long as the states retained their constitutional rights.[622] He argued that Switzerland served as an example of a multiethnic state that had achieved such a balance and thus offered a model for his reforms.[623] The central government authority would be divided between the Emperor and the *Reichstag* and contain ministries for war, foreign affairs, finance, and trade. These ministries would be responsible only to the center, but the states would have jurisdiction over all matters not assigned to the center.[624] The plan envisioned popularly elected legislatures at the state and federal levels to which the ministries would be responsible.[625]

---

620 Ibid., pp. 78–83.

621 József Eötvös, *Ueber die Gleichberechtigung der Nationalitäten in Oesterreich*, 3rd ed. (Pest: Moriz Ráth, 1871; orig., 1851), pp. 122–3, 127.

622 Eötvös, *Die Garantien der Macht und Einheit Oesterreichs*, pp. 50, 91–2.

623 Ibid., p. 51.

624 Ibid., p. 95.

625 Bödy, p. 65.

Eötvös argued that the Monarchy faced two discrete sets of problems: the struggle for the rights of the provinces within Austria, and the struggle for the rights of nationalities within each province. He believed that both of these problems needed to be solved, but contended that the reform of the whole Monarchy could only deal with the former. Only after the provinces received self-rule could each one individually, independent from the central government, work to achieve the equality of the peoples within its borders. He did not offer an overall formula for how each province should proceed, but the Nationalities' Law for Hungary he proposed in 1868 offered a strong indication of his views on this matter.

Eötvös' plan is noteworthy because, although it envisioned wide autonomy for the states, it represented the endorsement of a unified state structure for the whole Habsburg patrimony by a prominent, if moderate, Hungarian leader. Eötvös declared "Austria requires a constitution through which all individual parts of the state must be created **equally** [emphasis in original] with regard to their relationship to the whole....The warmest supporters of provincial autonomy must admit that a constitution in which one part of the Monarchy would occupy a special position can never create a unified state."[626] He specifically noted that the constitutional connection between Hungary and the overall Austrian state was no different from that of any other province because each relationship derived from the legitimate right of the dynasty to rule in that land.[627] Arguing that the autonomy he and his colleagues demanded for Hungary did not reflect a desire for special status, Eötvös hoped that "what we demand for Hungary as historical rights shall become the common property of all lands, and thus our nation's constitutional rights and self-government, formerly an object of envy, will be regarded as the guarantee of their own liberty by all citizens of the empire."[628]

On the one hand, Eötvös' endorsement of a single constitutional and parliamentary system for the whole Habsburg patrimony reflected

---

626 Eötvös, *Die Garantien der Macht und Einheit Oesterreichs*, p. 61.

627 Ibid., p. 26.

628 Letter of April 7, 1859 from Eötvös to Stephen Széchenyi, a fellow Magyar leader, cited in Bödy, p. 65.

the realities of the neo-absolutist era. However, he faced significant opposition from other leading liberal Magyar politicians such as Deák and Gyula Andrássy who refused to accept the existence of an Austrian state structure above the kingdom of Hungary.[629] Eötvös thus seriously risked his standing as a leader by taking such a position on this question.[630] Had he not sincerely believed in the need for a unified Austrian constitution, he could have simply remained quiet on the matter. During the period leading up to Austria's disastrous 1859 war, there existed some support among Hungarian politicians for a compromise solution that would have preserved a unitary state structure for the Monarchy, albeit perhaps not under the kind of constitutional regime Eötvös'endorsed in his 1859 publication. For example, on May 9, 1857, Emil Dessewffy, a political figure and President of the Hungarian Academy of Sciences (Eötvös was vice-President and Deák was a director), delivered a memorandum signed by 129 persons, including both high and lower-level nobles, senior clergy, and seven Pest merchants, that urged Franz Joseph to end the era of neo-absolutism by returning to the pre-1848 political system.[631]

Eötvös maintained his support for some kind of central legislative body until the spring of 1865, more specifically a system that divided the Monarchy into three states: the lands within the German Confederation, that is the hereditary Habsburg provinces plus the Bohemian lands; Hungary; and Galicia, Bukovina, and Venice, but also allowed for a common legislative body made up of delegates from the state diets to deal with the military, finance, and foreign affairs.[632] At that point he finally relented in the face of the steadfast opposition of Deák, by then the leader of the Hungarian movement, calling for a rein-

---

629 Király, p. 142. Before publishing *Die Garantien der Macht und Einheit Oesterreichs*, Eötvös had sent the proofs to Deák, who (presumably) read and then returned them without comment of any kind. Eötvös took this non-reaction to mean that Deák approved of his proposals. Deák later claimed that he did not approve, but had not commented because he did not want to stop the publication of opinions simply because he opposed them. (See Király, p. 143). Later on, in particular from the *Ausgleich* in 1867 until Eötvös' death, the two worked extremely closely on virtually every major political issue.

630 Bödy, pp. 73–5.

631 Király, p. 142.

632 Eötvös described this plan in a journal entry dated January 5, 1864, which was cited in Bödy, p. 91.

statement of the Hungarian Constitution of 1848 and backing away from his endorsement of a common parliament.[633] Had the Emperor accepted Eötvös' proposals in the early 1860s, thus before Austria's defeat in the Seven Weeks' War with Prussia, he could perhaps have had a powerful Magyar ally who supported his desire to preserve a unified constitutional system for the Monarchy. If he had been willing to compromise before the debacle of 1859, Franz Joseph may well have isolated the more radical Magyar nationalists by striking a deal with the not insignificant group of Magyars willing to accept a unitary state system in return for some form of autonomy for Hungary significantly narrower than that prescribed in the *Ausgleich*. Such a compromise might have preserved a single political structure for Austria and thus avoided the paralyzing effect dualism had on more comprehensive reform efforts in the decades that followed 1867.

Eötvös' proposals for constitutional reform were linked to his theoretical conception of nationalism. He defined nationality as based not on race or language, but on a consciousness of being one people separate from all others.[634] While language provided a basis for national differences, it alone could not create a national feeling.[635] What he referred to as race could not serve as a defining national characteristic, he claimed, because, with the exception of Jews, intermarriage had done away with any biological or genetic differences between the European nationalities by the mid-nineteenth century.[636]

For Eötvös, nationalism represented a potentially powerful and destructive force that, if unchecked, would clash with the notions of liberty and equality.[637] He maintained that nationalism contained a

---

633 József Eötvös, *Die Nationalitäten-Frage*, trans., Max Falk (Pest: Moriz Ráth, 1865), p. 175. See also Bödy, p. 75.

634 József Eötvös, *The Dominant Ideas of the Nineteenth Century and Their Impact on the State, Volume II: Remedy*, trans., D. Mervyn Jones (New York: Columbia University Press, 1996; orig., 1851), p. 476.

635 Eötvös, *The Dominant Ideas of the Nineteenth Century and Their Impact on the State, Volume I: Diagnosis*, trans., D. Mervyn Jones (New York: Columbia University Press, 1996, [original version appeared 1851]), pp. 193–4.

636 Ibid., p. 191. Eötvös left an extremely progressive record regarding Jews overall, and went on record supporting Jewish emancipation as early as 1840. See Bödy, p. 25.

637 Eötvös, *The Dominant Ideas of the Nineteenth Century and Their Impact on the State*, Vol. I, p. 109.

belief in the superiority of the nation over all others that inevitably led to a desire to dominate and oppress other groups.[638] Eötvös further contended that a system in which each nationality received its own state would not work because of differences in the size and strength of different peoples.[639] Such a system would initially require the destruction of almost every existing state, as well as the balance of power that kept peace among them. Afterwards, the larger nation-states, acting on the desire to dominate that was inseparable from nationalist principles, would immediately swallow their smaller neighbors, rendering the process of giving a state to each nationality useless in any case.[640] Yet, since nationalism was too powerful and too much a part of European thought to ignore, he sought to craft a set of principles that would guide the organization of states that balanced the rights of nationalities, religious groups and individuals.[641] Eötvös recognized the potential force of nationalism and wanted to blunt its destructive energies by protecting and extending the rights of nationalities to develop freely within existing states.[642]

Eötvös maintained that the different linguistic groups within the Hungarian kingdom could come together to form a Hungarian national community based on the rights and freedoms that state extended to its citizens. One can characterize this concept as a 'civic nationality' because it was a sense of nationhood based not on ethnicity or even culture but on the bonds created among people who shared a common citizenship. He defined nationality as "nothing other than the consciousness of belonging together which can be engendered in a large number of people through the commonality of their past, their present situation, and the commonality of interests and feelings that derive therefrom."[643] However, Eötvös rejected the notion that this Hungarian nation had to speak a common language or share a common culture. He opposed, albeit unsuccessfully, the policy of Magyarization, and remarked that

---

638 Ibid., pp. 109–112.

639 Ibid., pp. 203–4.

640 Ibid., pp. 125, 135.

641 Ibid., Vol. II, p. 494. See also Bödy, p. 6.

642 Eötvös, *The Dominant Ideas of the Nineteenth Century and Their Impact on the State*, Vol. II, pp. 494–5.

643 Eötvös, *Die Nationalitäten-Frage*, p. 11.

the nationalities problem in his country would not be solved "by supporting through special interest the Hungarian, Serbian, or Slavic nationalities, rather it can only be definitively worked out if we keep the common interest of our fatherland before our eyes."[644] Such a statement would apply to the overall Austrian situation as well. If different peoples could form a Hungarian civic nation around their shared rights, they could also form an Austrian civic nation in addition to their identification as Hungarians. This formula provided the basis for Eötvös' conception of an Austrian *Staatsidee*.

Unlike other reformers, Eötvös did not believe that Austria should make equality among the peoples its guiding principle. Throughout his writings in the 1850s and 60s, in which he remained remarkably consistent, he referred back to the principle of dynastic legitimacy, which had and would continue to provide the sole basis for Austria's existence.[645] Eötvös noted "Austria is one because the different parts of the Monarchy are all monarchic and because in all of them the legitimate law names the same person as ruler."[646] The only 'mission' he envisioned for the Habsburg Monarchy was that it serve as the bulwark of European civilization against what he described as Russian barbarism.[647]

Thus, a set of reforms based on purely on the concept of equality for the nationalities that altered the historic rights of the Habsburg province-kingdoms would throw into question the historic right of the dynasty to rule, and threaten the unity of the Austrian state. Eötvös claimed that the eradication of provincial borders in favor of a division along ethnic lines would surely destroy any feelings of patriotism and love of fatherland that citizens felt for Austria because they identified above all with their individual province directly rather than the overall state.[648] He further argued "if the interests of the common Monarchy are antagonistic towards those of the individual provinces, the so-called provincial patriotism will turn against the Empire."[649] Eötvös predicted

---

644 Ibid., p. x.

645 Eötvös, *Ueber die Gleichberechtigung der Nationalitäten in Oesterreich*, pp. 61–2.

646 Eötvös, *Die Garantien der Macht und Einheit Oesterreichs*, p. 90. Such a statement ignored territories won through wars and diplomacy such as Galicia, Bukovina, and Venetia.

647 Ibid., p. 107.

648 Eötvös, *Ueber die Gleichberechtigung der Nationalitäten in Oesterreich*, pp. 107–8.

649 Eötvös, *Die Nationalitäten-Frage*, p. 133.

that if the provinces disappeared (a thought that horrified him) and the peoples no longer could identify with them, they would then turn towards a deeper identification with their *Stamm*, a development that could endanger the integrity of Austria and plunge the region into bloody chaos.[650] A solution that preserved provincial rights and the peoples' identification with the provinces would save the Monarchy from the dangers of the ethnic nationality principle and encourage greater loyalty to Austria as the guarantor of those historic rights.[651]

In Eötvös' view, dynastic legitimacy and the common history of the Monarchy provided Austria with all the pre-conditions necessary to create unity among its disparate parts, as no state possessed true religious, ethnic or cultural homogeneity.[652] He contended that the "the bond that holds [a state] together in all cases is to be found in the commonality of the moral and material interests of the population."[653] According to Eötvös, although each was loyal to the dynasty, the provinces expressed strong resentments against one another.[654] He lamented "a general Austrian consciousness has not yet officially been created," while noting that the survival of the Monarchy through the times of Maria Theresa and the Napoleonic wars demonstrated at least "considerable elements of unity."[655] The development of a common spirit among Austrians was among Eötvös' fondest hopes, and he declared "I know of nothing more important for the future of Austria than that the different peoples of the Monarchy finally draw nearer to one another."[656] Eötvös acknowledged that the distinct constitutional status of Hungary vis-à-vis the other Austrian lands had worked against the development of a common Austrian consciousness in that kingdom.[657] In his analysis, Austria could have achieved "a solidarity of the

650 Ibid., pp. 134, 138–9.

651 Eötvös, *Ueber die Gleichberechtigung der Nationalitäten in Oesterreich*, pp. 112–17.

652 Eötvös, *Die Garantien der Macht und Einheit Oesterreichs*, pp. 37–38, 40–41. This point neglected the fact that differing degrees of homogeneity (or perceived homogeneity) could make it easier for some states to develop a sense of unity than others.

653 Ibid., p. 38.

654 Ibid., p. 51.

655 Ibid., p. 39.

656 Ibid., p. 51.

657 Ibid., p. 58.

interests and as a result a cohesion of all the parts of the Monarchy" merely by abolishing the Hungarian tariff barriers in an earlier period.[658]

A unified constitutional structure, as long as it respected the rights of the historic provinces, would create the bonds that Eötvös contended were necessary to hold a state together. He proclaimed "the best guarantee of the unity of Austria is a constitution."[659] Accordingly, the reforms he proposed would not only hold the state together but would encourage the Austrian peoples to see themselves as part of a single political nation.[660] Eötvös envisioned that an overall Austrian state patriotism would someday replace the provincial patriotism on which he placed such a high value as a stabilizing force for his time. He predicted that

> [Austrian patriotism] will spread further with the conviction that Austrian citizenship is synonymous with the ideas of constitutional freedom, it will finally permeate all classes when the newly unified Austria has one history, and the feeling which binds the individual to his province will fade into the background.[661]

Eötvös shared with Bloch a belief in the need to cultivate a civic identity to unify Austrians of all nationalities based on the rights they shared as citizens of a liberal, constitutional state. Eötvös, however, opposed the extension of democratic rights while Bloch not only supported this measure, but also considered it central to his understanding of equality and his vision for a vital civic nationalism based on a citizenry that takes an active part in governance.

In Central Europe by the end of the nineteenth century, a form of nationalism defined by the construct of race had eclipsed both Eötvös' definition of a civic nationality based on political rights, and to a large degree the linguistic definition he had once dismissed as unworkable. If anything, it would have been even harder to create nation-states in

---

658 Ibid., p. 76.

659 Ibid., p. 43.

660 Bödy, pp. 65, 72.

661 Eötvös, *Ueber die Gleichberechtigung der Nationalitäten in Oesterreich*, p. 108.

Central Europe based on a racial rather than a linguistic definition of nationhood because of the scattered presence of Jews, Gypsies-Roma, Germans, and many other groups whose members did not live in a compact territory free of other peoples. Nevertheless, racial nationalism grew more and more popular.

In many ways Eötvös was a classic nineteenth century liberal, in particular regarding his faith in the possibility of creating political bonds based on shared interests and rights. The decades that followed his death in 1871 did not bear out his faith on this matter. However, the implementation of a constitution in Austria that enforced real equality among the peoples and full political and civil rights might have created a vibrant civic nationality across ethno-cultural lines and prevented the kind of alienation that led by the early twentieth century to the final victory of an exclusivist, racial definition of nationhood.

Aurel Popovici

Aurel Popovici (1863–1917) was a leading Transylvanian Romanian politician in the two decades leading up the First World War. In 1885 he enrolled at the University of Vienna to study medicine, and transferred his studies to the University of Graz three years later. While in Graz he became involved in the Transylvanian Romanian nationalist movement, and by 1891 he emerged as one of the leaders of the Romanian National Party. He also served as editor of *Tribuna*, a leading journal of the movement.[662] Having returned to Hungary, in 1893 Popovici and his colleague Nicolae Roman each received a four year-prison term and a 5000 gulden fine for distributing *Replica* (The Rejoinder), a document Popovici had written in

662 For more details of Popovici's life, see Marius Turda, 1998. *Aurel C. Popovici's Nationalism and its Political Representation in the Habsburg Empire (1890–1910)* [online]. Budapest: Local Government and Public Service Reform Initiative, Database of Research papers on Ethnic relations in Central and Eastern Europe and Countries of the Former Soviet Union. Available from World Wide Web: (http://lgi.osi.hu/ethnic/relations/1/mariust.html).

1892 while in Graz that called for Romanian rights and attacked the oppressive policies of the Hungarian state.[663] After the verdict Popovici fled Hungary for Austria and continued his writing and political activities, which culminated in the 1906 publication of his *Die Vereinigten Staaten von Groß-Österreich*.[664] This book represented "the most influential statement" of the position of the Romanian leadership in Hungary, as represented by the Romanian National Party, on the nationalities question.[665] Furthermore, Popovici's approach to the reform of the Habsburg Monarchy became "the centre-piece of all subsequent Rumanian plans for political development until the First World War."[666]

Popovici's ideas found the ears of the heir apparent, Archduke Franz Ferdinand. The Archduke convened an unofficial advisory body on Hungary with representatives from all the major Hungarian nationalities: Magyars, Germans, Croats, Slovaks, and Romanians.[667] Some of these advisors, in particular Baron Paul Rauch, Ban of Croatia, did not represent the majority opinion of their nationality. However, Alexander Vaida, the Romanian representative, was a leader of the Romanian National Party, a parliamentary deputy in Budapest, and the editor of the Lupta, the party's newspaper, from its inception in January 1907.[668] Vaida wholeheartedly agreed with Popovici's proposals for the constitutional reorganization of the Habsburg Monarchy, presented them to the Archduke, and attempted for years to gain Franz Ferdinand's support for its basic formula: an end to dualism, a unitary federal state with autonomy for the nationalities based on ethnically drawn territorial units, and universal male suffrage by secret ballot.[669] Popovici's ideas therefore became the basic position of the Romanian

---

[663] Keith Hitchins, ed. *The Nationality Problem in Austria-Hungary: The Reports of Alexander Vaida to Archduke Franz Ferdinand's Chancellery* (Leiden, Netherlands: E.J. Brill, 1974), p. 141. See also Keith Hitchins, *Rumania, 1866–1947* (Oxford: Clarendon Press, 1994), p. 208.

[664] Kann, *The Multinational Empire*, Vol. II, p. 197.

[665] Hitchins, *The Nationality Problem in Austria-Hungary*, p. x.

[666] Hitchins, *Rumania, 1866–1947*, p. 212.

[667] Hitchins, *The Nationality Problem in Austria-Hungary*, p. x.

[668] Ibid., p. xii.

[669] Ibid., pp. xiii–xiv. According to Vaida, Popovici had "completed my political education." Ibid., p. 27.

nationalist leadership in Hungary.[670] According to Vaida, Popovici's ideas found acceptance among Romanian young people as well as leading politicians.[671] As for non-Romanians in Austria, *Reichsrat* members from a wide array of ethnic and party backgrounds expressed sympathy with some aspects of Popovici's reforms, in particular his call for a division of the Monarchy into ethnic territories without regard to crownlands.[672] Opposition arose from some aristocratic politicians who rejected any democratic reforms and, more importantly, from those with either German or Magyar nationalist leanings. Other reform-minded conservatives liked Popovici's program in general, in particular those who wanted to reform the dualist system and replace it with a unitary state. However, even these erstwhile supporters opposed the plan's complete abandonment of the historic provinces for ethnically defined territories as well as its embrace of equal male suffrage.[673]

The ideology of Popovici reflected the influence (among others) of all the other reformers studied in this chapter with the exception of Bauer, whose work appeared after Popovici's own. He quoted Fischhof's analysis of the nationalities strife, claimed that Palacký's ethnic-territorial federal plan of 1848 could have solved the Monarchy's national problems once and for all, and most importantly for Hungary, praised "the clear-seeing Eötvös" as having understood that Hungary could not be a Magyar state.[674] Popovici offered high praise for Karl Renner, recommending one of his works to "all friends of Great-Austria,"[675] and cited *Der Kampf der österreichischen Nationen um den Staat* on at least a dozen occasions.[676]

A Romanian living under the Magyarization policies of Budapest, Popovici rejected with a special vehemence the dualist structure erect-

---

[670] Ibid., p. xiv. So-called moderates such as Emil Babes and Vasile Mangra advocated the integration of Romanian social and political institutions into the Magyar mainstream, and opposed Popovici's territorial and constitutional reform proposals.

[671] Ibid., p. 173.

[672] Kann, *The Multinational Empire*, Vol. II, p. 205.

[673] Ibid., pp. 205–6.

[674] Aurel C. Popovici, *Die Vereinigten Staaten von Groß-Österreich* (Leipzig: Verlag von B. Elischer Nachfolger, 1906), p. 114. On Fischhof, see pp. 23–4, 247–8; Palacký, pp. 185, 265, 283, 313, 314; Eötvös, pp. 76–7, 113–4.

[675] Ibid., p. 168.

[676] See ibid., pp. 26, 33, 130, 149, 310, 313, 340, among others.

ed by the *Ausgleich*.[677] Dualism had proven to him that any system based on autonomy for the historic provinces would not lead to equality for the Habsburg peoples.[678] Thus, the situation of Romanians led him to endorse ethnic-territorial federalism as the organizing principle of constitutional reform in the Monarchy. He realized that national equality and autonomy within Hungary could only occur in conjunction with Empire-wide reform, and thus sought to gain support in Cisleithania among nationalities that had large numbers within Hungary, in particular the Germans, by calling attention to the threat Magyarization posed to their co-nationals.[679] Popovici proposed the creation of a unitary, federal state called 'The United States of Great-Austria' and divided Austria-Hungary into fifteen states: German Austria (the Alpine provinces), German Bohemia, German Moravia, Trentino (Italian South Tyrol), Trieste (the Italian Littoral), Carniola, Croatia, Voivodina (Serb territory), Transylvania, Hungary, Land of the Szekels (Magyar Transylvania), East Galicia (Ukrainian), West Galicia (Polish), Slovakia, and Bohemia (Czech).[680] He drew the boundaries with "the purpose of creating homogeneous national states within the Empire."[681]

Popovici sought to separate institutionally the concerns of individual nationalities from questions that related to the whole state. According to his model, the central government would handle military, diplomatic, and financial issues, as well as all common legislation regarding civil rights and the legal system.[682] The central Parliament would consist of members elected by direct, equal, and universal male suffrage, "so that above all the federation remains directly in touch with the people."[683] The individ-

[677] Popovici, p. 10 and throughout.

[678] Ibid., p. 27.

[679] Ibid., p. 16–17.

[680] Ibid., p. 119.

[681] Ibid., p. 297. Popovici provided a drawing of his new map of Great Austria in his book. A copy also appears in Kann, *The Multinational Empire*, Vol. II, p. 199. This copy has been reproduced in Appendix C.

[682] See ibid., pp. 317–27, where Popovici presented a draft of his new constitution that described the structure of the United States of Great Austria.

[683] Ibid., p. 271. He did not specify whether women would get the vote, but it is safe to say that he meant universal male suffrage, not truly universal suffrage, based on the time and place in which he wrote.

ual states would then have jurisdiction over all other issues, including those related to cultural and educational development. Popovici sought a system that was centralized enough to provide for the security and maintenance of a sovereign state and decentralized enough to provide for wide autonomy and the free development of all the peoples.[684]

Switzerland served as the archetype for Popovici's vision of multi-ethnic Austria, despite the incongruity between his ethnic federalism and the Swiss system of cantonal autonomy.[685] He also drew heavily on the US constitutional model. Popovici quoted directly from the Federalist papers and showed the depth of his knowledge by offering praise for the shift by the United States from the Articles of Confederation to the constitution adopted in 1789.[686]

In terms of a theoretical analysis of nationalism and of the nation in an abstract sense, a number of different and somewhat contradictory ideas informed Popovici's vision.[687] On the one hand, he endorsed a form of an inclusive *Kulturnation* concept based on a common language. Popovici defined as a nationality a group of people who "live on a co-terminous territory, speak the same language, have acquired a consciousness of their belonging together as a nation, and strive towards a common political-cultural ideal...The main characteristic of a nationality is...national consciousness."[688] However, he also displayed some interest in a racial definition of nationality. Popovici quoted so-called "race-scientists" about the detrimental effects of intermarriage, including Herbert Spencer and Houston Stewart Chamberlain, and cited the latter again on the dangers of the mixing of Jews into the Magyar nation.[689] Despite his

684 Ibid., pp. 242–3.

685 Ibid., p. 20.

686 Ibid., pp. 275–7.

687 See also Turda, *Aurel C. Popovici's Nationalism and its Political Representation in the Habsburg Empire (1890–1910).*

688 Ibid., p. 219.

689 Ibid., pp. 89, 91–2. In general, his attitude towards Jews was ambiguous. Although he criticized Jewish support for dualism, he attributed it to those Jews' lack of a "true national sensibility." (p. 238). He seemed to want Jews to assert an independent *Stamm* identity, and even proposed national autonomy for Habsburg Jews. However, he did not go into detail about how Jewish autonomy would be implemented or why he felt Jews should receive self-rule in the first place. (p. 310). See also Kann, *The Multinational Empire*, Vol. II, pp. 201–02.

recognition of race and then-current racialist theories, he nevertheless stated directly that a shared national consciousness was the most important criterion in defining the boundaries of a nation.[690]

Popovici's definition also linked national groups to defined territories, a position that revealed his ambivalence towards the assimilation of small minorities scattered within a relatively homogeneous area. His plan did offer some protection for ethnic minorities within states by creating constitutionally sanctioned "enclaves" where a people that formed a minority within a state inhabited a relatively large territorial area within that state, although he only specifically mentioned German enclaves within Hungary, Transylvania, and Bohemia (perhaps as a tactical move to gain German nationalist support). The proposal also endorsed, albeit without specifics, the creation of national curiae within the state parliaments "according to the famous recommendation of R. Springer [aka Renner]."[691] Furthermore, minority groups within any of the fifteen states would receive the rights spelled out in the hitherto unenforced Hungarian Nationalities Law, written in 1868 by Eötvös.[692] However, Popovici did not want to protect scattered minorities within the fifteen states from what he saw as their natural assimilation, and in fact put forth as a benefit of his plan that it would rapidly acculturate "insignificant enclaves" and create culturally homogeneous national states on the various territories within the Monarchy.[693] Popovici was a practical politician more concerned with preserving ethnic and cultural entities collectively than the cultural rights of each individual.

Popovici sought to achieve freedom for his people and to secure the future of the Habsburg Monarchy. He believed these two goals were intertwined and could not be achieved under the current constitutional structure and the *Staatsidee* that underlay it. Popovici argued that the Habsburg Monarchy could only guarantee its survival and unity by assigning more of its governmental authority to its peoples, albeit on an equal basis.[694] Furthermore, Austria-Hungary had to make the freedom and equality of

690 Hitchins, *Rumania, 1866–1947*, p. 211.

691 Ibid., pp. 309–310. He did not appear to know that Springer and Renner were the same man.

692 Ibid., p. 310.

693 Ibid., p. 367.

694 Ibid., p. 282.

all its peoples the ideological foundation of its existence. Popovici called on it to "seize its lofty calling in Southeastern Europe, to become a true haven for its constituent nations."[695] He described the need for "a new, Great-Austrian Empire idea," based on "the dynastic principle, military strength and above all equality among all the peoples that reside within."[696] The goal of his reform would be to convince the nationalities that "the Habsburg Empire is the only real guarantee of the preservation of national individuality."[697] Popovici called on all politicians to encourage the identification of the peoples with the state based on the rights provided by their citizenship in Great-Austria.[698]

According to Popovici, in order to preserve itself, multiethnic Austria-Hungary required a common civic consciousness binding together its various ethnic groups. He wanted the peoples to become "naturally intimate and irrevocably bound" to one another.[699] Popovici believed that the achievement of national equality would "work unconditionally towards the furthering and strengthening of Austrian patriotism, the feeling of community among all nationalities."[700] Finally, he proclaimed "when a Constitution as described here is implemented, we will not only become a state, but will be transformed into a true political nation."[701]

Popovici offered little original in the way of theory and analysis for the solution of Austria-Hungary's national problems. He drew on and combined various aspects of the proposals offered by Palacký, Fischhof, and Renner to create a comprehensive scheme that divided the whole Habsburg patrimony into relatively coherent ethnic territories. Most importantly, he supported the creation of a civic Austrian identity to unify all the peoples into, as he called it, "a true political nation." Popovici recognized the need for both an Austrian patriotism that would tie the citizen to the state, and the common, horizontal bonds based on shared rights and freedoms that would link citizens of all the nationalities.

---

695 Ibid., p. 243.

696 Ibid., p. 21.

697 Ibid., p. 247. He then cited "Fischhoff [sic!]" who had made the same argument forty years earlier.

698 Ibid., p. 236.

699 Ibid., p. 246.

700 Ibid., p. 248.

701 Ibid., p. 260.

Some important differences remain between Popovici's vision for Austria and that of Bloch. First, the latter's was not tied to military strength and traditional dynastic fealty. Furthermore, Popovici did not see the creation of an Austrian identity as part of a larger ideological battle against ethnic hatred and the nation-state principle to the same degree as Bloch. Despite his loyalty to Austria-Hungary, perhaps Popovici knew that Habsburg Romanians could always fall back on the national principle and unify with their co-nationals in the Romanian kingdom if the Monarchy ever did disappear. Bloch, on the other hand, realized that Habsburg Jews had no such attractive alternative without leaving en masse the countries they had inhabited for centuries, and thus he thought of himself as an Austrian in a deeper sense. Nevertheless, Popovici's writings demonstrated that the idea of an Austrian civic consciousness resonated with Romanian nationalists and, by extension, with the non-Magyar nationalities in Hungary.

Karl Renner

Karl Renner (1870–1950) was one of the leading figures within the Austrian Social Democratic Party and the overall political scene in Austria from the turn of the century until his death. He was the first chancellor of the first Austrian Republic in 1918–1919, and served as the second Austrian Republic's first president from 1945 to 1950.[702] Renner, along with Otto Bauer, was one of a handful of thinkers who formulated the ideology known as Austro-Marxism, an adaptation of Marxist theory to Austrian circumstances.[703]

---

702 For a recent biography, see Walter Rauscher, *Karl Renner, ein österreichische Mythos* (Vienna: Ueberreuter, 1995).

703 For an analysis of the personalities in this group, which also included, among others, Max Adler and Friedrich Adler, see Mark E. Blum, *The Austro-Marxists, 1890–1918: A Psychobiographical Study* (Lexington, KY: University Press of Kentucky, 1985). See also Tom Bottomore and Patrick Goode, eds., *Austro-Marxism* (London: Clarendon, 1978), pp. 1–45. The classic analysis of the SDP and the Habsburg nationalities issue is Hans Mommsen, *Die Sozialdemokratie und die Nationalitätenfrage im habsburgischen Vielvölkerstaat* (Vienna: Europa-Verlag, 1863). For a more concise version see Mommsen, *Arbeiterbewegung und nationale Frage: ausgewählte Aufsätze* (Göttingen: Vandenhoeck und Ruprecht, 1979), pp. 127–217.

After becoming acquainted with members of the various ethnic groups during his years in the Habsburg army, Renner developed a deep interest in the Austrian nationalities question.[704] He and Bauer put forth similar, although not identical analyses of the Austrian nationalities question.

Renner's writings reveal an intimate acquaintance with the reform plans put forth by Palacký, Eötvös, Fischhof, and his own contemporary, Popovici. In a "Literature Overview" of works on the national question he listed works by Eötvös, Fischhof, and Palacký.[705] Renner called Palacký the "father of the ethnic *Reichsidee*" for his 1848 plan to divide the whole Monarchy along ethnic lines,[706] and lauded Fischhof as an early proponent of the idea of national curiae that, in an altered form, were at the center of his own plan.[707] Renner also offered the highest level of praise for Fischhof's ideas in general: "Of all the Austrian politicians of German nationality, only one, Fischhof, recognized the needs of the Austrian Germans and the Empire...he was the only great political mind among the German bourgeoisie in the entire constitutional epoch. Only he saw further into the future."[708]

---

704 Bottomore and Goode, *Austro-Marxism*, p. 290.

705 Karl Renner (pseudonym: Synopticus), *Zur österreichischen Nationalitätenfrage: Staat und Nation* (Vienna: Josef Dietl, 1899), "Literature Overview" following the essay's completion on p. 39. The overview consisted of three topics. Under the topic 'Peoples, Ethnic groups and Nationality-Nation and State' Renner listed Eötvös' *Über den Einfluss der herrschenden Ideen des 19. Jahrhunderts auf den Staat*, and *Die Nationalitätenfrage* as well as Fischhof's *Die Sprachenrechte in den Staaten gemischter Nationalität*. Under the topic 'Austria in General' he lists Eötvös' *Über die Gleichberechtigung der Nationalitäten in Österreich*, Fischhof's *Österreich und die Bürgschaften seines Bestandes*, and *Der österreichische Sprachenzwist*, and Palacký's *Österreichs Staatsidee*. He also lists Palacký's *Politisches Vermachtnis* in his section 'Bohemia in particular.' This book appeared before Popovici's treatise.

706 Karl Renner (pseudonym: Rudolf Springer), *Grundlagen und Entwicklungziele der Österreichisch-Ungarischen Monarchie* (Vienna: Franz Deuticke, 1906), p. 191. He also quoted Palacký's dictum on the necessity of Austria's existence (p. 3).

707 Karl Renner (pseudonym: Rudolf Springer), *Der Kampf der oesterreichischen Nationen um den Staat* (Leipzig: Franz Deuticke, 1902), p. 37.

708 Ibid., p. 150. Later in this work Renner quoted from W. Lustkandl's Föderation oder Realunion? (Vienna, 1870), a centralist critique of Fischhof, but noted that he only accepted criticisms of Fischhof's individual suggestions, and did not endorse Lustkandl's conception of a centralized state (pp. 175–6).

Renner referred to Eötvös as "one of the greatest Magyars," and argued that the latter's *Die Garantien der Macht und Einheit Oesterreichs* "demonstrates how far removed the dualistic form of Empire was even in Hungary in 1859. Eötvös included Hungary under Austria, and represented this inclusion as self-evident."[709] Perhaps Renner hoped to find some elements within Magyar politics that would support the reform of dualism, and praised Eötvös because he provided historical justification for such a measure.

Some aspects of Popovici's ideas on the Habsburg nationalities question also appealed to Renner, although he did not advocate the Romanian's ethnic-territorial federalism.[710] Renner referred to Popovici as a source on the evils of Magyarization in Hungary.[711] Popovici's *Die Vereinigten Staaten von Groß-Österreich* impressed Renner, who characterized it as a "highly interesting, very instructive great work," and its author as one "who fought unremittingly for his people, and not on an irredentist, but rather on an Austrian basis."[712] He also noted that the book was banned in Hungary because it proved that "the Hungarian nationalities are not poor cultureless barbarians, as the Magyars would like to describe them."[713]

Renner expressed his disgust with the situation in Hungary on many occasions, and condemned the dualist system, which he felt promoted the dominance of the Germans in Austria, with the Poles as junior partners, and the dominance of the Magyars, with the Croats in the analogous junior rule, in Hungary.[714] Dualism prevented the achievement of equality and autonomy for all the Habsburg nationalities, as well as full democracy and equal rights for all citizens.

As an alternative to the status quo Renner rejected both federalism based on the devolution of power to the historic crownlands as well as federalism that sought to divide the Monarchy's territory along purely

---

[709] Renner, *Grundlagen und Entwicklungziele der Österreichisch-Ungarischen Monarchie*, pp. 29–30.

[710] Ibid., p. 246.

[711] Ibid., p. 183, n. 2.

[712] Ibid., p. 192. He also characterized it as a "warm apologia for the Austrian Empire idea." (p. 7).

[713] Ibid., p. 192, n. 1.

[714] Ibid., p. 47.

ethnic lines. Too many regions within the state, in particular the cities that drove the economy, contained inhabitants of more than one ethnic group. For Renner, this heterogeneity rendered unfeasible any reform that sought to solve the nationality problem largely through territorial division, whether based on provincial or ethnic borders. Neither concept could provide equality for all the members of each nationality, in particular those who inhabited small enclaves within another people's geographic homeland.[715] Unlike Popovici, Renner did not support the assimilation of these small enclaves into the surrounding *Stamm.*

Renner proposed instead a reform plan based on what he called "the personality principle," through which all Habsburg citizens "can participate in the national cultural products, in the rights and duties of the nation without consideration of the accidents of residence, the circumstances of territorial mixing; any majority dominance, any forced nationalization is precluded."[716] In Renner's conception, the cultural and linguistic rights of the members of each *Stamm* would not be tied to any particular territory, but would rather rest in each individual and be portable throughout the state.[717] This portable form of personal cultural autonomy would benefit in particular those who had migrated from one part of the Monarchy where their nationality was the majority to another area where that group was a distinct minority, many of whom were workers (and thus potential SDP voters) moving from the countryside to the cities looking for factory employment.[718]

Renner's reform plan called for a separation of governmental authority into two structures, one to deal with nationality issues, which he defined as those related to culture, education, and language, and another to handle all other political, economic, and material questions. All legislative bodies in both systems would be elected by direct, equal, and universal male suffrage. Each *Stamm* would receive full autonomy to govern the nationality issues listed above according to a multilayered formula. At the federal level, the members of each people, no matter where in the Monarchy they lived, would vote for members of a nation-

715 Ibid., pp. 195–7.

716 Ibid., p. 198.

717 Renner, *Der Kampf der Oesterreichischen Nationen um den Staat*, pp. 35–44.

718 Kann, *The Multinational Empire*, Vol. II, p. 162.

al chamber, which he referred to as "the cultural parliament of the nation."[719]

In addition, individuals would elect regional and local bodies for their nationality so as to achieve maximum autonomy both for each ethnic group and each locality. These 'cultural legislatures' would have the authority to tax and raise funds that could be used only for the cultural and educational programs for which they were responsible. Like Fischhof, he argued that the *Kreis* was the most appropriate level of self-rule, and sought to devolve as much power as possible to the district level so that each locality could administer its own programs. Renner sought to create districts that were as small as possible in order to ensure the maximum level of both local autonomy and ethnic homogeneity within each district. He predicted that 90% of districts would consist of one *Stamm*, but recommended that ethnically mixed districts create two (or more) separate state sanctioned bodies known as *Gemeinden* to govern ethnic/cultural issues for each nationality within that district.[720]

Renner's plan also envisioned a parallel, territorially organized federal system to deal with economic and social issues. There would be a federal parliament and administration, which he claimed, "must be fully independent from all national and provincial influence."[721] In this plan the federal *Reichsrat*, no longer forced to deal with ethno-cultural questions, would act in the best interests of the state as a whole. As Renner put it, "here, the totality of the state, the people as a political-social idea, rather than nationality, must predominate."[722] Equivalent legislative bodies would also exist for the four regions and the eight sub-regions within each region. The proposed regions were based on geographic divisions and included: the Alpine lands, the Sudeten lands (Bohemia, Moravia, Silesia), the Carpathian lands and the Adriatic littoral.[723]

---

719 Renner, *Der Kampf der Oesterreichischen Nationen um den Staat*, p. 200.

720 Ibid., pp. 145–54.

721 Ibid., p. 214.

722 Renner, *Zur österreichischen Nationalitätenfrage: Staat und Nation*, p. 26.

723 For a detailed blueprint of this entire system, see Renner, *Der Kampf der Oesterreichischen Nationen um den Staat*, pp. 180–209. See also Vincent J. Knapp, *Austrian Social Democracy, 1889–1914* (Washington, D.C.: University Press of America, 1980), pp. 96–8, and Kann, *The Multinational Empire*, Vol. II, pp. 158–64.

Although Renner did not include Hungary in this plan, he believed that the reforms in Cisleithania would inevitably, through force of public opinion, lead to reform in Hungary.[724] He refuted the notion of the one thousand-year-old Hungary upon which that kingdom's leaders based its historic territorial integrity. Renner argued instead that Hungary had only been reconquered at the end of the 17th century by the combined forces of the whole Monarchy, and thus Hungary had no historic right to a special status because its territorial integrity was "a gift of the Emperor, that is, of Austria and its peoples."[725] On another occasion he proclaimed that the a reformed state should be the Austria "of the *Kaiseridee* of 1804."[726] This reference implies that he wanted to return to the concept of a unified Habsburg state under a single administrative and executive authority, although democratic and decentralized rather than autocratic in nature.

Because class interests cut across ethnic lines, Renner believed that economic and material questions could be separated from those relating to the nationalities. This separation would be most easily achieved in the more politically powerful and economically developed peoples whose very development created greater class diversification within their communities.[727] He displayed great optimism that his reform could solve the Austrian nationalities problem. He pointed out that the 1849 Kremsier Constitution had demonstrated that Austrians could, if given the chance, come to an agreement that balanced the need for equality and autonomy for each of the nationalities with the need for a central government strong enough to defend the borders and protect their freedoms.[728] Indeed he felt that, with the exception of the Magyars, all the Habsburg peoples "cry out today for national autonomy, for the federal state of nationalities."[729]

---

724 Renner, *Grundlagen und Entwicklungziele der Österreichisch-Ungarischen Monarchie*, p. 247. See also Kann, *The Multinational Empire*, Vol. II, p. 160.

725 Renner, *Grundlagen und Entwicklungziele der Österreichisch-Ungarischen Monarchie*, p. 13, see also pp. 9–12, 19–20.

726 Ibid., p. 248.

727 Renner, *Zur österreichischen Nationalitätenfrage: Staat und Nation*, p. 29–30.

728 Renner, *Grundlagen und Entwicklungziele der Österreichisch-Ungarischen Monarchie*, p. 236.

729 Ibid.

Renner's reform plan, in particular his disavowal of territorial federalism as a solution for Austria-Hungary, reflected his conception of the nation and nationalism. He defined the nation as "an intellectual and cultural community with a recognizable national literature as the expression of this community of culture."[730] He did not believe that national rights and desires could only be satisfied with sovereignty over a specific piece of land, or even that "national consciousness possesses...a necessary relationship with a particular territory."[731] Such a territorial definition of the nation would omit those who were minorities in outlying areas of the national homeland.[732] His characterization of the nation as extra-territorial fitted well with his definition of the Austrian German people, according to which "we are not all-German (*allDeutsch*), we are the East German vanguard...East German are we, but all-East German (*all-ostdeutsch*).[733] Once again crossing the border that separated the Austrian and Hungarian halves of the Empire, Renner proclaimed, "we want to reunite with our Transylvanians, our Banaters, with all Germans of the Monarchy wherever they reside...all Germans between Bodenbach and Orszova should build one legal cultural community."[734] Like the other reformers discussed here, Renner developed a vision for Austrian reform that reflected both the needs of the state as well as his understanding of the needs of his ethnic group. His Germans were both the most powerful *Stamm* in the Monarchy, dominating a number of wealthy Alpine provinces in which they were the overwhelming majority, and yet, next to the Jews, the most territorially dispersed of the major nationalities.[735]

In addition to his extra-territorial definition of the nation, Renner argued that there could be no objective criteria for membership in a national community such as race, mother tongue, or even language of daily use

---

730 Renner, *Zur österreichischen Nationalitätenfrage: Staat und Nation*, p. 8.

731 Renner, *Der Kampf der Oesterreichischen Nationen um den Staat*, p. 55.

732 See, for example, his discussion of a German-speaker in Prague, Ibid., p. 60.

733 Renner, *Grundlagen und Entwicklungziele der Österreichisch-Ungarischen Monarchie*, pp. 238. This notion of the Austro-Germans as a vanguard hinted at Renner's German cultural chauvinism, which will be discussed later in this section.

734 Ibid., pp. 238–9.

735 See also Beller's "Germans and Jews as 'Mitteleuropäisch' Elites," in which he explores the similarities between the two groups in their vision of a unified Central Europe based on their territorial dispersion throughout the region.

(*Umgangsprache*). Instead, each individual should remain free to choose his or her national affiliation. Renner proclaimed "this right to self-determination for the individual serves as a corollary to the right to self-determination for each nation...What criterion can be given for belonging to an intellectual and cultural community other than the consciousness of this belonging?"[736]

Renner remained true to his non-racial definition of Germanness when, for example, he characterized Fischhof as a German without any qualifications based on his Jewishness. Renner was, however, more ambiguous when he discussed a hypothetical black German-speaking Viennese. While he argued that the state must recognize him as a German with equal rights, Renner also pragmatically noted that other Germans would not accept him as one of them. He ambiguously stated that "lawyers" would clarify the man's status by calling him a "quasi-German," although such a statement carefully avoided a direct statement of what Renner himself would consider such a person.[737] When compared to his contemporaries, Renner's statements placed him among the most tolerant and inclusive. He did prescribe full legal rights for a black man even as he waffled on the more philosophical question of whether he could be a true German.

Renner's definition of the nation as cultural rather than territorial and/or racial dovetailed with his rejection of the idea that each state must correspond to a particular nation. He recognized that such a principle would mean the end of Austria-Hungary.[738] Renner admitted that the nation-state principle was perhaps preferable in an ideal world, but argued that demographic and historical circumstances had rendered this ideal impossible in Central Europe.[739]

Although he rejected the idea that all polities must be nation-states, Renner did not seek to create a denationalized cosmopolitanism that would destroy the national consciousness of peoples.[740] He sought a balance between the ethnic interests of individuals, which related to their

---

736 Renner, *Zur österreichischen Nationalitätenfrage: Staat und Nation*, pp. 8–9.

737 Renner, *Der Kampf der Oesterreichischen Nationen um den Staat*, p. 8. See also Blum, pp. 56–7.

738 Renner, *Grundlagen und Entwicklungziele der Österreichisch-Ungarischen Monarchie*, p. 3.

739 Ibid., pp. 186–7.

740 Karl Renner, *Die Nation als Rechtsidee und die Internationale* (Vienna: Ignaz Brand, 1914), p. 15.

cultural and linguistic heritage, and their transethnic,—or to use his term "international"—interests, those relating to material and social conditions that transcended ethnicity. Renner believed that individuals could separate these sets of interests, and thus he crafted a reform plan that assigned cultural responsibilities to autonomous, ethnically defined legislative bodies and economic affairs to multiethnic legislative bodies. He argued that individuals possessed different layers of identity: economic, social, religious, ethnic, cultural, civic, etc., each of which created horizontal ties (*Verbände*) with others who shared it.[741] His analysis of nationalism centered on his contention that "the national as well as the international are relative rather than absolute communities and the problem of organizing the world is how to divide control between the international and the nation."[742] Renner, like Bloch, explicitly relied on a multi-layered or hyphenated understanding of identity when discussing his vision for a reformed multiethnic Austria.

The desire to achieve this balance between the national and "international" also informed Renner's conception of a supraethnic Austrian identity. Like many other reformers, he utilized Switzerland as a model for a future Austria, which was to become "a Switzerland writ large."[743] Renner did not, however, see Switzerland as a model because of its federal constitution, and in fact he rejected the territorial federalism enshrined in the Swiss canton system. Instead Austria was to emulate what Renner saw as Switzerland's greatest accomplishment, the creation of a supraethnic civic consciousness. As Renner described it, "the Swiss are sociologically three nations; politically they are one nation."[744] Through his reforms the peoples of Austria would become, like the Swiss, one political nation even as they remained separate cultural nations.

Renner pointed to the achievements of Britain, Australia, and Canada in forging political unity, a civic nation, out of their diverse populations, and claimed that a reformed Austria would be able to do the same.[745] In addition, his writings attest to his detailed knowledge of the multiethnic

---

741 Renner, *Der Kampf der Oesterreichischen Nationen um den Staat*, pp. 30–31.

742 Renner, *Die Nation als Rechtsidee und die Internationale*, p. 19–20.

743 Ibid., p. 59.

744 Renner, *Der Kampf der Oesterreichischen Nationen um den Staat*, p. 8.

745 Ibid., p. 78.

American society. Renner suggested a clause for the Austrian constitution that he wrote to mirror the preamble of the Virginia state constitution: "We the Germans, Czechs, Poles, Ukrainians, Slovenes, Croats, Serbs, Romanians, and Italians of Austria pledge to live in peace with one another, are bound in this commonwealth, will attend to our common interests through a collective government and reserve our particular interests to our particular governments..."[746]

Alongside the existing, separate ethnic consciousness of each people, Renner hoped for the emergence of a supraethnic Austrian identity, what he described as "a conscious constitutional internationalism... not nationless or opposed to nations, thus neither anational nor antinational....Proletarian internationalism does not declare nationalism null and void, rather it assumes it."[747] This common, "international" identity could only develop as a result of reforms that solved the nationality crisis. Renner demanded "we must have an international constitution and must be governed with a clearly international consciousness...Our constitutional order must make us into...'The United Danube Peoples.'"[748]

Renner placed great faith in the ability of constitutionally guaranteed equality to create civic ties across ethnic lines. A federal parliament elected by universal, direct and equal suffrage would provide all Austrians with "a shining example that a house of many peoples is possible, one that signifies their peace and progress; so will it be a model for the future Empire and as well for the constituents of the Empire!"[749] He further declared that "the nation shall form an organized unity, polit-

---

[746] Karl Renner, *Oesterreichs Erneuerung*, 3 vols. (Vienna: Ignaz Brand, 1916), Vol. I, p. 63. This was a collection of previously published articles. The article cited here originally appeared November 5, 1915. Renner did not offer any ideological explanation of why he chose the Virginia constitution. Presumably, the rhetoric of that document suited the statement he was trying to make. Perhaps he also sought to demonstrate to Americans, whose country was then neutral in the war being fought in Europe, the affinities between the Austrian state and their own.

[747] Renner, *Grundlagen und Entwicklungziele der Österreichisch-Ungarischen Monarchie*, pp. 59–60.

[748] Renner, *Oesterreichs Erneuerung*, Vol. III, p. 8. Originally appeared July 4, 1915.

[749] Renner, *Grundlagen und Entwicklungziele der Österreichisch-Ungarischen Monarchie*, p. 137. He also believed that the Habsburg dynasty had played and would continue to play a symbolic role as a unifying force, along with the desire of the peoples to remain free from their more powerful neighbors.

ical rights will be the foundation for this and for the ties that organically bind together the whole Austrian state."[750] Renner envisioned much more than a pragmatic but shallow alliance of peoples. On many occasions he wrote about "we Austrians" in reference to all the people of Cisleithania, usually in opposition to the Magyar leadership of Hungary. This phrase demonstrated his inclusion of many ethnic groups into a single Austrian identity.[751] On another occasion Renner proclaimed his clear support for an inclusive sense of nationhood that included all the Habsburg peoples, including the Magyars, when he asked "Why should the Monarchy not become a single people of peoples…each free in its circle, all equal, under a centuries old, yet now strong once again parliamentary dynasty?"[752] The terms he used above, in particular "a single people," "organized unity," and "organically bind," suggest that Renner envisioned that the peoples of Austria could form a deep, meaningful bond with one another, perhaps deeper than the various national leaders could have imagined at that time. Such bonds would develop slowly after the implementation of reforms; a common identity did not have to precede constitutional changes.

The new supraethnic identity Renner envisioned for the citizenry went hand in hand with the new *Staatsidee* upon which a reformed Austria would rest. He proclaimed "the only possible state idea (*Staatsgedanke*) for Austria can be: Austria as a modern economic and legal-constitutional state, domestically interconfessional and international, unparalleled with regard to the material well being and political freedom of its citizens."[753]

Renner devoted so much time to developing his constitutional reform proposals because he believed that his personal mission was to discover "the legal structure that is required for the peaceful coexistence of many nations in one state organization."[754] That same search

---

[750] Renner, *Der Kampf der Oesterreichischen Nationen um den Staat*, p. 12.

[751] For two examples see Renner, *Grundlagen und Entwicklungziele der Österreichisch-Ungarischen Monarchie*, pp. 212, 223.

[752] Ibid., p. 237.

[753] Renner, *Der Kampf der Oesterreichischen Nationen um den Staat*, p. 173.

[754] Karl Renner, *Das Selbstbestimmungsrecht der Nationen in besonderer Anwendung auf Oesterreich* (Leipzig: Franz Deuticke, 1918), Vorrede, 2nd page, written in Vienna, December 14, 1917. According to the text on the title page, this work was a second, completely reworked edition of *Der Kampf der österreichischen Nationen um den Staat*.

provided the Austrian state with its mission as well. Austria would provide an example to the world that different nationalities could come together peacefully and on an equal basis in a single polity.[755] Renner explained that the problems Austria faced

> affect the whole world. Austria is merely the typical state of nationalities or peoples, and serves as illustration material...[Austria] has undisputedly made the first and most interesting attempt at a law of peoples within a state. It can be seen as a field of experimentation for internationalism within a state.[756]

These statements, written in December 1917, demonstrated that Renner continued almost until the very end to believe that Austria's problems could still be solved through reform, and that the multiethnic state remained the best solution for the peoples of Central Europe. Austria would demonstrate that multiethnic states were viable and able to provide equality for all the nationalities within their borders.

Leaders at the highest levels of government and politics offered praise for Renner's program.[757] Renner claimed that his book enabled him to meet with high-ranking officials in the bureaucracy, including Minster-President Koerber and Finance Minister Bilinski, and the military, as well as leaders of various nationalities such as Karl Kramár, Masaryk and Vaida.[758] Although it never won official approval at a party congress,[759] his reform proposal gained support from various quarters within the party as well as across party lines.[760] However,

---

755 See also Bottomore and Good, p. 31.

756 Renner, *Das Selbstbestimmungsrecht der Nationen in besonderer Anwendung auf Oesterreich*, Vorrede, 2nd page.

757 Blum, p. 48.

758 Karl Renner, *An der Wende Zweier Zeiten* (Vienna: Danubian, 1946), p. 597, cited also in Blum, p. 48.

759 In its 1899 Brünn program, the Social Democratic Party embraced traditional ethnic-territorial federalism, and did not incorporate Renner's non-territorial concept of personal autonomy. Only later did this idea gain wider support in the party. See Kann, *The Multinational Empire*, Vol. II, pp. 155–56.

760 Knapp, p. 98.

some members of the party, mostly Czechs and other Slavs who strongly identified with their ethnicity, criticized Renner for ignoring the deeply held desire of many for their nationality to have a constitutionally recognized territory to call their national home.[761] Oskar Jászi, who like Renner had sought a solution to Austria-Hungary's problems during the life of the Monarchy, offered a similar criticism.[762] Indeed Jászi charged that Renner's reform proposals "indirectly (though not outspokenly)" affirmed German hegemony in Austria.[763]

The plan never became law, and so it remains impossible to determine whether Jaszi's verdict is fair. However, one can examine what Renner said about the role of Germans in Austria as well as how he understood his German identity. Renner proposed that local administrative offices should operate in the language of the people it served, an important point in a system that maximized local autonomy. He nevertheless believed that the use of German as a state language at the federal level and for communication between administrative offices was necessary because it was the only common language between Austrians of different nationalities.[764] Renner acknowledged the objections to this point by non-Germans. He countered, however, that such a policy could not serve as a tool for Germanization because only the highest officials and politicians would need to learn German, and this only as a second language. Renner insisted that this "cream of the nationality will not be denationalized by the use of a foreign language."[765]

On another occasion, Renner warmly endorsed the growth of bilingual schools, calling them "true good fortune for the state."[766] He encouraged German fathers in Vienna to send their sons to schools that

761 Ibid.

762 Jászi, *The Dissolution of the Habsburg Monarchy*, p. 180.

763 Ibid. A more recent scholar has argued that, in particular after 1907, Renner's stance on questions of culture and language was "the same as that of every German nationalist" (Blum, p. 55). Blum also stated that Renner's German nationalism became even more pronounced during the First World War (Ibid., pp. 169–79). Blum's analysis goes too far by characterizing Renner as no better than any German nationalist.

764 Renner, *Grundlagen und Entwicklungziele der Österreichisch-Ungarischen Monarchie*, p. 186.

765 Renner, *Zur österreichischen Nationalitätenfrage: Staat und Nation*, p. 37.

766 Renner, *Der Kampf der Oesterreichischen Nationen um den Staat*, p. 69.

would teach them Czech, Polish, and all the languages of the country, and comforted his readers that learning other languages would not lead to the denationalization of Germans. Rather, he predicted, the Germans would be able to maintain their political leadership of Austria much longer if they spoke some of the other languages of the Monarchy's peoples.

In his writings Renner expressed a certain level of ambiguity regarding about the Germans of Austria and their relationship to the other Habsburg peoples. In addition to the reform plan itself, his call for bilingualism certainly placed him among the most tolerant politicians of German background in Austria. Nevertheless, Renner was unable to separate his support for learning a second language from his desire to preserve of a leading role for his people within a reformed, democratic Austria.

Renner condemned the failed German bourgeois national-liberal conception of Austria because, among its other flaws, it had damaged the German position within the Monarchy's political system. German liberal nationalists had repeatedly retreated over the previous half-century. They began by seeking a Germanized state covering the whole Monarchy, then merely Cisleithania, then Cisleithania minus Dalmatia and Galicia, and their vision finally collapsed in the wake of the Badeni crisis.[767] Renner lamented that the bourgeois nationalist conception seemed to operate along the axiom "the Fatherland must be smaller."[768] Through his reforms, however, "Austria will be reborn, not the old German-centralized bureaucratic Austria, less still the anarchic feudal Austria, rather a strong democratic Austria, the powerful union of powerful peoples who stand not under the rule of a caste of Germans, rather under level-headed German leadership."[769] Renner made this point more clearly in another passage:

> The German Austrian once was the ruling race in Austria. That rule has ended, but they will always be the **leading** [emphasis his] people. And it is better to lead seven nations

---

767 Karl Renner, *Der deutsche Arbeiter und der Nationalismus* (Vienna: Ig. Brand, 1910), pp. 59–60.

768 Ibid.

769 Renner, *Der Kampf der Oesterreichischen Nationen um den Staat*, pp. 91–2.

> than to serve as a hinterland for the Hohenzollerns. Furthermore every insightful German Austrian and even more so each Reich German knows that the place of Germandom in Europe is better served by the German Austrian manning his post, holding the door to the West open to the Southern and Eastern Slavs, whatever the cost, so that these peoples are not all absorbed into the arms of Russia. Each German Austrian irredentum is a flight from his post; it is national and cultural desertion.[770]

Despite his goal—the achievement of legal equality and cultural autonomy for all the Habsburg peoples—Renner revealed a belief in German cultural superiority that cannot be ignored. Renner is, in many ways, a legatee of the Fischhofian branch of German liberalism and, like Fischhof, attests to the validity of Judson's analysis of Austro-German liberals. Fischhof, too, argued for complete legal equality and the preservation of cultural differences, but, like Renner, saw those concepts as a means for preserving both the Austrian state and the leading role of Germans within it. Fischhof and Renner both rejected the explicit desire to Germanize that was inherent in the dominant strain of German liberalism. Nevertheless, neither abandoned the belief in the superiority of German culture and the German people on some level when discussing his vision of Austria's future. On balance, Fischhof appeared to be the most tolerant German liberal of his time, and one can say the same about Renner in his.

Like Fischhof, Renner could not separate his call for equality among all the Austrian peoples from his desire to maintain political leadership for the German Austrians. Bloch, on the other hand, did not seek to preserve a special position for the Germans or any other ethnic group in the Monarchy and thus differed from Renner as well as Fischhof. Despite this profound difference, some similarities remain between Renner and Bloch on the issue of identity.[771]

Although Renner did not explicitly state it until late 1917, his call for Austria to serve as a model for multiethnic states everywhere was

---

770 Ibid., p. 170.

771 See Lander, who stated that the Social Democrats' Brünn party program had "characteristics analogous to those of Bloch's Austria model." (p. 132).

reminiscent of Bloch's Austrian mission. Furthermore, Renner's concept of "constitutional internationalism" paralleled Bloch's call for the cultivation of constitutional patriotism and civic Austrian identity. Both ideas referred to an identification on the part of citizens with the common state based on the civil rights and freedoms guaranteed by a constitutional order, and also the creation of civic bonds across ethnic lines among all those citizens who shared those rights and freedoms. Both Renner and Bloch described an Austrian identity that preserved *Stamm* consciousness while attempting to build a broader set of ties alongside it. These parallels make more sense when one considers that Renner's non-territorial definition of nations was in some measure an outgrowth of his understanding of the collective interests of Austro-Germans, who, with the exception of Jews, were scattered territorially throughout Austria-Hungary more widely than any other numerically significant ethnic group.[772] Although Renner identified strongly as a German, and Bloch as a Jew, both did so in a way that was divorced from any particular territory within the state. Furthermore, Renner's socialist ideology relied on the ability of workers of different nationalities to understand their shared interests and proletarian identity without losing their cultural distinctiveness. Thus, both Renner and Bloch envisioned a dual-layered identity based on ties between individuals who shared a nationality, and then a broader set based on participation in a constitutional state without any intermediate territorial identification with either a crownland or an ethnic territory.

Otto Bauer

Otto Bauer (1881–1938) was another major figure within the Austrian Social Democratic Party during the last decade before the

[772] In fact, the Zionists, in their 1906 Cracow Program, called for a Rennerian reorganization of the Monarchy into a federation of autonomous nationalities organized according to the principle of personal, not territorial, autonomy. See Marsha L. Rozenblit, "The Dilemma of Identity: The Impact of the First World War on Habsburg Jewry," in Ritchie Robertson & Edward Timms, eds., *The Habsburg Legacy: National Identity in Historical Perspective* (Edinburgh: Edinburgh University Press, 1994), pp. 144–57, esp. p. 148.

First World War, and officially led the party during the interwar period.[773] He accepted Renner's constitutional reform proposals and supported them in the pre-1914 period.[774] However, Bauer criticized some of Renner's ideas, and he also believed that peoples possessed a specific character and had a collective ethos in a more profound way than did Renner.[775] Unlike Renner, who remained committed to multiethnic Austria down to November 1918, Bauer, along with the left wing of the Austro-German Social Democrats, endorsed the breakup of the Monarchy into national states in late 1917.[776] Furthermore, unlike Renner, whose highest priority seemed to be the successful reorganization of the multiethnic state, Bauer gave primacy to the needs of the proletariart, which a resolution of the Habsburg nationalities strife happened to serve.[777] Finally, although both identified themselves as Germans, Bauer was also Jewish, and the way he felt about his Jewishness affected his view of nationalism in the abstract. Bauer cited Renner's works profusely in his own major theoretical work, *Die Nationalitätenfrage und die Sozialdemokratie*, and did not offer his own constitutional scheme apart from that of Renner.[778] Like Renner, Bauer displayed his familiarity with other leading reformers, and referred directly to Palacký, Fischhof, and Popovici.[779]

Bauer undertook his detailed analysis of the nationalities question, which culminated in *Die Nationalitätenfrage und die Sozialdemokratie*,

---

773 For a biography of Bauer, see Otto Leichter, *Otto Bauer, Tragodie oder Triumph* (Vienna: Europa Verlag, 1970).

774 Knapp, pp. 102.

775 Knapp, pp. 102. See also Norbert Leser, "Otto Bauer und Karl Renner," in Erich Fröschl, Helge Zoitl, Hg., *Otto Bauer (1881–1938), Theorie und Praxis* (Vienna: Europa-Verlag, 1985), pp. 25–38; and Bottomore and Goode, pp. 31–2.

776 Kann, *The Multinational Empire*, Vol. II, pp. 170, 175.

777 Ibid., p. 168.

778 Otto Bauer, *Die Nationalitätenfrage und die Sozialdemokratie* (Vienna: Verlag der Wiener Volksbuchhandlung Ignaz Brand, 1908).

779 For references to Palacký, see Ibid., pp. 150, 253, 384–5; for Popovici, p. 378; for Fischhof, p. 378, and also a 1911 book review on Fischhof, in which Bauer offered both criticism and compassion towards his subject. See Otto Bauer, "Buecherschau," *Der Kampf* 4 (January, 1911), pp. 191–2, cited in Blum, pp. 107–8. Although Bauer did not mention Eötvös by name, the fact that Renner had done so combined with Bauer's intimate familiarity with Renner's writings and with Austrian history in general strongly suggested Bauer's knowledge of Eötvös' ideas.

at the request of fellow Austro-Marxist Viktor Adler, who had asked him to develop a Marxist analysis of the nationalities question.[780] Bauer believed in the absolute necessity of reform, and proclaimed that "Austria will be transformed into a federal state of autonomous nations or it will cease to exist."[781] He recognized that national hatreds were often directly linked to class oppression, which made the nationalities question even more explosive.[782] Only a federal system could satisfy the peoples because a centralized governmental system, no matter how democratic, only recognized the state and the individual. Such a system ignored the need of each ethnic group to gain control over the institutions vital to its collective existence.[783] Both absolutist and dualist Austria, despite their obvious differences, were centralized systems that ignored the rights of nationalities.[784] Bauer also rejected crownland federalism because it would have done nothing more than create a number of individual territories in which the majority nationality dominated the smaller one(s) without creating the equality for all the peoples necessary to end the strife among them.[785]

Bauer proposed instead reform based on Renner's personality principle, which recognized the rights of each nationality but separated those rights from specific territory.[786] He maintained that only such a system could create a constitution that "gives each nation the power to develop its culture... [yet] forces no nation to take and hold this power only through a struggle against the state authority...and supports the power of no nation in the rule of a minority over the majority."[787]

---

780 Bottomore and Good, p. 287.

781 Otto Bauer, *Geschichte Oesterreichs* (Vienna: Verlag von Robert Danneberg, 1913), p. 48.

782 Bauer, *Die Nationalitätenfrage und die Sozialdemokratie*, p. 200. He cited as examples German nobles vs. Czech and Slovene peasants, Poles vs. Ukrainians in Galicia, and Italians vs. South Slavs along the Adriatic coast. Ibid., p. 246.

783 Ibid., p. 239.

784 Ibid., p. 242.

785 Ibid., p. 252. In fact, Bauer rebuked Palacký for abandoning his position of 1848, in which he championed ethnic-based federalism, in favor of crownland federalism, and accused him of selling out to win the backing of the feudal aristocracy. Ibid., p. 253.

786 Ibid., pp. 308–318.

787 Ibid., p. 277.

As for Hungary, Bauer believed that the reforms he proposed should cover the whole Habsburg patrimony, not just Cisleithania. He predicted and even urged Franz Joseph to use force if necessary to reunify Austria and Hungary under a unified, federal, and democratic constitution.[788] Bauer laid out an almost surreal scenario in which the Emperor would send the army into Hungary under the banner of "direct, universal, and equal suffrage! Right of assembly for workers! National autonomy!"[789] According to Bauer, the victorious Emperor should then

> counter the idea of an independent Hungarian national state with the idea of a United States of Great-Austria, the idea of a federal state in which each nation can independently pursue its national concerns and all nations unite towards the realization of their common interests. Necessarily, unavoidably, the idea of the federal state of nationalities will become the tool of the Crown to destroy the dualism that has decayed its Empire.[790]

He argued that all the national groups in Cisleithania except the Poles had oppressed brethren in Hungary, and would thus support such a move, as would clericals and pro-imperial conservatives.[791] Bauer contended that his reforms would make Austria-Hungary an irresistible magnet that would attract and eventually absorb the Balkan states that had co-nationals already within the Monarchy's borders, such as Romania and Serbia, and cited both Fischhof and Popovici in support of this claim.[792] Despite his enthusiastic description of the process, Bauer made clear that the reintegration of Hungary into Austria in and of itself was not the program of the proletariat, but rather would provide an opportunity for the implementation of his and Renner's democratic federalization plan.[793] He noted "the description of this difficult tactical mission lies outside the realm of this work."[794] .

788 Ibid., pp. 373–75.

789 Ibid., p. 373.

790 Ibid.

791 Ibid., pp. 376–77.

792 Ibid., p. 378.

793 Ibid., p. 381.

794 Ibid

Bauer endorsed Renner's personality principle and his reform scheme, but did so for reasons that reveal a subtle difference between them. Bauer argued that "national autonomy must necessarily be the program of all nations, classes, and parties that have an interest in Austria's preservation."[795] According to Bauer, it was necessary to preserve the multiethnic Habsburg state because a large common economic area served the material needs of Central European workers and capitalists, and, along the lines of Palacký, because the geo-political conditions of Central and Eastern Europe required political cooperation among the small nations.[796]

Renner had viewed the creation of a multiethnic democracy in Austria as a great achievement because it would demonstrate that different peoples could come together to form a political community, an event that was for him equally or perhaps more important than the creation of a socialist state itself. Bauer, on the other hand, focused more on the functional purpose of creating political cooperation across ethnic lines, the overriding purpose of which was to clear the path for socialism and nurture the development of the national cultures.[797] He wanted to bring an end to the nationalities strife so that the working classes of all ethnicities would be free of the perceived need to ally with the non-proletarian elements within their own *Stamm* in a struggle among the peoples. The workers of the various nationalities would then be ready to join together, albeit as discrete units, within a large class-based coalition against the ruling classes.[798]

Bauer believed that nationalities not only had the legal right to equality, but also that each had a life force and individual character of its own built around its common culture and language.[799] Renner, on the other hand, focused largely on the specifics of reform and did not examine the nation as a metaphysical concept in the same way.[800] Although Bauer contended that each people had a separate existence,

---

[795] Ibid., p. 438.

[796] Ibid., pp. 384–5.

[797] See Kann, *The Multinational Empire*, Vol. II, p. 176; Bottomore and Goode, p. 32.

[798] Bauer, *Die Nationalitätenfrage und die Sozialdemokratie*, p. 461.

[799] Ibid., pp. 98–100.

[800] Bottomore and Goode, p. 31.

he rejected the argument that each one should have its own state because the need for economic viability required states to be of a certain size.[801]

According to Bauer, the founding of a socialist order would greatly aid the cultural development of each nationality. In addition to the creation of material equality, socialism sought to bring the cultural fruits of each nation to its proletariat.[802] Capitalism had begun to sharpen the differences between the nationalities by increasing access to education, but socialism would bring this process to its full fruition.[803] Such an analysis contradicted Marx's analysis of nationalism.[804]

By the turn of the century, it had become clear to Austrian Social Democrats such as Renner and Bauer that differences among the nationalities were not disappearing in the Habsburg Monarchy. Unlike Marx and Engels, Renner and Bauer could not have cavalierly dismissed nationalism as a distraction that international proletarianism would simply overcome. In fact they did not want to see the peoples dissolve into a cosmopolitan proletariat in part because of their own sense of German identity. Furthermore, they realized that such an ideological position would have been unacceptable to the non-German members of the SDP, who had no interest themselves in abandoning ethnic consciousness.

Bauer wanted not only to nurture the individual consciousness of each nationality, but also to create a spirit of cooperation across ethnic lines, and achieve a balance between the two. He described how class oppression had warped ethnic consciousness. Because the capitalist classes of Austria were German, the German workers, who were not oppressed as Germans *per se*, became too cosmopolitan. Bauer criti-

---

[801] Bauer, *Die Nationalitätenfrage und die Sozialdemokratie*, p. 383.

[802] Ibid., pp. 88, 94.

[803] Ibid., p. 135.

[804] Marx and Engels had argued that national differences would simply fade away as industrial capitalism and global commerce brought the world into closer contact. Furthermore, national differences were nothing more than bourgeois inventions devised to keep the workers of various countries and language groups from realizing their common interests. Marx and Engels believed that when the world communist revolution succeeded, nations would disappear because they would no longer seek to exploit one another. Karl Marx and Friedrich Engels, *The Communist Manifesto* (Boston: Bedford, 1999), p. 82.

cized the many German socialists who, following a more traditional Marxist analysis of nationalism, wrongly dismissed legitimate national feelings as "bourgeois prejudice."[805] He dubbed this phenomenon "naive cosmopolitanism."[806] Bauer also lamented the "naive nationalism" of the non-German workers who reacted against the Germanness of the capitalist class and saw all Germans as their enemies.[807] An end to the nationalities strife, he hoped, could transform these naive ideologies into what he called the

> internationalism of the mature working classes...its politics rooted in the clear recognition that the interests of the working classes of the individual nation cannot be supported in any way other than by supporting the struggle of the workers of other nations. It springs forth no longer from the idea of humanity, rather from the recognition of the international solidarity of class.[808]

Any kind of de-nationalized cosmopolitan socialism based on the unity of the human race conflicted with Bauer's belief in the uniqueness and worth of each nation's character. He endorsed a politics that was both socialist-international and national, a concept he referred to as "conscious internationalism."[809] Bauer did not place a great emphasis on the creation of a common Austrian consciousness. His concept of conscious internationalism was as close as he came to an endorsement of the type of dual-layered, civic-ethnic identity espoused by Bloch.

In another area, however, the views of Bauer and Bloch collided head on. Bauer was Jewish, and his grandparents on both sides had been *Ostjuden*. His family, however, had acculturated into German culture after moving to Moravia a generation before his birth, and he almost exclusively identified himself culturally and politically as a German, not a Jew.[810]

---

805 Bauer, *Die Nationalitätenfrage und die Sozialdemokratie*, p. 270.

806 Ibid., p. 266.

807 Ibid.

808 Ibid., p. 270.

809 Ibid., p. 457.

810 Blum, p. 73. In Bauer's time this was, in fact, a relatively standard position among Jewish socialists in German-speaking areas.

Bauer was thus the type of Jew that Bloch targeted when he called for Jews to abandon their delusion of belonging to the German *Volk* and return to a Jewish *Stamm* identity.

A Jew who had experienced his own family's adoption of a German identity, Bauer was strongly committed to a cultural definition of nationality because such a definition provided legitimacy to his Germanness. He believed not only that each individual could choose his nationality, but also that national character, the force that binds a people together, could actually evolve over time. Bauer explained that "national character changes....The nation of today is in no way linked to the ancestors of two or three hundred years earlier. Where we speak of a German national character, we mean the common characteristics of the German during a specific hundred years or decade."[811] He thus implied that anyone, including Jews, could become Germans, and more importantly that the entry of large numbers of Jews into Germandom had transformed the national character into something new, something to which Jewish and Christian Germans had contributed. Bauer's belief in the malleability of national character made his Germanness legitimate, at least to himself. Since he never rejected his German identity, which was a product of at least partial assimilation, he must have seen assimilation in a positive light, a view that had to have colored his view of nationalities in general and the Austrian nationalities question in particular.

Bauer's writings on the topic of assimilation were inconsistent and ambiguous. He declared that Jews were not a nation, would not receive autonomy even under the Renner-Bauer reform plan, and should assimilate into the surrounding cultures.[812] However, on another occasion he

---

811 Bauer, *Die Nationalitätenfrage und die Sozialdemokratie*, p. 1. Also cited in Blum, p. 91.

812 Bauer, *Die Nationalitätenfrage und die Sozialdemokratie*, pp. 328–31. These views were consistent with the official position of his party. In October 1904, after several years of seeing their proposals for autonomy within the Polish Social Democratic Party of Galicia (PPSD) rejected, Galician Jewish Socialists finally decided to establish an independent party, the *Zydowska Partja Social-demokratyczna* (ZPS-Jewish Social Democratic Party). Until 1897 the PPSD had been known as the Galician Social Democratic Party. Its name change made clear its identification of Galician proletarians as Polish and contradicted the previous name's implication that it was regional party that represented both Poles and non-Poles. The PPSD, with the support of the Austrian party executive in Vienna, denounced the Jewish organization's call for autonomy as separatist

described how Jews, because of their different racial origin, remained Jews even after German acculturation whereas a Czech could actually become indistinguishable from other Germans because those two groups shared a similar, if not identical, racial background.[813] Bauer could not deny his Jewish origin to himself, and the inner doubts he, as a Jew, must have had about his Germanness had an impact on his ideological motivations. He expressed, at times, a clear German cultural chauvinism and implied on a few occasions that Germanization of the other Austrian peoples was a possibility, although not in his major work, which remained consistently in favor of cultural equality and the preservation of individual nationalities.[814] It is, of course, impossible to know what was in Bauer's innermost thoughts, but the insecurity of his German identity in light of the increased belief among Germans in a racially defined nationhood may well have been responsible for the chauvinistic German outbursts scattered throughout his writings. As a Germanized Jew arguing for equality but yet unable to shake his belief in German cultural superiority, Bauer, in a different way than Renner, also served as a legatee of Fischhof.

****

and injurious to the interests of a united proletariat. Both the PPSD and the overall Austrian Social Democratic Party refused to recognize the ZPS as an autonomous entity within the party. The PPSD argued that differences of language and religion were not grounds for the Galician Jews to seek autonomy within the organization. However, the pan-Austrian party was in fact organized along such *Stamm* lines, with each section having exactly the autonomy from the center that the Jews of Galicia had demanded. The PPSD's condemnatory report won the approval of the executive in Vienna. Ultimately, the Galician Jewish Socialists remained in the Polish organization, and received nothing more than a statement from the party leadership that they represented the Galician Jewish proletariat. The PPSD leadership had welcomed Jews into the Polish party, but wanted them to acculturate themselves as Poles. For more on this affair, see Robert Wistrich, "Austrian Social Democracy and the Problem of Galician Jewry, 1890–1914," *Leo Baeck Institute Yearbook*, 26 (1981), pp. 89–124. See especially pp. 111–15. For a broader discussion of Austrian Social Democracy and the Jews of the Monarchy, see Wistrich, *Socialism and the Jews: The Dilemmas of Assimilation in Germany and Austria-Hungary* (Rutherford [N.J.]: Fairleigh Dickinson University Press, 1982).

813 Otto Bauer, "Die Bedingungen der Nationalen Assimilation," *Der Kampf* 5 (March, 1912), pp. 247–59; cited in Blum, p. 98. Blum does a good job analyzing the inconsistent and tortured twists in Bauer's writings on assimilation, Jews, and Germans, pp. 91–101.

814 Blum, p. 98.

Each of the reformers discussed here proposed reforms and put forth a vision of Austria that reflected the political circumstances and interests of the nationality with which he identified. Like Fischhof before them, Renner and Bauer could not separate their calls for equality and the preservation of individual cultures from their desire to maintain a position of political primacy for Germans Austria. Holovatskyj and Popovici represented ethnic groups that were oppressed as much if not more by neighboring nationalities than by the central government in Vienna in terms of their cultural development, and thus endorsed ethnic-territorial rather than provincial federalism as the proper basis for reform (although certainly there were disagreements within each ethnic group on individual questions). Eötvös, whose Magyars dominated the kingdom of Hungary, espoused reform based on the preservation of historic rights and provincial autonomy. Palacký's Czechs occupied a position between these two extremes. They were the majority *Stamm* in an extremely important province-kingdom with a historic tradition rivaling that of Hungary, yet found themselves suffering under a governmental and bureaucratic system that favored the language and, by extension, culture of its province's powerful German minority. Depending on how confident the Czechs were about their own position at a given moment, either provincial federalism or ethnic-territorial federalism might make sense. This helps explain why Palacký switched his support from the former to the latter in 1848, and back again in the mid-1860s. Even Bloch's call for the creation of a political Austrian nation reflected most urgently the alienation Jews felt in an era of increasing ethnic prejudice and hatred that threatened the multiethnic society in which they felt most secure.

It is not surprising that tensions and contradictions existed among the proposed constitutional schemes. Each of them reflected in some measure the needs of one nationality, and often conflicted with those of another. Although the idea of an Austria with a German mission might never be reconciled with the rhetoric of Austro-Slavism, it might have been possible to compromise over the degree of centralization vs. decentralization members of each nationality was willing to accept. Institutional reforms could have preceded a concerted effort by a reformed Austrian state to cultivate a culturally neutral Austrian identity. Peoples that felt secure in their existence thanks to such reforms might have been more receptive to such a notion.

Politicians such as those examined here, all of whom endorsed a liberal, constitutional system of government, had to expect to compromise from their initial positions to some degree. Each proposal may have served as a statement of an individual reformer's ideal, but not necessarily as a final offer. By the very act of proposing a specific set of reforms, each of these political thinkers confirmed his belief that Austria could find a solution to its nationalities question with which his group could live. Furthermore, these proposals demonstrated that leading politicians from virtually every ethnic group, as well as from the largest multiethnic political party, the Social Democrats, took a public position that endorsed the continued existence of a multiethnic state in the Danube region. An examination of other groups within Austrian society reveals that the Christian Social Party favored a continuation of the Monarchy, as did the Catholic Church and the aristocracy. In fact, the Catholic 'Austrian idea' shared with the *Staatsidee* envisioned for Austria by Bloch, Fischhof, and even Renner the notion that the Austrian state would serve as a non-national mediator bringing together many peoples under one roof, although the Catholic version exalted the dynasty's role on explicitly religious grounds.[515] Furthermore, individuals and organizations within the Austrian artistic and intellectual community sought to promote a supraethnic Austrian identity, including among others Hugo von Hofmannsthal, Egon Schiele, the geographer Erwin Hanslike, art historian Alois Riegl, and the Association for Austrian Folklore, which did so by promoting the study of the folk art of all the Monarchy's peoples as a way to emphasize that Austria was a state in which a multitude of peoples could live together and develop their cultures.[516] The Galician Poles

[515] This idea can be seen in an early form as far back as Friedrich Schlegel, and in such later politicians as Heinrich Lammasch and Ignaz Seipel. See Schlegel's 1804–6 Cologne lectures in *Kritische Friedrich-Schlegel-Ausgabe, Vol. 13* (Munich: Schöningh, 1964), p. 165. See Seipel's proposal for a reformed Austria in, Ignaz Seipel, *Nation und Staat* (Vienna: Braumuller, 1916). See also Kann, *The Multinational Empire*, Vol. II, p. 208–19.

[516] See Kimberly Smith, "Schiele, Hanslike, and the Allure of the Natural Nation," *Austrian History Yearbook* 33 (2002), pp. 176–7. For more on the Association for Austrian Folklore, see Diana Graham Reynolds, "Alois Riegl and the Politics of Art History: Intellectual Traditions and Austrian Identity in *Fin-de-Siècle* Vienna" (Ph. D. Diss., University of California, San Diego, 1997), p. 172, cited also in Kimberly Smith, p. 177. On Hofmannsthal, see LeRider, "Hugo von Hofmannsthal and the Austrian Idea of Central Europe."

did not formulate a reform plan after the enactment of the *Ausgleich* because they, like the Hungarians after 1867, were generally satisfied with the existing arrangement, especially in comparison to the circumstances faced by Poles in Germany and Russia. In 1848 Franz Smolka had issued a plan that typified the attitude of the Galician Polish leadership at that time toward the larger Austrian state. He called for the Monarchy to renounce Lombardy and Venetia, restore the Hungarian constitution and give that kingdom full autonomy, and create a fully separate government for Galicia with the express purpose of that province forming the core of a future reunited Poland. Galicia, the future Poland, and Hungary would be linked to the rest of Austria by a personal union. The rest of Austria would then be joined with Germany to recreate the Holy Roman Empire. Such a plan evinced little concern for the interests and rights of the other Cisleithanian Slavic peoples, either the Ukrainians of Galicia or the Czechs and Slovenes consigned once again to a 'German' Empire; the main concern was self-rule for a Galicia politically dominated by the Polish nobility. Although neither the Holy Roman Empire nor an independent Poland reappeared as a result of the *Ausgleich*, after 1867 the political organization of the Habsburg Monarchy itself strongly resembled Smolka's proposal, with autonomy for Hungary and (unofficially) Galicia and thus most Polish leaders in the province felt satisfied.[517] The Galician electoral compromise of 1914, although never implemented before the war, nevertheless demonstrated that by that time Polish leaders were ready to make concessions to the Ukrainians in the interest of solving the nationalities problem and preserving the Monarchy, which, while not quite as attractive as an independent Poland, certainly seemed to be the best available situation for Galician Poles in the near-term. The Italians were perhaps the only group without any interest in preserving Austria for the long term, although even here the city of Trieste served as an exception to this absolute.[518]

As for post-1867 Hungary, the ideas of Popovici did to a large degree coincide with the interests of the non-Magyar nationalities, including the

---

817 See Namier, p. 97.

818 See Angelo Ara, "The 'Cultural Soul' and the 'Merchant Soul': Trieste between Italian and Austrian Identity," in *The Habsburg Legacy*, Ritchie Robertson and Edward Timms, eds. (Edinburgh: Edinburgh University Press, 1994), pp. 58–66.

Croats whose province possessed some autonomy from Budapest according to its own compromise, the 1868 *Nagobna.* Widespread support existed across class lines among Croats for an end to dualism and a continuation of the Austrian state.[819] The Croat peasant party, which developed a mass following before 1914, endorsed "the Austrian idea," and its leader, Stjepan Radic, sounded like Popovici when he called for an Austria that was "neither German nor Magyar nor Slav but Christian, European and democratic."[820] Among the Magyar noble leadership, it is unclear whether any of Eötvös' moderate legacy, in particular his opposition to state-sponsored Magyarization, survived the *Ausgleich.* Nevertheless, perhaps some democratic elements within the Magyar nobility, and even more likely, the disenfranchised Magyar masses, would have supported equality for the nationalities if it had been combined with greater democratic rights for all citizens of Hungary.

The array of reform proposals discussed in this chapter demonstrates that broad support existed among political leaders for reform, not the overthrow of Austria. These proposals, offered across six decades, envisioned different constitutional structures for a reformed Austria; some called for ethnic federalism of various stripes and others for provincial autonomy. Perhaps the political leaders of the nationalities could not have reconciled their differences even if Franz Joseph had been willing to let them try. However, the Kremsier Constitution demonstrated that the representatives of the nationalities of the Austrian half of the Monarchy, on that occasion at least, were able come to a compromise on paper. It was Franz Joseph who prevented them from trying to implement it.

Any comparison of the ideas of reformers ranging from the pre-1848 period through the first decades of the twentieth century must recognize that changes in the political arena made elements of compromise that may have been acceptable to one or another of the peoples in 1848 no longer acceptable by 1900. Equally certainly, it was much eas-

---

819 Sked, *The Decline and Fall of the Habsburg Empire*, p. 217. Sked argued that universal suffrage in Croatia would have produced a majority for the peasant party, and that only among the small middle class did the 'Yugoslav' idea so feared by the Habsburgs have any support.

820 Quoted in Ibid.

ier for the Kremsier Parliament to negotiate a solution to the nationalities question in 1848, when liberals and moderate nationalists dominated the Cisleithanian political scene, than it was for Austria-Hungary or even Cisleithania to do so by the time of the Badeni crisis, when more strident nationalists had asserted leadership within the political spheres of most of the nationalities, most importantly among the Czechs and Germans, the two most powerful peoples in Cisleithania. However, we can also recognize that the changed situation a half-century after Kremsier resulted in large part from the policies of the Habsburg regime itself. If Franz Joseph's government could not solve the nationalities problem in 1897, much of the blame for that lay with the actions of Franz Joseph's government in 1849 and 1867.

The Monarchy clung to dualism in the years leading up to 1914. It proved unable and/or unwilling to enact comprehensive reforms and begin to treat its peoples equally. Thus, the Austrian nationalities never developed the common civic consciousness that is necessary to ensure the survival of a state, in particular a multiethnic state. Bloch recognized that Austria was failing in this all-important task, and publicly called on his state's leaders to take action to rectify that failure. He remained committed to this goal throughout his long career in a way that separated him from other Austrian reformers, including those discussed in this chapter. Furthermore, Bloch alone rejected the national state as the ideal form of government and argued that the main purpose of Austria's existence was to demonstrate the moral superiority of the multiethnic state to the nation-state idea. Although none of the other reformers examined here rejected the idea of creating a sense of peoplehood across ethnic lines, neither did they make it a priority to the same degree as did Bloch. Most of them simply stated that, as a result of reforms that solved the nationalities question, a common state patriotism and cooperative spirit would arise among the peoples, with Renner displaying the greatest enthusiasm for such a development. Nevertheless, the other reformers' acceptance of and/or support for the creation of a supraethnic identity along the lines envisioned by Bloch demonstrated that such a concept would have been viable in a reformed Austria that allowed for the autonomy and equality of all its peoples. Although unique in its own right, Bloch's vision for an Austrian nation thus complemented the calls for constitutional change made by prominent reformers who represented virtually all the nationalities as well as the working classes.

Each of the reformers examined in this study, as well as many of their colleagues throughout the Monarchy accepted a few fundamental premises: the need for a constitutional form of government, the principle of legal equality for citizens of any nationality, the right of each people to preserve and develop its culture, and the need for some form of representative legislature. Most reformers as well as most Habsburg politicians in general accepted these basic tenets of liberalism, although each colored these universal assumptions based on the different needs of the time period in which he operated, as well as his nationality and/or class, the two of which were often related.

Each reformer offered a different blueprint; some had different definitions from the others of autonomy for each people and even democracy itself. Nevertheless, a level of consensus existed across ethnic lines as well as across the decades that suggested that a solution was possible, even if it is impossible to know whether the peoples could have compromised if given the chance. Perhaps the nationalities would have never come to an agreement on the reform of Austria-Hungary. The Emperor, however, never gave them that opportunity, and instead chose to use the rivalry among them to preserve as much power as possible in his own hands. As a result, the peoples of Austria never developed the common civic identity and supraethnic consciousness that could, perhaps, have held them together in some form of cooperation or confederation even after the fall of the Habsburgs.

Some might ask whether the creation of such an identity was even possible in light of the bewildering diversity of the Habsburg population. Certainly much of the older Habsburg historiography, the so-called 'doomed Austria' school, believed that its diversity foreordained the Monarchy's destruction in age of nation-states. However, Judson questioned how strongly Austria-Hungary differed from European nation-states such as France, Germany, and Italy, noting that government policy had played a large role in creating national identities in those countries during the nineteenth century.[821] He asked "Is it not

[821] Judson, *Exclusive Revolutionaries*, pp. 7–8. See also Kimberly Smith, "Schiele, Hanslike, and the Allure of the Natural Nation," p. 174.

finally time to see the Habsburg Monarchy in the same terms as those other states?" Revising the picture of an inevitably doomed Austria does not seek to whitewash its past or apologize for its mistakes. If anything, the fact that Austria-Hungary could have survived and did not earns an even harsher judgment for those who governed it.

A multiethnic Austrian nation could have been built on the foundation of the Austrian state, just as a French nation was so created, a British nation was so created, and an American nation was so created.[822] The Emperor and the men who held power chose not to try. Their choice, not its diversity, condemned Austria-Hungary to dissolution. More importantly, their choice helped push the citizens of the region to define nationhood in racial and biological terms, a definition at the heart of the unspeakable crimes Nazi Germany and its collaborators committed against the peoples they considered genetically inferior. It did not have to be so.

---

822 While the British and American national identities are more obvious examples of diverse populations becoming a single nation, as has been discussed by Linda Colley and Liah Greenfeld (see Chapter 1) among others, the creation of French identity was equally dependent on the state as well as social and economic development. See Eugen Weber, *Peasants into Frenchmen: The Modernization of Rural France* (Stanford: Stanford University Press, 1976).

CONCLUSION

This book makes two overarching historiographical arguments. First, it seeks to place Bloch's ideas within the broader discussion among reform-minded Habsburg politicians on how to solve the Monarchy's nationalities question. His ideas have for too long appeared in any detail only in the works of historians of Habsburg Jewry. Bloch's conception of an Austrian civic consciousness is a part of Austrian as well as Jewish history, and a historiography that ignores it is incomplete.

Second, this book argues that Austria's failure to create a common sense of nationhood for its peoples bears directly on the central question of Habsburg historiography: Why did Austria-Hungary disappear in November 1918? I have argued here that, in addition to ethnically conscious Jews such as Bloch, leaders across lines of class and nationality supported the existence of a reformed Austrian state. Despite their different approaches to reform, these leaders either actively urged or were willing to accept the creation of some kind of supraethnic identity to bring together the Habsburg peoples. However, the state never took advantage of this opportunity. During his long and crucial reign, Franz Joseph and his government never undertook a large scale effort to build such a consciousness among the citizenry as a whole, and thus a supraethnic Austrian nation remained only an idea. This fact undercuts the attempt by some recent historians who, while correctly rejecting the idea that Austria-Hungary's demise was inevitable, have identified within the pre-1914 Austrian state 'viable' institutions and sectors in order to argue that it was a sound and stable polity that disappeared simply because it lost the First World War. Austria-Hungary could exist only as long as the Habsburg dynasty ruled because it possessed no other justification for its existence. As the example of the Habsburg Monarchy has shown, a state that cannot survive the overthrow of its rulers possesses only a limited lifespan. In the twentieth century, virtually all European monarchies have either democratized or disappeared.

Austria-Hungary fell apart with the overthrow of the Habsburgs because its peoples saw no reason to continue their political association without the dynasty that had brought them together in the first place. The disintegration of the multiethnic Habsburg state does not mean that multiethnic states are inherently unstable or somehow doomed to fail. If the citizens of a state see themselves as a nation, even a nation made up of distinct peoples, they are much more likely to continue their political association in another form after the fall of any particular political order. However, any multiethnic, multilinguistic, multireligious state that lacks a common identity binding together its population simply lacks long-term viability. That conclusion is unavoidable.

BIBLIOGRAPHY

Primary Sources:

Bauer, Otto. *Geschichte Oesterreichs*. 2nd ed. Vienna: Verlag von Robert Danneberg, 1913.

_________.*Die Nationalitätenfrage und die Sozialdemokratie*. Vienna: Verlag der Wiener Volksbuchhandlung Ignaz Brand, 1908.

Bloch, Joseph Samuel. *Aus der Vergangenheit für die Gegenwart: Social und Literarhistorische Vorträge und Essays*. Vienna: Engel, 1886.

_________.*Ein Besuch beim Judenthum in New-York und Umgebung*. Vienna: Verlag der 'Oesterreichischen Wochenschrift,' 1912.

_________.*Documente zur Aufklärung: Talmud und Judenthum in der Österreichischen Volksvertretung: Parliamentsreden*. Vienna: Oester-reichische Wochenschrift, 1900.

_________.*Erinnerungen aus meinem Leben*, Vol. III. Morris Bloch, ed. Vienna: Appel, 1933.

_________.*Gegen die Anti-Semiten: Eine Streitschrift*. Vienna: D. Lowy, 1882.

_________.*Israel and the Nations*. Berlin: Benjamin Harz, 1927.

_________.*My Reminiscences*, 2 vols. Vienna: R. Lowit, 1923.

_________.*Der Nationale Zwist und die Juden in Österreich*. Vienna: M. Gottlieb, 1886.

_________.ed, *Österreichische Wochenschrift*. Vienna, 1884–1920.

Eötvös, József. *The Dominant Ideas of the Nineteenth Century and Their Impact on the State*, 2 vols., trans., D. Mervyn Jones. New York: Columbia University Press, 1996; orig., 1851.

_________.*Die Garantien der Macht und Einheit Oesterreichs*. Leipzig: F.A. Brockhaus, 1859.

_________.*Die Nationalitäten-Frage*, trans., Max Falk. Pest: Moriz Ráth, 1865.

________. *Ueber die Gleichberechtigung der Nationalitäten in Oesterreich*, 3rd ed. Pest: Moriz Ráth, 1871; orig., 1851.

Fischhof, Adolf. *Ein Blick auf Oesterreichs Lage*. Vienna: Wallishauser, 1866.

________. *On the Reduction of Continental Armies*, translated by Humphry William Freeland. London: Williams and Norgate, 1875.

________. *Österreich und die Bürgschaften seines Bestandes*. Vienna: Wallishauser, 1869.

________. *Der Österreichische Sprachenzwist*. Vienna: Manz, 1888.

________. *Die Sprachenrechte in den Staaten gemischter Nationalität*. Vienna: Manz, 1885.

________. *Zur Erweiterung der Municipal-Autonomie*. Vienna: Wallishauser, 1868.

Grunwald, Max, ed. *Dr. Josef S. Bloch, Auswahl aus seiner Briefsammlung*. Vienna: Ludwig Hirschfeld, 1930.

________. "Josef Bloch." in *Festschrift zum 75jährigen Bestehen des jüdischen-theologischen Seminars Fraenckelscher Stiftung*, Vol. 2. Vienna: n.p., 1930.

Helfert, Joseph Alexander. *Oesterreich und die Nationalitäten: Ein offenes Wort an Herrn Franz Palacký*. Vienna: C. Gerold, 1850.

________. *Über Nationalgeschichte und den gegenwärtigen Stand ihrer Pflege in Oesterreich*. Prague: Calve, 1854.

Holovatskyj, Iakiv. (pseudonym: Havrylo Rusyn) "Zustände der Russinen in Galizien." in *Jahrbücher für Slavische Literatur, Kunst und Wissenschaft*. Leipzig, 1846.

Jaques, Heinrich. *Denkschrift über die Stellung der Juden in Oesterreich*. Vienna: C. Gerold, 1859.

Kopp, Josef. *Zur Judenfrage nach den aktenprozesses Rohling-Bloch*. Leipzig: J Klinkhardt, 1886.

Masaryk, Thomas G. *Palacký's Idee des Böhmischen Volkes*. Prag: Verlag von IUC Aug. Zalud, 1899.

Palacký, Frantisek. *Oesterreichs Staatsidee*. Prag: n.p. 1866.

Popovici, Aurel C. *Die Vereinigten Staaten von Groß-Österreich*. Leipzig: Verlag von B. Elischer Nachfolger, 1906.

Renner, Karl. *An der Wende Zweier Zeiten*. Vienna: Danubian, 1946.

________.*Der deutsche Arbeiter und der Nationalismus*. Vienna: Ig. Brand, 1910.

________.(pseudonym: Rudolf Springer) *Grundlagen und Entwicklungziele der Österreichisch-Ungarischen Monarchie*. Vienna: Franz Deuticke, 1906.

________.(pseudonym: Rudolf Springer) *Der Kampf der Oesterreichischen Nationen um den Staat*. Leipzig: Franz Deuticke, 1902.

________.*Die Nation als Rechtsidee und die Internationale*. Vienna: Ignaz Brand, 1914.

________.*Oesterreichs Erneuerung*, 3 vols. Vienna: Ignaz Brand, 1916.

________.*Das Selbstbestimmungsrecht der Nationen in besonderer Anwendung auf Oesterreich*. Leipzig: Franz Deuticke, 1918.

________.(pseudonym: Synopticus) *Zur österreichischen Nationalitätenfrage: Staat und Nation*. Vienna: Josef Dietl, 1899.

Schalit, Isidor. "Erinnerungen von Ehrenburschen Medizinalrat Isidor Schalit." in *Festschrift zur Feier des 100 Semesters der akademischen Verbindung Kadimah*. Ludwig Rosenhek, ed. Mödling: n.p., 1933.

Selected Secondary Sources:

Agnew, Hugh L. *Origins of the Czech National Renaissance*. Pittsburgh: University of Pittsburgh Press, 1993.

Anderson, Benedict. *Imagined Communities*. London: Verso, 1983.

Ara, Angelo. "The 'Cultural Soul' and the 'Merchant Soul': Trieste between Italian and Austrian Identity." In *The Habsburg Legacy*. Ritchie Robertson and Edward Timms, eds. Edinburgh: Edinburgh University Press, 1994.

Arendt, Hannah. *On the Origins of Totalitarianism*. New York: Harcourt, Brace, 1951.

Aschheim, Steven. *Brothers and Strangers: the East European Jews in German and German-Jewish Consciousness*. Madison: University of Wisconsin Press, 1982.

Barry, Brian. "Self-Government Revisited." in *Theorizing Nationalism*. Ronald Beiner, ed. Albany: State University of New York Press, 1999.

Bartal, Israel. "'The Heavenly City of Germany' and Absolutism à la mode Autriche: The Rise of the Haskalah in Galicia." in *Toward Modernity: The European Jewish Model.* Jacob Katz, ed. New Brunswick, NJ: Transaction, 1986.

Bartal, Israel and Polonsky, Antony, eds. *Focusing on Galicia: Jews, Poles, and Ukrainians, 1772–1918.* London: The Littman Library of Jewish Civilization, 1999.

Bato, Ludwig. *Die Juden im alten Wien.* Vienna: Phaidon-Verlag, 1928.

Beller, Steven. *Francis Joseph.* London: Longman, 1996;

_________. "Germans and Jews as Mitteleuropäisch' Elites." in *Mitteleuropa*, Peter Stirk, ed. Edinburgh: Edinburgh University Press, 1994.

_________. *The Jews of Vienna, 1867–1938: A Cultural History.* Cambridge: Cambridge University Press, 1989.

_________. "Kraus's Firework: State Consciousness Raising in the 1908 Jubilee Parade in Vienna and the Problem of Austrian Identity," in *Staging the Past: The Politics of Commemoration in Habsburg Central Europe, 1848 to the Present*, Maria Bucur and Nancy Wingfield, eds. West Lafayette, IN: Purdue University Press, 2001.

_________."On Jewish DNA, Ethnonationalism and the Law of the Included Middle: Problems of Jewish Identity in Modern Central European History," in *Jüdische Identitäten: Einblicke in die Bewusstseinslandschaft des österreichischen Judentums*, Klaus Hödl, ed., Innsbruck: Studien-Verlag, 2000.

_________."Patriotism and the National Identity of Habsburg Jewry, 1860–1914." *Leo Baeck Institute Year Book* 16. (1996).

_________.ed. *Rethinking Vienna 1900.* New York: Berghahn Books, 2001.

_________. "The Tragic Carnival: Austrian Culture in the First World War," in *European Culture during the Great War: The Arts, Entertainment, and Propaganda, 1914–1918.* Aviel Roshwald and Richard Stites, eds. Cambridge: Cambridge University Press, 1999.

_________. "The World of Yesterday Revisited: Nostalgia, Memory, and the Jews of Fin-de-Siècle Vienna." *Jewish Social Studies* 2 (1996).

Beiner, Ronald, ed. *Theorizing Citizenship.* Albany: State University of New York Press, 1995.

_________.ed. *Theorizing Nationalism.* Albany: State University of New York Press, 1999.

Bihl, Wolfdieter. "Die Juden." in *Die Habsburgermonarchie 1848–1918.* Adam Wandruszka and Peter Urbanitsch, eds. Vol. 3. *Die Völker des Reiches.* part II. Vienna: Österreichische Akademie der Wissenschaften, 1973.

Berlin, Isaiah. "The Bent Twig: On the Rise of Nationalism." in Berlin. *The Crooked Timber of Humanity.* London: John Murray, 1990, pp. 238–261.

Blanning, T.C.W. *Joseph II.* London: Longman, 1994.

Bled, Jean-Paul. *Franz Joseph.* Cambridge: Blackwell Publishers, 1992.

_________. "Les Allemandes d'Autriche et la Question Nationale (1850–1918)." *Revue d'Allemagne et des pays de langue allemande* 28 (1996).

Bloch, Chaim. "Theodor Herzl and Joseph S. Bloch." *Herzl Yearbook* 1 (1959).

Blum, Mark E. *The Austro-Marxists, 1890–1918: A Psychobiographical Study.* Lexington, KY: University Press of Kentucky, 1985.

Bödy, Paul. *Joseph Eötvös and the Modernization of Hungary, 1840–1870.* 2nd ed. New York: Columbia University Press, 1985; orig., 1972.

Bohachevsky-Chomiak, Martha. *The Spring of a Nation: The Ukrainians in Eastern Galicia in 1848.* Philadelphia: Shevchenko Scientific Society, 1967.

Bottomore, Tom and Patrick Goode, eds. *Austro-Marxism.* London: Clarendon, 1978.

Boyer, John. *Culture and Political Crisis in Vienna: Christian Socialism in Power, 1897–1918.* Chicago: University of Chicago Press, 1995.

_________.*Political Radicalism in Late Imperial Vienna: Origins of the Christian Social Movement, 1848–1897.* Chicago: University of Chicago Press, 1981.

Brubaker, Rogers. *Citizenship and Nationhood in France and Germany.* Cambridge: Harvard University Press, 1992.

Bruckmüller, Ernst. *Nation Österreich.* Vienna: Bohlau, 1984.

Cahnmann, Werner J. "Adolf Fischhof als Verfechter der Nationalität und seine Auswirkung auf das jüdisch-politische Denken in Österreich." in *Studia Judaica Austriaca.* Wolfgang Häusler, ed. Vol. I. Vienna: Verlag Herold, 1974.

________."Adolf Fischof and his Jewish Followers." *Leo Baeck Institute Yearbook* 4 (1959).

Charmatz, Richard. *Adolf Fischhof: Ein politisches Lebensbild.* Stuttgart: Cotta, 1910.

Cohen, Gary. *Education and Middle-Class Society in Imperial Austria, 1848–1918.* West Lafayette, IN: Purdue University Press, 1996.

________."Jews in German Society: Prague, 1860–1914." *Central European History* 10 (1977).

________."Neither Absolutism nor Anarchy: New Narratives on Society and Government in Late Imperial Austria" *Austrian History Yearbook* 29 (1998).

________.*The Politics of Ethnic Survival: Germans in Prague, 1861–1914.* Princeton: Princeton University Press, 1981.

Colley, Linda. *Britons: Forging the Nation, 1707–1837.* New Haven, Yale University Press, 1992.

Connor, Walker. *Ethnonationalism: The Quest for Understanding.* Princeton: Princeton University Press, 1994.

Cornwall, Mark. "The Dissolution of Austria-Hungary." in *The Last Years of Austria-Hungary.* Cornwall, ed. Exeter: University of Exeter Press, 1990.

________. "Disintegration and Defeat: The Austro-Hungarian Revolution" in *The Last Years of Austria-Hungary* 2nd (revised) ed., Cornwall, ed. Exeter: University of Exeter Press, 2002.

Deák, István. *Beyond Nationalism, A Social and Political History of the Habsburg Officer Corps, 1848–1918.* New York: Oxford, 1990.

________."Comparing Apples and Pears: Centralization, Decentralization and Ethnic Policy in the Habsburg and Soviet Armies." in *Nationalism and Empire: The Habsburg Monarchy and the Soviet Union.* Richard L. Rudolph and David F. Good, eds. New York: St. Martin's Press, 1992.

Denitch, Bogdan. *Ethnic Nationalism: The Tragic Death of Yugoslavia.* Minneapolis: University of Minnesota Press, 1994.

Drabek, Anna, et. al., eds. *Das Österreichische Judentum: Voraussetzungen und Geschichte*. Vienna: Jugend und Volk, 1974.

Fraenkel, Josef. *The Jews of Austria: Essays on their Life, History and Destruction*. London: Vallentine, Mitchell, 1967.

Fröschl, Erich and Helge Zoitl, eds. *Otto Bauer, 1881–1938, Theorie und Praxis*. Vienna: Europa-Verlag, 1985.

Gagliardo, John. *Reich and Nation: The Holy Roman Empire as Idea and Reality,1763–1806*. Bloomington, IN: Indiana University Press, 1980.

Gaisbauer, Adolf. *Davidstern und Doppeladler*. Vienna: Böhlau, 1988.

Garver, Bruce. *The Young Czech Party and the Emergence of a Multi-Party System*. New Haven: Yale University Press, 1978.

Gay, Peter. *Freud, Jews and Other Germans*. New York: Oxford University Press, 1978.

Geehr, Richard S. *Karl Lueger, Mayor of Fin de Siècle Vienna*. Detroit: Wayne State University Press, 1990.

Gellner, Ernest. *Conditions of Liberty: Civil Society and its Rivals*. London: Hamish Hamilton, 1994.

_________.*Language and Solitude: Wittgenstein, Malinowski and the Habsburg Dilemma*. Cambridge: Cambridge University Press, 1998.

_________.*Nations and Nationalism*. Oxford: Blackwell, 1983.

Gerő, András. *Emperor Francis Joseph, King of the Hungarians*. Boulder, CO: Social Science Monographs, 2001.

_________. *The Hungarian Parliament, 1867–1918: A Mirage of Power*. Boulder, CO: Social Science Monographs, 2001.

Good, David. *The Economic Rise of the Habsburg Empire, 1750–1914*. Berkeley: University of California Press, 1984.

Gordon, Milton. *Assimilation in American Life: The Role of Race, Religion and National Origins*. New York: Oxford University Press, 1964.

Götz, Thomas. *Bürgertum und Liberalismus in Tirol 1840–1873. Zwischen Stadt und 'Region,' Staat, und Nation*. Cologne: SH-Verlag, 2001.

Greenfeld, Liah. *Nationalism: Five Roads to Modernity*. Cambridge: Harvard University Press, 1992.

Gross, Feliks. *The Civic and the Tribal State: The State, Ethnicity, and the Multiethnic State*. Westport, CT: Greenwood Press, 1998.

Grunwald, Max. "Josef Bloch." in *Festschrift zum 75jährigen Bestehen des jüdischen-theologischen Seminars Fraenckelscher Stiftung*. Vol. 2. Vienna: n.p., 1930.

_________. *Vienna*. Philadelphia: The Jewish Publication Society of America, 1936.

Habermas, Jürgen. "Citizenship and National Identity: Some Reflections on the Future of Europe." In *Theorizing Citizenship*. Ronald Beiner, ed. Albany: State University of New York Press, 1995.

_________."Historical Consciousness and Post-Traditional Identity: The Federal Republic's Orientation to the West." in Habermas, *The New Conservatism: Cultural Criticism and the Historians' Debate*. Shierry Weber Nicholsen, ed. and trans. Cambridge: MIT Press, 1989.

Hacohen, Malachi. "Dilemmas of Cosmopolitanism: Karl Popper, Jewish Identity and 'Central European Culture.'" *Journal of Modern History* 71 (1999).

Hahn, Hans Joachim. *The 1848 Revolutions in German-Speaking Europe*. Harlow: Longman, 2001.

Hall, John, ed. *The State and the Nation: Ernest Gellner and the Theory of Nationalism*. Cambridge: Cambridge University Press, 1998.

Hanak, Peter. *The Garden and the Workshop: Essays on the Cultural History of Vienna and Budapest*. Princeton: Princeton University Press, 1998.

_________. "Problems of Jewish Assimilation in Austria-Hungary." in *The Power of the Past: Essays for Eric Hobsbawm*. Peter Thane, Geoffrey Crossick, Roderick Floud, eds. Cambridge: Cambridge University Press, 1984.

Handler, Andrew. *Blood Libel at Tiszaeszlár*. New York: Columbia University Press, 1980.

Hanisch, Ernst. *1890–1990: Der lange Schatten des Staates: Österreichische Gesellschaftsgeschichte in 20. Jahrhundert*. Vienna: Ueberreuter, 1994.

Hann, Chris. "Nationalism and Civil Society in Central Europe: From Ruritania to the Carpathian Euroregion." in *The State and the Nation: Ernest Gellner and the Theory of Nationalism*.

John Hall, ed. Cambridge: Cambridge University Press, 1998.

Hantsch, Hugo. *Die Nationalitätenfrage im alten Oesterreich: das Problem der Konstruktiven Reichsgestaltung*. Vienna: Verlag Herold, 1953.

Häusler, Wolfgang. "Toleranz, Emanzipation und Antisemitismus: Das österreichische Judentum des bürgerlichen Zeitalters, 1782–1918." in *Das Österreichische Judentum: Voraussetzungen und Geschichte*. Anna Drabek, et. al., ed. Vienna: Jugend und Volk, 1974, pp. 83–134.

Heindl, Waltraud. *Gehorsame Rebellen: Bürokratie und Beamte in Österreich 1780 bis 1848*. Vienna: Böhlau, 1991.

Heer, Friedrich. *Der Kampf um die Österreichische Identität*. Vienna: Bohlau, 1981.

Himka, John-Paul. "Dimensions of a Triangle: Polish-Ukrainian-Jewish Relations in Austrian Galicia," in *Focusing on Galicia: Jews, Poles, and Ukrainians, 1772–1918*. Bartal, Israel and Polonsky, Antony, eds. London: The Littman Library of Jewish Civilization, 1999.

_________.*Galician Villagers and the Ukrainian National Movement in the 19th Century*. Edmonton: Macmillan Press, 1988.

_________.*Religion and Nationality in Western Ukraine. The Greek Catholic Church and the Ruthenian National Movement in Galicia, 1867–1900*. Montreal: McGill-Queen's University Press, 1999.

Hitchins, Keith, ed. *The Nationality Problem in Austria-Hungary: The ReportsofAlexander Vaida to Archduke Franz Ferdinand's Chancellery*. Leiden, Netherlands: E.J. Brill, 1974.

_________.*Rumania, 1866–1947*. Oxford, Clarendon Press, 1994.

Hobsbawm, Eric. *Nations and Nationalism*. Cambridge: Cambridge University Press, 1990.

Hödl, Klaus, ed. *Jüdische Identitäten: Einblicke in die Bewusstseinslandschaft des österreichischen Judentums*. Innsbruck: Studien-Verlag, 2000.

_________.*Als Bettler in die Leopoldstadt: Galizische Juden auf dem Weg nach Wien*. Vienna: Böhlau, 1994.

Iggers, Wilma A., ed. *The Jews of Bohemia and Moravia: A Historical*

Reader. Detroit: Wayne State University Press, 1992.

_________. *Women of Prague: Ethnic Diversity and Social Change from the Eighteenth Century to the Present*. Providence: Berghahn Books, 1995.

Ignatieff, Michael. *Blood and Belonging: Journeys into the New Nationalism*. New York: Farrar, Straus and Giroux, 1994.

Ingrao, Charles. *The Habsburg Monarchy, 1618–1815*. Cambridge: Cambridge University Press, 1994.

Janik, Allan and Toulmin, Stephen. *Wittgenstein's Vienna*. New York: Simon and Schuster, 1973.

Jászi, Oskar. *The Dissolution of the Habsburg Monarchy*. Chicago: University of Chicago Press, 1929.

Jenks, William. *Austria under the Iron Ring, 1879–1893*. Charlottesville: University Press of Virginia, 1965.

The Jews of Czechoslovakia: Historical Studies and Surveys. Vol. 1. Philadelphia: The Jewish Publication Society of America, 1968.

John, Michael. "Obdachlösigkeit-Massenerscheinung und Unruheherd in Wien des Spätjahrhundertzeit." In *Glücklich ist, Wer vergiss-?; das andere Wien um 1900*. Hubert Ehalt, Gernot Heiss, Hannes Stekl, eds. Vienna: Böhlau, 1986.

Johnston, William. *The Austrian Mind*. Berkeley: University of California Press, 1983.

Judson, Pieter. *Exclusive Revolutionaries: Liberal Politics, Social Experience and National Identity in the Austrian Empire, 1848–1914*. Ann Arbor: University of Michigan Press, 1996.

Kann, Robert A. "German Speaking Jewry during Austria-Hungary's Constitutional Era, 1867–1918." *Jewish Social Studies* 10 (1948).

_________. *The Habsburg Monarchy: A Study in Integration and Disintegration*. New York: Praeger, 1957.

_________. *The Multinational Empire: Nationalism and National Reform in the Habsburg Monarchy, 1848–1918*. 2 vols. New York: Columbia University Press, 1950.

Katz, Jacob. *Out of the Ghetto: The Social Background of Jewish Emancipation, 1770–1870*. Cambridge: Harvard University Press, 1973.

_________.ed. *Toward Modernity: The European Jewish Model.* New Brunswick, NJ: Transaction Books, 1986.

Katzenstein, Peter. *Disjoined Partners: Austria and Germany since 1815.* Berkeley: University of California Press, 1976.

Kemiläinen, Aira. *Nationalism: Problems Concerning the Word, Concept and Classification.* Jyväskylä: Kustantajat, 1964.

Kestenberg-Gladstein, Ruth. "Jews between Czechs and Germans in the Historic Lands 1848–1918." in *The Jews of Czechoslovakia: Historical Studies and Surveys.* Vol. I. Philadelphia: The Jewish Publication Society of America, 1968.

Kieval, Hillel. *The Making of Czech Jewry.* New York: Oxford University Press, 1988.

Knapp, Vincent J. *Austrian Social Democracy, 1889–1914.* Washington, D.C.: University Press of America, 1980.

Kohn, Hans. *The Idea of Nationalism: A Study in Its Origins and Background.* New York: Macmillan, 1946.

Kornberg, Jacques. *Theodor Herzl.* Bloomington: Indiana University Press, 1993.

Kozik, Jan. *Ukrainian National Movement in Galicia, 1815–1849.* Edmonton: Macmillan Press, 1986.

Kymlicka, Will. "Misunderstanding Nationalism." in *Theorizing Nationalism.* Ronald Beiner, ed. Albany: State University of New York Press, 1999.

Landau, Saul R. *Der Polenklub und seine Hausjuden.* Vienna: n.p., 1907.

Lander, Katja. "Joseph Samuel Bloch und die Österreichisch-Israelitische Union: Initiativen zur Begrundung einer Judischen Politik im Spaten 19. Jahrhundert." Ph.D. diss., Universität des Saarlandes, 1993.

Laqueur, Walter. *A History of Zionism.* London: Weidenfeld and Nicolson, 1972.

Leichter, Otto. *Otto Bauer, Tragodie oder Triumph.* Vienna: Europa Verlag, 1970.

Leitsch, Walter. "East Europeans Studying History in Vienna, 1855–1918. in *Historians as Nation-Builders: Central and South-East Europe.* Dennis Deletant and Harry Hanak, eds. London: Macmillan, 1988.

LeRider, Jacques. "Hugo von Hofmannsthal and the Austrian Idea of

Central Europe." in *The Habsburg Legacy*. Edinburgh: Edinburgh University Press, 1994.

Leser, Norbert. "Otto Bauer und Karl Renner." in *Otto Bauer, 1881–1938, Theorie und Praxis*. Erich Fröschl and Helge Zoitl, eds. Vienna: Europa-Verlag, 1985.

Lindemann, Albert S. *Esau's Tears: Modern anti-Semitism and the Rise of the Jews*. Cambridge: Cambridge University Press, 1997.

Ljiphardt, Arend. *Democracy in Plural Societies*. New Haven: Yale University Press, 1977.

Macartney, C.A. *The Habsburg Empire, 1790–1918*. New York: MacMillian, 1969.

Magris, Claudio. *Der Habsburgische Mythos in der österreichische Literatur*. Salzburg: O. Müller, 1966.

Markovits, Andrei and Frank Sysyn, eds. *Nationbuilding and the Politics of Nationalism, Essays on Austrian Galicia*. Cambridge: Harvard University Press, 1982.

May, Arthur J. T*he Hapsburg Monarchy, 1867–1914*. Cambridge: Harvard University Press, 1951.

Mayer, Sigmund. *Die Wiener Juden, 1700–1900: Kommerz, Kultur, Politik*. Vienna: R. Lowit, 1917.

McCagg, William. *A History of Habsburg Jews, 1670–1918*. Bloomington: Indiana University Press, 1989.

McGrath, William J. *Dionysian Art and Populist Politics in Austria*. New Haven: Yale University Press, 1974.

_________."Student Radicalism in Vienna." *Journal of Contemporary History* 2 (1967).

Miller, Nicholas J. *Between Nation and State: Serbian Politics in Croatia Before the First World War*. Pittsburgh: University of Pittsburgh Press, 1997.

Mintz, Matityahu. "Jewish Nationalism in the Context of Multinational States," in *Jewish Nationalism and Politics: New Perspectives*. Jehuda Reinharz, Gideon Shimoni, Yosef Salmon, eds. (Hebrew, with English summary). Jerusalem: Zalman Shazar Center for Jewish History, 1996.

Mommsen, Hans. *Arbeiterbewegung und nationale Frage: ausgewählte Aufsätze*. Göttingen: Vandenhoeck & Ruprecht, 1979.

_________.*Die Sozialdemokratie und die Nationalitätenfrage im habs-*

burgischen Vielvölkerstaat. Vienna: Europa-Verlag, 1963.

Morava, Georg J. *Franz Palacky: eine Fruhe Vision von Mitteleuropa*. Vienna: Österreichische Bundesverlag, 1990.

_________.*Palacký: Cech, Rakusan, Evropan*. Prague: Vysehrad, 1998

Mosse, George L. *German Jews beyond Judaism*. Bloomington, IN: Indiana University Press, 1985.

Namier, Lewis B. *1848: The Revolution of the Intellectuals*. London: Geoffrey Cumberlege, 1944.

Nielsen, Kai. "Cultural Nationalism, Neither Ethnic nor Civic." in *Theorizing Nationalism*. Ronald Beiner, ed. Albany: State University of New York Press, 1999.

Okey, Robin. *The Habsburg Monarchy*. New York: St. Martin's Press, 2001.

Oxaal, Ivar. "The Jews of Young Hitler's Vienna." in *Jews, Antisemitism and Culture in Vienna*. Ivar Oxaal, Michael Pollak, Gerhard Botz, eds. London: Routledge and Kegan Paul, 1987.

Patai, Raphael. *The Jews of Hungary: History, Culture, Psychology*. Detroit: Wayne State University Press, 1996.

Paupie, Kurt. *Handbuch der österreichischen Pressegeschichte 1848–1959*. 2 vols. Vienna: Wilhelm Braumüller, 1960–6).

Poppel, Stephen. *Zionism in Germany: the Shaping of a Jewish Identity*. Philadelphia: The Jewish Publication Society of America, 1976.

Pulzer, Peter. "The Austrian Liberals and the Jewish Question, 1867–1914." *Journal of Central European Affairs* 23 (1963).

_________.*The Rise of Political Anti-Semitism in Germany and Austria*. New York: Wiley 1964.

Rath, R. John. *The Viennese Revolution of 1848*. New York: Greenwood Press, 1957.

Rauscher, Walter. *Karl Renner, ein österreichische Mythos*. Vienna: Ueberreuter, 1995.

Rechter, David. *The Jews of Vienna and the First World War*. London: The Littman Library of Jewish Civilization, 2001

_________."Kaisertreu: The Dynastic Loyalty of Austrian Jewry," in *Jüdische Identitäten: Einblicke in die Bewusstseinslandschaft des österreichischen Judentums*, Klaus Hödl, ed., Innsbruck: Studien-Verlag, 2000.

Redlich, Joseph. *Emperor Francis Joseph of Austria: A Biography.* New York: Macmillan, 1929.

Reifowitz, Ian. "An Austrianist and a Zionist: The Ideas of Joseph Samuel Bloch and Theodor Herzl on National Identity and the Multinational State." in Hildegard Kernmayer, ed. Moritz Csáky, series ed. *Zerfall und Rekonstruktion. Identitäten und ihre Representation in der österreichischen Moderne. Studien zur Moderne.* Vol. 5. Vienna: Passagen Verlag, 1999.

_________."Threads Intertwined: German National Egoism and Liberalism in Adolf Fischhof's Vision for Austria," *Nationalities Papers* 29 (2001), No. 3.

_________."'To become Jews once again': Antisemitism and the Call to Embrace a Jewish Identity in fin-de-siècle Austria," *Transversal* 2 (2001), No. 2.

Renan, Ernest. "What is a Nation?" in *The Dynamics of Nationalism.* L.L. Snyder. D. Van Nostrand: Princeton, 1964.

Reynolds, Diana Graham. "Alois Riegl and the Politics of Art History: Intellectual Traditions and Austrian Identity in *Fin-de-Siècle* Vienna." Ph. D. Diss., University of California, San Diego, 1997.

Robertson, Ritchie and Edward Timms, eds. *The Habsburg Legacy.* Edinburgh: Edinburgh University Press, 1994.

Rosenfeld, Max. *Die Polnische Judenfrage.* Vienna: R. Löwit, 1919.

Roshwald, Aviel. *Ethnic nationalism and the unraveling of empires: Central Europe, Russia, and the Middle East, 1914–1923.* London: Routledge, 2001.

_________."Jewish Cultural Identity in Eastern and Central Europe during the Great War," in *European Culture during the Great War: The Arts, Entertainment, and Propaganda, 1914–1918.* Roshwald and Richard Stites, eds. Cambridge: Cambridge University Press, 1999.

Roth, Joseph. *The Radetzky March.* Woodstock: Overlook Press, 1983.

Rozenblit, Marsha L. "The Dilemma of Identity: The Impact of the First World War on Habsburg Jewry." in *The Habsburg Legacy.* Ritchie Robertson and Edward Timms, eds. Edinburgh: Edinburgh University Press, 1994.

_________."Jewish Identity and the Modern Rabbi: The Cases of Isak

Noa Mannheimer, Adolf Jellinek and Moritz Güdemann in Nineteenth-Century Vienna." *Leo Baeck Institute Yearbook* 35 (1990).

_________. *The Jews of Vienna, 1867–1914: Assimilation and Identity*. Albany: State University of New York Press, 1983.

_________. *Reconstructing a National Identity: The Jews of Habsburg Austria during World War I*. Oxford: Oxford University Press, 2001.

_________. "Review Article: The Jews of the Dual Monarchy." *Austrian History Yearbook* 23 (1992).

Rudnytsky, Ivan. "The Ukrainians in Galicia under Austrian Rule." in *Nationbuilding and the Politics of Nationalism, Essays on Austrian Galicia*. Andrei Markovits and Frank Sysyn, eds. Cambridge: Harvard University Press, 1982.

Rudnytsky, Leonid, "The Image of Austria in the Works of Ivan Franko." in *Nationbuilding and the Politics of Nationalism, Essays on Austrian Galicia*. Andrei Markovits and Frank Sysyn, eds. Cambridge: Harvard University Press, 1982.

Rudolph, Richard and David Good, eds. *Nationalism and Empire: The Habsburg Monarchy and the Soviet Union*. New York: St. Martin's Press, 1992.

Rusinow, Dennison. "Ethnic Politics in the Habsburg Monarchy and Successor States: Three Answers to the National Question." in *Nationalism and Empire: The Habsburg Monarchy and the Soviet Union*. Richard L. Rudolph and David F. Good, eds. New York: St. Martin's Press, 1992.

Schorske, Carl. *Fin-de-Siècle Vienna: Politics and Culture*. New York: Vintage Books, 1981.

Scruton, Roger. "In Defense of the Nation." in Scruton. *The Philosopher on Dover Beach*. Manchester, U.K.: Carcanet, 1990.

Shedel, James. "Fin de Siècle or Jahrhundertwende: The Question of an Austrian Sonderweg." in Steven Beller, ed. *Rethinking Vienna 1900*. New York: Berghahn Books, 2001.

Silber, Michael. "The Historical Experience of German Jewry and Its Impact on Haskalah and Reform in Hungary." in *Toward Modernity: The European Jewish Model*. Jacob Katz, ed. New Brunswick, NJ: Transaction Books, 1986.

Simon, Walter B. "The Jewish Vote in Austria." *Leo Baeck Institute Year Book* 16 (1971).

Sked, Alan. *The Decline and Fall of the Habsburg Empire, 1815–1918.* London: Longman, 1989.

Smith, Anthony. *The Ethnic Origins of Nationalism.* New York: Basil Blackwell, 1986.

_________.*Nationalism and Modernism: A Critical Survey of Recent Theories of Nations and Nationalism.* London: Routledge, 1998.

Smith, Kimberly. "Schiele, Hanslike, and the Allure of the Natural Nation," *Austrian History Yearbook* 33 (2002), pp. 163– 205.

Sorkin, David. *The Transformation of German Jewry, 1780–1840.* New York: Oxford University Press, 1987.

Stauter-Halstead, Keely. *The Nation in the Village: The Genesis of Peasant National Identity in Austrian Poland, 1848–1914.* Ithaca: Cornell University Press, 2001.

Stepan, Alfred. "Modern Multinational Democracies: Transcending a Gellnerian Oxymoron." in *The State and the Nation: Ernest Gellner and the Theory of Nationalism.* John Hall, ed. Cambridge: Cambridge University Press, 1998.

Stourzh, Gerald. "Ethnic Attribution in Late Imperial Austria: Good Intentions, Evil Consequences." in *The Habsburg Legacy.* Ritchie Robertson and Edward Timms, eds. Edinburgh: Edinburgh University Press, 1994.

_________."Galten die Juden als Nationalität Altösterreichs?" in *Prag, Czernowitz, Jerusalem: der österreichische Staat und die Juden vom Zeitalter des Absolutismus bis zum Ende der Monarchie.* Anna Drabek, Mordechai Eliav, Gerald Stourzh, eds. Eisenstadt: Edition Roetzer, 1984.

_________.*Die Gleichberechtigung der Nationalitäten in der Verfassung und Verwaltung Österreichs, 1848–1918.* Vienna: Österreichische Akademie, 1985.

_________."The Multinational Empire Revisited—Reflections on late Imperial Austria." *Austrian History Yearbook* 23 (1992).

_________."Der Nationale Ausgleich in der Bukowina, 1909/1910." in *Die Bukowina, Vergangenheit und Gegenwart.* Ilona Slawinski, Joseph P. Strelka, eds. Bern: Peter Lang, 1995.

Sugar, Peter, ed., *A History of Hungary.* Bloomington: Indiana University Press, 1990.

Tamir, Yael. *Liberal Nationalism*. Princeton: Princeton University Press, 1993.

Taylor, A.J.P. *The Habsburg Monarchy, 1809–1918*. University of Chicago Press, Chicago, 1948.

Thaler, Peter. *The Ambivalence of Identity: The Austrian Experience of Nation-Building in a Modern Society*. West Lafayette, IN: Purdue University Press, 2001.

Tietze, Hans. *Die Juden Wiens: Geschichte-Wirtschaft-Kultur*. Leipzig: E.P. Tal, and Co., 1933.

Todorova, Maria N. *Imagining the Balkans*. New York: Oxford University Press, 1997.

Toury, Jacob. "Josef Samuel Bloch und die Jüdische Identität im österreichischen Kaiserreich." in *Jüdische Integration und Identität in Deutschland und Österreich, 1848–1918*. Walter Grab, ed. Tel Aviv: Nateev, 1984.

_________. *Die Jüdische Press im österreichische Kaiserreich: ein Beitrag zur Problematik der Akkulturation, 1802–1918*. Tübingen: Mohr, 1983.

_________. "Troubled Beginnings: The Emergence of the Österreichisch-Israelitische Union." *Leo Baeck Institute Year Book* 30 (1985).

_________. Years of Strife: The Contest of the Österreichisch-Israelitische Union for the Leadership of Austrian Jewry," *Leo Baeck Institute Year Book* 33 (1988).

Turda, Marius, 1998. *Aurel C. Popovici's Nationalism and its Political Representation in the Habsburg Empire (1890–1910)* [online]. Budapest: Local Government and Public Service Reform Initiative, Database of Research papers on Ethnic relations in Central and Eastern Europe and Countries of the Former Soviet Union. Available from World Wide Web: (http://lgi.osi.hu/ethnic/relations/1/mariust.html).

Unowsky, Daniel. "Creating Patriotism: Imperial Celebrations and the Cult of Franz Joseph." *Österreichische Zeitschrift für Geschichtswissenschaften* 9 (1998) No. 2.

Vardy, Steven B. *Baron Joseph Eötvös, A Literary Biography*. Boulder, Co: Social Sciences Monographs; distributed by Columbia University Press, 1987.

Vermes, Gábor. *István Tisza: the Liberal Vision and Conservative State-*

craft of a Magyar Nationalist. New York: East European Monographs; distributed by Columbia University Press, 1985.

Vick, Brian E. *Defining Germany: The 1848 Frankfurt Parliamentarians and National Identity.* Cambridge: Harvard University Press, 2001.

Walz, Stefan. *Staat, Nationalität, und Jüdische Identität in Österreich vom 18. Jahrhundert bis 1914.* Frankfurt am Main: Peter Lang, 1996.

Wandruszka, Adam and Peter Urbanitsch, eds. *Die Habsburgermonarchie 1848–1918.* Vols. 1–3. Vienna: Österreichische Akademie der Wissenschaften, 1973–80.

Wandycz, Piotr S. *The Lands of Partititoned Poland, 1795–1918.* Seattle: University of Washington Press, 1974.

Wank, Solomon. "Pessimism in the Austrian Establishment at the Turn of the Century." in *The Mirror of History: Essays in Honor of Fritz Fellner.* Solomon Wank, Heidrun Maschl, Brigitte Mazohl-Wallnig and Reinhold Wagleitner, eds. Santa Barbara: ABC-Clio, 1988, pp. 295–314.

_________. "Some Reflections on the Habsburg Empire and Its Legacy in the Nationalities Question." *Austrian History Yearbook* 28 (1997).

Weber, Eugen. *Peasants into Frenchmen: The Modernization of Rural France.* Stanford: Stanford University Press, 1976.

Weber, Johann. *Eötvös und die ungarische Nationalitätenfrage.* Munich: Oldenbourg, 1966.

Weitzmann, Walter. "Politics of the Viennese Jewish community." *Jews, Antisemitism and Culture in Vienna.* London: Routledge and Kegan Paul, 1987.

Whiteside, Andrew. *Austrian National Socialism Before 1918.* The Hague: Martinus Nijhoff, 1962.

_________. *The Socialism of Fools: Georg Ritter von Schoenerer and Austrian Pan-Germanism.* Berkeley: University of California Press, 1975.

Williams, C.E. *The Broken Eagle: The Politics of Austrian Literature from Empire to Anschluss.* New York: Barnes & Noble, 1974.

Williamson, Samuel R. *Austria-Hungary and the Origins of the First World War*. New York, St. Martin's Press, 1991.

Wistrich, Robert. "Austrian Social Democracy and the Problem of Galician Jewry, 1890–1914." *Leo Baeck Institute Yearbook* 26 (1981).

_________."The Jews and Nationality Conflicts in the Habsburg Lands." *Nationalities Papers* 22 (1994).

_________.*The Jews of Vienna in the Age of Franz Joseph*. Oxford: Oxford University Press, 1989.

_________.*Socialism and the Jews: The Dilemmas of Assimilation in Germany and Austria-Hungary*. Rutherford [N.J.]: Fairleigh Dickinson University Press, 1982.

Yack, Bernard. "The Myth of the Civic Nation." in *Theorizing Nationalism*. Ronald Beiner, ed. Albany: State University of New York Press, 1999.

Zacek, Joseph F. Palacký: *The Historian as Scholar and Nationalist*. The Hague: Mouton, 1970.

Zeman, Z.A.B. *The Break-Up of the Habsburg Empire, 1914–1918*. London: Oxford University Press, 1961.

Zollner, Erich. *Geschichte Oesterreichs: von den Anfängen bis zur Gegenwart*. Oldenbourg: Verlag Munchen, 1979.

APPENDIX A: Great Austrian Empire Federation Plan of Aurel Popovici
Shaded areas show minority (mostly German) enclaves which are potential regions of territorial autonomy.

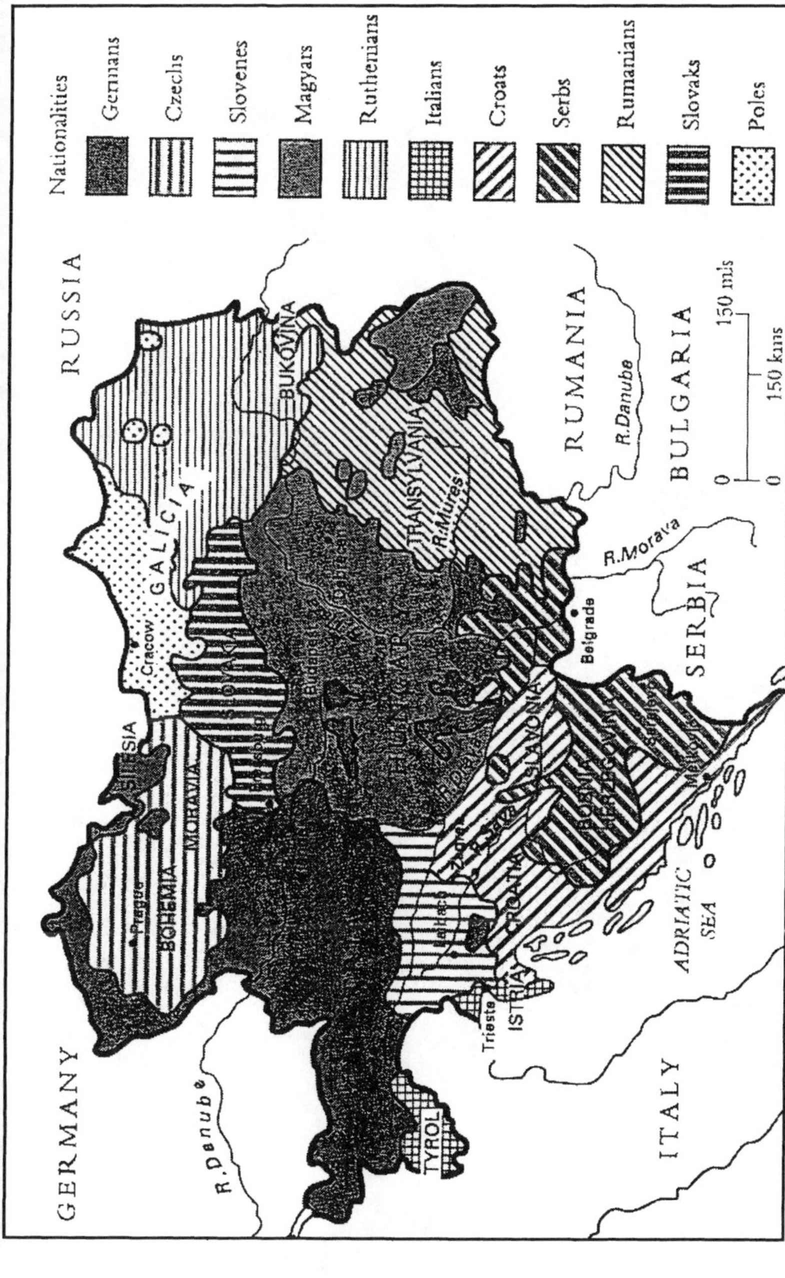

APPENDIX B: Nationalities of the Habsburg Monarchy
(Printed with the permission of Cambridge University Press)